China Currents
2015 Special Edition

China Currents
2015 Special Edition

Penelope B. Prime and James R. Schiffman, Editors

China Research Center, Atlanta, Georgia
www.chinacenter.net

Cover design: Vanessa F. Garver

For electronic browsing and ordering of this, and other China Research Center titles, visit www.chinacenter.net

For more information, please contact:
China Research Center
Atlanta, Georgia
info@chinacenter.net

China Currents: 2015 Special Edition
Penelope B. Prime and James R. Schiffman, Editors

ISBN: 978-0-9826415-4-5

Published in the United States by China Research Center

Design and Production: Carbon Press LC
Manufactured in the United States of America

First Edition

Contents

Business

Politics and International Relations

Third Plenum of the Eighteenth Party Congress

Preface

Economic reform and development in China are reshaping the global system in the 21st century and fueling an unprecedented social transition within China itself. China Currents is a forum for thoughtful, concise articles analyzing society in contemporary China, published by the China Research Center at ChinaCurrents. com. Periodic printed special editions include selections from past issues, organized by topic. The 2015 Special Edition includes articles covering social change, economic transition, the environment, business issues, international relations and a special section updating the progress on the Decisions of the Third Plenum of the Eighteenth Party Congress.

The Center would like to gratefully acknowledge financial support from East West Manufacturing and Project Success as Gold sponsors. We would also like to thank Lisa Guthrie for her editorial contribution. The views expressed in these articles are those of the authors.

Founded in 2001, the China Research Center's mission is to promote understanding of greater China based on research and experience, and to work collaboratively on events and projects with the public and private sectors. The Center draws much if its expertise from the universities and institutions around the southeast U.S., including Agnes Scott, the Carter Center, the Centers for Disease Control, Dalton State, Emory, Georgia College & State University, Georgia Institute of Technology, Georgia State, Kennesaw State, Mercer, Oglethorpe, the University of Georgia and University of North Carolina at Greensboro. The Center is currently based at Georgia State University, with institutional sponsorship from the Institute of International Business in the J. Mack Robinson College of Business.

The associates of the Center believe that favorable U.S.-China relations will be critical to supporting economic development in the U.S. and greater China, and to promoting peace in the region. One of the foundations of favorable relations is mutual understanding based on knowledge and open communication. The associates specialize in the study of a wide variety of aspects of Chinese society, including language, culture, history, politics, society, international relations, demographics, geography, the environment, the economic system and the business environment. The Center's goal is to make knowledge and expertise available to a wide variety of constituents within and beyond our academic communities, as well as to enhance our academic work via cross-disciplinary and cross-institutional collaboration.

Penelope B. Prime, Ph.D.
James R. Schiffman, Ph.D.
February 2015

The Development of China's Developmental State: Environmental Challenges and Stages of Growth

Brian Woodall and Siqi Han

Vol. 13, No. 1
2014

China's political leaders are grasping for ways to clean up a notoriously polluted environment without sidetracking economic growth plans. For longtime observers of the East Asia scene, this evokes a sense of déjà vu replete with flashbacks to South Korea in the 1990s and Japan two decades earlier. Despite geographic proximity and many cultural commonalities, China, South Korea, and Japan are distinctly dissimilar countries. China's large, diverse citizenry inhabits a vast, resource-abundant subcontinent ruled by a "communist state" in a semi-marketized economy. Located on a peninsula still divided by Cold War machinations, South Korea is a small, homogenous, and resource-poor country with an advanced economy and a presidential-style democracy. Also homogenous and resource-poor, Japan boasts a mature market economy and a stable parliamentary democracy. South Korea and China were numbered among the second and third waves of developers, while Japan was the first Asian country to cross the industrial divide. Nevertheless, at comparable stages of advancement, these dissimilar states responded in broadly similar ways to common challenges. Why is this so?

Outward dissimilarities aside, China, South Korea, and Japan are exemplars of the East Asian "developmental state." Allowing for case-specific variations, we posit that the developmental state has three structural components. First, it requires a stable policy environment to insulate government bureaucrats from political demands that might derail state-led guidance of a market-driven economy.[1] Japan's Ministry of International Trade and Industry (MITI, the organizational predecessor of today's Ministry of Economy Trade and Industry), South Korea's Economic

Planning Board, and China's National Development and Reform Commission played the part of pilot planning agencies in their respective economies. Second, the economic bureaucracy must be "embedded" in a set of ties that bind the state to society and open channels for ongoing negotiation and renegotiation of goals and policies.[2] And, third, the long-term success of the developmental state requires a relatively equitable distribution of national wealth to ensure the social quiescence needed to endure the rigors of forced-march industrialization.[3] Japan industrialized while simultaneously narrowing the gap between rich and poor, and South Korea did so without expanding that gap. China's increasing income inequality – which, in theory, allows a "few to get rich first" – is rationalized as a temporary expedient to achieve the socialist ideal of income equality.[4]

Similarities in institutional responses at comparable levels of advancement suggest that the East Asian developmental state evolves through discernible stages. To test this premise, we explore the state of affairs in post-1978 China by focusing on a key subset of the broad set of consequences produced by the obsessive pursuit of profit and improved productivity. Specifically, we focus on the institutional responses of Chinese state actors to pressure to address environmental degradation, which is an inevitable social cost of the developmental state's business-first growth strategy. In this way, the institutional response of Chinese state actors to environmental protest represents a crucial case study of the sorts of forces that punctuate the development of the East Asian developmental state into discernible stages of growth.

Environmental Challenges and Stages of Growth

The developmental state is constructed of institutions, which we define as humanly devised constraints that structure behavior and carry power-distributional consequences.[5] Viewing institutional choices in this way draws attention to their "social costs," which, in the case of the developmental state, includes all of the losses imposed on domestic and foreign interests as a result of a business-first economic strategy. For example, under China's developmental state, "producers have been favored over consumers, state companies…over private firms, and production of export goods…over provision of household services."[6] In other words, the developmental state's institutional arrangements give favored interests an implicit license to pollute, and, in so doing, create potential change agents among those who must suffer in a degraded environment.

While the East Asian developmental state is the focal point in a contentious debate, little effort has been made to explain how and why its institutional arrangements change over time. We argue that the developmental state progresses through a process that, to paraphrase W.W. Rostow, can be understood as a "sequence of stages rather than merely a continuum."[7] During Stage 1, the primary task is to erect the institutional scaffolding to nurture strategic industries and sectors. In Stage 2, export-led growth brings industrialization along with predictable consequences, including a badly degraded environment and friction with trading partners. As a result, during Stage 3, state actors must decelerate the high-growth machine and liberalize some of its mercantilist components. If and when a developmental state arrives at the frontier of technological and economic advancement – and, in so doing, enters Stage 4 – state actors will be pressed to address the challenges of globalization and sustainable development. To be clear, there is considerable room for case-specific variation within these broad stages (e.g., the relatively greater powers of local Chinese authorities), and consequently, there is no reason to assume an exact convergence of developmental processes or outcomes.

We argue that Japan and South Korea have progressed to the fourth hypothesized stage, while China is just now crossing the threshold of the penultimate stage. In the analysis that follows, we explore China's progression through these stages of growth, focusing intensively on the response of political leaders to pressure from domestic and international interests negatively impacted by a polluted environment.

Stage 1: "Crossing the River by Feeling the Stones," 1978-1992
China's developmental state began to emerge in December 1978 at the Third Plenum of the Eleventh Central Committee of the Chinese Communist Party (CCP). With annual per capita income at around $155, trade volume at a mere trickle, and China's lagging development brought into sharp relief by the normalization of relations with the United States and Japan, CCP leaders were incentivized to experiment with institutions to guide in the gradual transition to socialist modernization. In his famous "Emancipate the Mind, Seek Truth from Facts, and Unite as One in Looking to the Future" speech, Deng Xiaoping made the case for pragmatic change. Not surprisingly, leftist critics lambasted Deng's reform program, arguing – correctly, as it turned out – that it would transform China "from a planned economy to a semi-market one."[8] While questions were voiced about the suitability of Maoist institutions for the tasks at hand, when properly modified these institutions provided political leaders with "an impressive array of policy instruments and political capacity."[9]

Reforms were enacted to increase agricultural production, nurture the growth of township and village enterprises (TVEs), and expand foreign trade. The first clear sign of change appeared Anhui Province, where peasants reaped a bumper crop after taking the liberty of decollectivizing farmland. In 1982, after initial misgivings, central authorities established the "household responsibility system" to permit decollectivization nationwide.[10] Subsequent reforms targeted the fiscal system and nurtured TVEs, whose contribution to GDP leaped from six percent in 1978 to 26 percent by 1996.[11] By allowing firms to compete in markets while continuing to fulfill obligations under central planning, gradual market liberalization spurred growth in the non-agricultural sector.

In 1979, Shenzhen, Zhuhai, Shantou, and Xiamen were designated "Special Economic Zones" (SEZ), and, by 1985, an additional 14 coastal cities and three delta regions had been added to the list. While these SEZs were becoming growth engines, many state-owned enterprises (SOEs) floundered. Officials began looking to Japan – a potentially attractive reference model because of its interventionist state and a hegemonic ruling party – for solutions to China's problems.[12] In 1988, an "industrial policy" (chanye zhengce) division was established under the State Planning Council, and the transportation, coal, oil, and steel industries were singled out for developmental nurturing. However, these early industrial policy experiments produced mixed results.

China's full-speed-ahead growth strategy produced badly sullied air and waterways, just as had been the case in Japan and South Korea. Although China established its first national-level organ for environmental protection in 1973, a half dozen years would pass before a nationwide environmental law was promulgated and another decade would elapse before the law was fully implemented.[13] In 1982, the authorities established an Environmental Protection Commission under the Ministry of Urban and Rural Construction and Environmental Protection. Political leaders set a target year of 2000 to harmonize environmental protection and socioeconomic development, and had, by 1993, almost a dozen laws relating to environmental and natural resource protection were on the books.[14] However, local governments and SOE managers were incentivized to grow the economy and not curb pollution, which translated into lax enforcement. Fearful of an authoritarian state and with no environmental NGOs to turn to, Chinese citizens were left with few channels through which to voice their complaints.

Stage 2: "Blind Pursuit of GDP Growth": 1993-2007
Deng attempted to respond to critics who claimed that his reforms displayed "disregard of the difference between socialism and capitalism," but the People's Daily refused to publish the op-ed.[15] So, in the spring of 1992, the 87-year-old retiree ventured to southern China to visit the reform "laboratories" that "lit the fire for further market opening and faster growth."[16] In a series of speeches, Deng called for a "socialist market economy," and warned that "leftist" elements posed the greatest impediment to progress. Afterward, Jiang Zemin and Zhu Rongji – Deng's handpicked successors – took the baton and pressed a broad reform package that included price liberalization. While the reforms granted local governments greater leeway in steering economic policy, a centralized Leninist regime continued to function.

In November 1993, at the Third Plenum of 14th Party Congress, the CCP embraced Deng's vision, and proceeded to institute tax and financial system reforms. The 1994 Outline of Industrial Policy proposed measures to grow the electronics, machinery, construction, automobile, and petrochemical industries. Other industries were subsequently added to the list, while central authorities invited the inflow of FDI that would transform China into the "world's factory." Although the non-state sector was confined to only a few industries, its total factor productivity expanded twice as fast as the state sector, which, between 1995 and 2002, shed 38 million workers as a result of restructuring (gaizhi) and layoffs (xiagang).[17] Although China was now deeply enmeshed in the world economy, the accumulation of large reserves of foreign currency enabled the country to avoid the worst effects of the 1997 Asian Financial Crisis.

In December 2001, after 15 years of lobbying, China finally became a member of the World Trade Organization. Henceforth, state actors would have to respond to accusations of "unfair" trade practices from foreign governments whose markets were now awash in Chinese exports.[18] By reducing tariffs that restricted Chinese exports and opening the door to the increased inflow of FDI, WTO membership accelerated the pace of growth, and the world took note of a Chinese economic machine that displayed characteristics of the East Asian developmental state.

The reforms pressed by Deng and his successors produced a system of decentralized authoritarianism that employed concrete measures of growth in GDP and foreign direct investment as yardsticks for assessing the effectiveness of local officials.[19] Officials whose metrics were positive stood to gain promotions and their localities might be upgraded in administrative status, say, from county to city level. Meanwhile, poor performing officials could expect demotions or less desirable postings.[20] By inducing a sort of "best practices" competition among local authorities, China's reformist leaders created a gigantic "laboratory, with different economic experiments taking place all over the land."[21]

China got its pilot planning agency in 1998 when the State Development Planning Commission (SDPC) replaced the State Planning Commission. Five years later, the SDPC morphed into the National Development and Reform Commission (NDRC), which became a superagency with responsibility for formulating and implementing policies affecting all aspects of socioeconomic development. Nicknamed the "mini State Council" because as many as four members of the CCP's powerful Central Committee were recruited from its ranks (as opposed to the solitary representatives from most other ministries and departments), the NDRC became the cockpit for national-level economic planning, price setting, and industrial policy coordination. While its formal powers rivaled those of Japan's MITI or South Korea's Economic Planning Board at comparable levels of development, in practice the NDRC was obliged to share power with local authorities in China's decentralized authoritarian system. Like their counterparts at MITI and the EPB, however, many NDRC officials – as well as senior CCP leaders – were alumni of prestigious educational institutions such as Tsinghua University and Beijing University.

The double-digit growth rates of the 1990s reshaped China's industrial structure into one founded upon consolidating the commanding heights sectors of iron, steel, energy, chemical and heavy machinery, while encouraging an emerging high technology sector led by telecom. Still, much of the growth was driven by labor-intensive exports, which, between 1992 and 2002, expanded from 19 percent to 25 percent of GDP, elevating China to fifth place among trading nations. As economic growth picked up, more and more motor vehicles appeared on roadways, especially in large cities such as Beijing, where the number of cars quadrupled between 1990 and 2002.[22] In the Seventh Five-Year Plan (2001-2005), central authorities aimed to produce a Chinese family car that would encourage mass ownership. The rapid increase in auto ownership contributed to heightened levels of airborne pollutants and CO_2 emissions, which had already jumped from 2.7 million kt (thousand metric tons) to 3.7 million kt in the decade that began in the early 1990s.[23] China now found itself numbered among the major culprits in the global campaign to combat climate change.

As had been the case in South Korea and Japan, Chinese state actors did almost nothing to prevent environmental pollution, even as favored firms reaped windfall profits. For the most part, those actions taken – e.g., the 1998 decision to grant the National Environmental Protection Agency vice-ministerial status – were not accompanied by a corresponding expansion of enforcement authority. It is not coincidental, therefore, that the first troubling reports of hundreds of so-called "cancer villages" (aizheng cun) appeared at this juncture.[24] Meanwhile, local Environmental Protection Bureaus (EPBs) were hamstrung in their enforcement efforts by local governments committed to economic growth.[25] Although Friends of Nature – China's first environmental non-governmental organization – was established in 1994, it and similar groups mainly advocated for protection of endangered species and nature preservation. Citizens voiced their discontent over environmental issues by submitting letters and petitions, filing civil lawsuits, and staging demonstrations. In 2006, authorities received 600,000 protest letters, a six-fold increase from the 1997 figure, and, beginning in the early 1990s, an average of 80,000 citizens submitted petitions each year.[26] While protests took place in localities, fear of harsh treatment by an authoritarian state kept a nationwide protest movement from congealing, in contrast to the large-scale protests that erupted in late 1960s Japan and in South Korea two decades later.[27]

Stage 3: Deceleration and Structural Change, 2007 to present

As China's experiment with the developmental state model enters its fourth decade, central authorities retain control of capital investment and labor mobility. After peaking at a rate of 14.2 percent in 2007, the Chinese economic juggernaut began to decelerate, leading to predictions of five to seven percent growth over the forthcoming two decades. Some observers believe that Premier Li Keqiang's 7.5 percent growth target for 2014 is overly optimistic.[28] Despite an expanding private sector, SOEs continue to dominate the economy. Ninety-five of the world's 500 largest companies are Chinese, and most of them are SOEs in "pillar industries" (zhizhu chanye) such as petrochemicals, steel, telecommunications, and banking. With their strong ties to state actors, the SOEs are positioned to exploit rent-seeking opportunities.[29] Although South Korea and Japan realized economic miracles in spite of – or, perhaps, because of – "structural corruption," rent-seeking poses a grave threat to the legitimacy of the CCP's claim to be the "people's party."[30]

The "cost side" of the Chinese economic miracle includes a dangerously damaged environment, and state actors must find a way to decouple economic growth and pollution control. Today, China is home to 16 of the world's 20 most polluted cities, and energy inefficiency is a major cause of the problem. To produce goods worth $10,000, it is estimated that China has to consume seven times the energy needed by Japan, six times more than the U.S., and three times the requirement for India.[31] In 2006, 36 percent of China's sulfur dioxide pollution was the result of export production, more than one-fifth of which found its way to U.S. markets. Ironically, the outsourcing of "dirty manufacturing" to China improved air quality in America's eastern states, but pollution from Chinese factories now pollutes the air in western states.[32] In response to international and domestic outcry, the CCP pledged in its Eleventh Five-Year Plan (2006-2010) to improve monitoring, enforcement, and assessment of environmental protection regulations. China's first-ever comprehensive air pollution prevention and control strategy was proposed in the current Twelfth Five-Year Plan (2011-2015).

Despite some reforms and much oratory, economic growth continues to trump environmental protection. Local officials and company managers are rewarded for promoting economic growth, not for rigorously enforcing environmental regulations. In 2007, central authorities launched a study of China's "Green GDP," but scrapped the project upon discovering that the costs of pollution negated more than 3 percent of 2004's GDP. In 2008, the State Environmental Protection Administration (SEPA) became the Ministry of Environmental Protection (MEP), but the new ministry remains relatively weak in the State Council. That same year, the central government began experimenting with "environmental courts" in the hope of keeping protests from mushrooming out of control.[33] Local EPBs continue to lack enforcement power, and are obliged to compromise with local authorities obsessed with growing GDP and expanded tax revenues.[34] This message was conveyed to an EBP director by a high-ranking local government official who made it clear that: "If you don't change your mind, we will change your place."[35] Some local EPBs are said to view the trivial fines paid by local businesses caught violating environmental protection regulations as an important revenue stream.

In recent years, large-scale environmental protests broke out in major Chinese cities.[36] To address the problem, the SEPA (MEP's predecessor) issued a 2006 report entitled "Tentative Measures for Public Participation in Environmental Impact Assessments," which advocates roles for ordinary citizens, developers, and NGOs in environmental impact assessment. In addition, Chinese authorities are being pressured to take action by media reporting and foreign governments. In 2011, the U.S. Embassy began publishing hourly air quality monitoring data for Beijing using an index based upon particulate matter with aerodynamic diameter smaller than 2.5 micrometers.[37] Prior to this, the Beijing Municipal Government had assured citizens that "fine particulate matter" poses no harm. Consequently, in June 2012, central authorities ordered foreign embassies to stop their reporting on domestic air quality.[38] On September 12, 2013, the State Council announced 10 broad measures to curb pollution, including a 30 percent pollution reduction in heavy polluting industries by 2017 and greater accountability for local governments.[39] Meanwhile, protests are becoming larger and more frequent, and surveys show that a majority of Chinese people favor environmental cleanup over economic growth.[40]

Stage 4: China's Road Ahead?

When the East Asian developmental state arrives at the frontier of technological and economic advancement – the threshold of Stage 4 – policymakers must address the challenges of globalization and sustainable growth. Currently, Japanese and South Korean state actors have put these issues at the forefront of policy, and, although China has yet to embark upon this stage, its leaders are under pressure to curb emissions while sustaining growth. Combating climate change was not the policy agenda when Japan decoupled pollution control and economic growth, and it was only on the distant horizon when South Korea tackled the challenge. Japan accomplished the objective by enacting a raft of laws that created incentives (e.g., low-interest loans, tax breaks, mandatory appointment of an "energy manager" in factories and workplaces, etc.) to encourage energy efficiency, establishing a cabinet-level Environment Agency (later given ministerial status), and expanding reliance on nuclear power and renewable energy.[41] Yet the challenge is even more daunting for Chinese leaders, who must reduce pollution while pondering policies to cut greenhouse gas emissions.

China's leaders must orchestrate environmental cleanup efforts in a context in which globalization and advances in information technology make it difficult to muzzle demands for reform from an increasingly affluent citizenry, as well as from the international community. Authorities succeeded in making Beijing's air somewhat more breathable in advance of the 2008 Olympics, although, in truth, many heavy polluters merely shifted operations outside the capital. Meanwhile, although state authorities are able to shut down groups that fail to do as they are told, the emergence of environmental NGOs and anti-pollution protests in major cities seems to indicate that China's store of "social capital" is growing.[42] Nevertheless, by the time the CCP embraced sustainable development in its Tenth Five-Year Plan (2001 – 2005), China had already overtaken the U.S. to become the world's largest CO_2 emitter.[43] Only time will tell whether Prime Minister Li Keqiang's declaration of "war against pollution" is a signal of genuine governmental resolve.[44]

In the final analysis, the East Asian developmental state model can be adapted to settings as dissimilar as those presented by China, South Korea, and Japan. Many unique aspects of China's institutional arrangements are the product of path dependence and situational imperatives, including the fact that the country is more akin to an empire than to a typical nation-state. Going forward, the stability of China's developmental state will depend on how well its leaders respond to the challenges of decoupling economic growth and environmental cleanup, curbing corruption while resisting the temptation to prop up politically potent but inefficient firms, and narrowing the gap between rich and poor. The well-being of the world economy hinges on the success of the Chinese leaders in addressing these critical challenges. Although China has ascended a developmental staircase broadly comparable to that trodden by Japan and South Korea, there is no reason to assume that development cannot beget decay or that the road ahead inexorably leads to a common terminus. Indeed, the institutional framework of China's developmental state remains fragile, and concrete steps must be taken if it is to survive and prosper in an uncertain future.

Notes

[1] *Johnson 1982, 315-6*
[2] *Evans 1995, 12*
[3] *Johnson 1995, 29*
[4] *Prime 2012, 693*
[5] *North 1990, 3; Mahoney and Thelen 2010, 7, 14*
[6] *Prime 2012, 688*
[7] *1959: 2; italics added*
[8] *Prime 2012, 694*
[9] *Oi 1995, 1133*
[10] *Oi 1995, 137*
[11] *Naughton 2007, 271*

[12] *Heilmann and Shih 2013, 6*
[13] *Jing 2010, 198*
[14] *China 1994, 7*
[15] *Peng and Chen 2008, 375*
[16] *Vogel 2011, 664*
[17] *Brandt et al 2008, 687*
[18] *Prime 2012, 695*
[19] *Oi 1995, 1136*
[20] *Xu 2011; Knight 2012, 8*
[21] *Coase and Wang 2012, 149*
[22] *Tang 2004*
[23] *World Bank 2013*
[24] *The Guardian, June 4, 2013*
[25] *Economy 2005, 92*
[26] *Jing 2010, 197*
[27] *Economy 2007, 47-8; Broadbent et al 2006*
[28] *Bloomberg BusinessWeek, April 3, 2014*
[29] *Nee et al 2007, 43; Xia 2000*
[30] *Wedeman 2012, 9*
[31] *Economy 2007, 40*
[32] *Lin et al, 2014*
[33] *Jing 2010, 197*
[34] *Chow 2013, 6; Ma and Schmitt 2008, 99*
[35] *personal communication, May 24, 2013*
[36] *Xie 2011, 210; Zaobao 2013*
[37] *Wall Street Journal, February 1, 2013*
[38] *CNN, June 6, 2012*
[39] *Xinhua, September 12, 2013*
[40] *The Guardian, May 16, 2013*
[41] *Woodall 2013, 154-7*
[42] *Ma and Schmitt 2008, 102; Economy 2007, 54*
[43] *Economy 2007, 45*
[44] *New York Times, March 25, 2014*

References

Brandt, Loren et al. 2008. "Growth and Structural Transformation in China." In *China's Great Transformation*. (Loren Brandt and G. Thomas Rawski, eds.). Cambridge: Cambridge University Press. Pp 683-728.

Broadbent, Jeffrey, Jun Jin, Yu-Ju Chien and Eunhye Yoo. 2006. "Developmental States and Environmental Limits: Regime Response to Environmental Activism in Japan, Taiwan, South Korea and China." *EAI Working Paper Series 6*. (available online at: http://www.eai.or.kr/data/bbs/kor_report/200905271123153.pdf; accessed November 11, 2013).

China. 1994. *China – Environmental Action Plan of China 1991-2000*. World Development Sources, WDS 1997-2. China: National Environmental Protection Agency and State Planning Commission. (available online at: http://documents.worldbank.org/curated/en/1994/03/698551/china-environmental-action-plan-china-1991-2000; accessed November 10, 2013).

Chow, Gregory. C. 2013. "China's Environmental Policy: A Critical Survey." In *China's Environmental Policy and Urban Development* (Joyce Yanyun Man, ed.). Cambridge, MA: Lincoln Institute of Land Policy.

Coase, Ronald and Ning Wang. 2012. *How China Became Capitalist*. New York: Palgrave Macmillan.

Economy, Elizabeth C. 2007. "The Great Leap Backward? The Costs of China's Environmental Crisis," *Foreign Affairs*, Vol. 86 (No. 5): 38-59.

Economy, Elizabeth. 2005. *The River Runs Black: The Environmental Challenge to China's Future*, New York: Cornell University Press.

Evans, Peter B. 1995. *Embedded Autonomy: States and Industrial Transformation.* Princeton: Princeton University Press.

Heilmann, Sebastian, and Lea Shih. 2013. *The Rise of Industrial Policy in China, 1978-2012 (Harvard-YenChing Institute Working Paper Series).* Cambridge: Harvard-Yenching Institute. (available online at: this link; accessed January 25, 2014).

Jing, Jun. 2010. "Environmental Protests in Rural China." In *Chinese Society: Change, Conflict and Resistance, Third Edition* (Elizabeth J. Perry and Mark Selden (eds.). London: Routledge. Pp. 97-214.

Johnson, Chalmers. 1995. *Japan: Who Governs? The Rise of the Developmental State.* New York: W.W. Norton.

Johnson, Chalmers. 1982. *MITI and the Japanese Miracle: The Growth of Industrial Policy, 1925-1975.* Stanford: Stanford University Press.

Knight, John. 2012. *China as a Developmental State (CSAE Working Paper No.2012-13).* Oxford: Centre for the Study of African Economies, University of Oxford. (available online at: http://www.csae.ox.ac.uk/workingpapers/pdfs/csae-wps-2012-13.pdf; accessed November 19, 2013).

Knight, John, and Sai Ding. 2012. "The Role of Structural Change: Trade, Ownership, Industry," in *China's Remarkable Economic Growth.* Oxford: Oxford University Press. Pp.131-54.

Lin, Jintai et al. 2014. "China's international trade and air pollution in the United States," *Proceedings of National Academy of Sciences:* 201312860.

Ma, Li, and Francois G. Schmitt. 2008. "Development and Environmental Conflicts in China," *China Perspectives,* Vol. 2, 94-101.

Mahoney, James, and Kathleen Thelen. 2010. "A Theory of Gradual Institutional Change." In *Explaining Institutional Change: Ambiguity, Agency, and Power* (James Mahoney and Kathleen, eds.). Cambridge: Cambridge University Press. Pp., 1-37.

Naughton, Barry. 2007. *The Chinese Economy: Transition and Growth.* Cambridge, MA: MIT Press

North, Douglass C. 1990. *Institutions, Institutional Change, and Economic Performance.* Cambridge: Cambridge University Press.

Oi, Jean C. 1995. "The Role of the Local State in China's Transitional Economy," *China Quarterly,* No. 144: 1132-1149.

Peng, Shen and Li Chen. 2008. *Zhongguo Jingji Tizhi Gaige Zhongda Shijian [Major Events during China's Economic System Reform].* Beijing: People's University Press.

Prime, Penelope B. 2012. "Sustaining China's Economic Growth: New Leaders, New Directions?" *Eurasian Geography and Economics,* Vol. 53 (No. 6): 688-701.

Prime, Penelope B. 2002. "China Joins the WTO: How, Why, and Now What?" *Business Economics* (April): 26-32.

Rostow, W.W. (1959) "The Stages of Economic Growth," *The Economic History Review,* 12 (No. 1), 1-16.

Tang, Xiaoyan. 2004. "The Characteristics of Urban Air Pollution in China." In *National Research Council, Urbanization, Energy, and Air Pollution in China: The Challenges Ahead — Proceedings of a Symposium.* Washington, DC: The National Academies Press. Pp 47-54. (available online at: http://www.nap.edu/catalog.php?record_id=11192; accessed November 20, 2013).

Vogel, Ezra F. 2011. *Deng Xiaoping and the Transformation of China.* Cambridge: Harvard University Press.

Wedeman, Andrew. 2012. "Growth and Corruption in China," *China Currents,* Vol. 11 (No. 2), available at www.chinacenter.net/growth-and-corruption-in-china/.

Woodall, Brian. Forthcoming. "The Development of Japan's Developmental State: Stages of Growth and the Social Costs of Energy and Export Promotion Policies," book chapter in a forthcoming edited volume.

Woodall, Brian, and Siqi Han. 2014. "Stages of Growth in the Developmental State, Social Costs and Change in Japan, South Korea, and China." Paper presented at the Annual Meeting of the Southeast Conference of the Association for Asian Studies, Duke University, Durham, North Carolina, January 18.

Woodall, Brian. 2013. "Japan: Energy Efficiency Paragon, Green Growth Laggard,"Can Green

Sustain Growth? From the Religion to the Reality of Sustainable Prosperity (John Zysman and Mark Huberty, eds.). Stanford, CA: Stanford University Press. Pp. 150-169.

World Bank. 2013. *World Development Indicators 2013.* Washington, DC: World Bank. (available online at: http://data.worldbank.org/indicator/; accessed November 20, 2013).

Xu, Chenggang. 2011. "The Fundamental Institutions of China's Reforms and Development." *Journal of Economic Literature.* 49(4):1076-151.

The concept of "developmental stages" of the East Asian developmental state is more fully explored in Woodall (forthcoming) and Woodall and Han (2014).

Brian Woodall is a tenured member of the faculty of Georgia Tech's Sam Nunn School of International Affairs and the recipient of a 2014-2015 Fulbright U.S. Scholar grant to Japan. Siqi Han graduated from Georgia Tech's Sam Nunn School of International Affairs.

Toward a New Social Contract in China: Overcoming the Legacy of the Old Regime

Thomas F. Remington
Vol.12, No.1
2013

In early 2012, China's government, in cooperation with the World Bank, issued a major white paper on the economic and social challenges facing the country in the period through 2030. The report called for a new model of economic growth and a fundamental reorientation of social policy.[1] The report called for moving up the global value chain, promoting innovation, raising efficiency, increasing consumption, increasing production of services, and reducing reliance on exports.

It also called for fundamental reforms in social policy, urging higher overall spending and improved benefits; measures to reduce income inequality; expanded investment in human capital and infrastructure; widened social pooling of risks, costs, and gains from growth; a more efficient balance between state and private provision; and better quality of services. It tacitly urged democratization to give society more voice over policy.

Coincidentally, a group of experts convened by Russia's government issued a report at almost the same time with very similar content.[2] Russia's challenge is to diversify the economy away from its resource dependency. But its solution is much the same as China's: to invest substantially more resources in upgrading skills and technology, expanding opportunity for entrepreneurship, reducing social inequities, and increasing public participation in decision-making. What explains the remarkable similarity in the two white papers? I would contend that many of the dilemmas China and Russia face in changing their economic and social policy models owe to the continuing impact of the common legacy of the old socialist "social contract." Like other post-Communist states, both China and Russia have had to adapt inherited systems of entitlements to a market-driven, globalized environment. Unlike their East Central European counterparts, however, Russia and China have seen growing levels of informal employment, rising income inequality, and increasing deficits in their pension funds despite high payroll tax rates in the formal sector.

Often China's social policies are explained by the pressure of globalization.[3] But China's rapid economic development is inextricably linked to its transition from a communist economic structure. This fact is particularly pertinent to the transformation of the urban industrial sector.[4] Therefore it is relevant to note that other post-Communist states with similar levels of foreign trade exposure and foreign direct investment exhibit far lower levels of inequality and dualism in their labor markets, and higher income replacement levels in their welfare regimes. Other studies emphasize specific characteristics of Chinese society, such as the enormous flow of China's surplus rural labor to the cities after market reforms began in the late 1970s.[5] These perspectives need to be complemented, however, with consideration of the way the old regime shaped the distribution of political interests and resources.

Most observers would agree that Russia and China represent diametrically opposite strategies of transition from communism to capitalism. For China specialists, it is axiomatic that Russia's record demonstrates the failure of its model of reform. Most would agree with Susan Shirk that "the Soviet strategy of political reform before economic reform produced political chaos and disintegration and a decline in living standards and growth rates," or Dali Yang's assessment that "Russia's shock therapy did not produce a sound market economy but instead a sort of anarchic capitalism riddled with corruption."[6]

However, valid these arguments may be in fact, it certainly is the case that the Chinese leadership believes the Russian model to have failed.[7] Deng Xiaoping, according to his son, thought Gorbachev was an "idiot" for trying to reform the political system before the economy: "He won't have the power to fix the economic problems and the people will remove him."[8] The chaos of the Soviet and Russian experience is treated as an object lesson in how not to conduct reform — "fanmian jiaocai" — negative teaching material.[9] Many Western scholars agree. For example, Mary Gallagher argues that China's "integration into the global economy, the increased use of legal institutions to mediate conflict, and the influence of a small but growing middle class may together slowly build up a more stable societal foundation for democratization...there may be benefits to continued authoritarianism."[10]

Yet despite the differences, Russia and China share three marked similarities in the social sphere: high social taxes but rising pension fund deficits; a growing share of informal employment; and rising income inequality.

In China, as in Russia, the government has converted state-funded, state-provided services to social insurance schemes for pensions and health care. With respect to pensions, beginning with a pay-as-you-go system of pension coverage for urban state-sector workers funded through enterprises in the 1950s, in 1984 China began reforming its pension system, adopting a three-tier scheme for state-sector workers in the cities. (Except for state employees in the countryside, the rural population was outside the state pension system. 11) Since then, the pension system has been steadily extended to wider categories of the population. In 1997 it was broadened to cover individual entrepreneurs and temporary workers. The current plan consists of public and individual accounts, both funded by social security taxes. Employers pay the equivalent of 20% of wages into the public account and employees pay another 8% into their individual accounts. Together with other social insurance contributions, the total payroll tax is effectively about 45% of the wage fund, which is one reason evasion is high.12 By 2010, all provinces had a province-wide pension insurance fund for old-age incomes. As of July 2011, the government had enacted a pension plan nominally covering all urban residents, including those without jobs or covered by other programs, which was gradually being implemented.[13]

Although the pension and other social contributions levels are relatively high, the pension system in China faces rising deficits. As is true of Russia as well, China's government is meeting current pension obligations by raiding the individual accounts funded through the mandatory insurance contributions and through large transfers from the state budget.[14] In China in 2011 the central government budget transferred about 180 billion yuan (about $30 billion) to make up shortfalls in the provincial pension funds of 13 provinces. Province-level governments also subsidize their funds; Shanghai had to spend more than 10 billion yuan to make up the deficit in its pension fund.[15]

Like Russia, China still relies heavily on taxes that are administratively less costly to collect but regressive. Although payroll tax rates are relatively high, they are capped at relatively low ceilings, imposing a proportionately greater tax burden on low and middle-income individuals in the formal sector. They are also highly variable depending on local arrangements between firms and governments. Income tax revenues do not form a large part of government revenues (consumption taxes, including the VAT, comprise more than half of total tax revenue in China). The personal income tax yields only 7%-8% of total tax revenue in China, and it is principally a source of revenue for subnational governments.[16] Tax declarations are voluntary for the highest income groups, contributing to widespread evasion. As a result, the richest pay a much lower share of overall income tax than other groups.[17] The relatively low income ceilings on payroll taxes mean that high-end earners pay a much lower share of their total earnings into the social insurance system than lower-income groups, while informal labor is not paying in at all. This fact imposes a substantial burden on middle-income earners in the formal sector, and on state enterprises, where compliance with payroll taxes tends to be higher.

The basic problem is that, as in Russia, the current three-tier pension system was built on top of the old socialist model that was based on state control of labor and capital. That system could offer generous pension benefits to all state employees and urban state-sector workers because wages were low and budget constraints soft. Even though wages and pensions were in cash form, cash could only make limited claims on goods and services. When the economies were put on a market footing, and budget constraints hardened, the government needed to finance its social spending obligations through new taxes that required substantial administrative capacity to collect. Wages became an important regulator of the labor market, so employers wanted to raise wages but minimize the taxes paid on the wage fund. Employees had little trust in the system and often preferred to receive the full amount of wages in cash. Tax evasion and labor market dualism — i.e. the divide between those "inside the system" and "outside the system" ("tizhi nei" vs. "tizhi wai") —followed. Many migrant workers in China prefer to receive all their wages in cash because they do not believe that they will benefit from the retirement benefits system.[18] Evasion of social insurance taxes by workers and firms at the micro-level aggregates up to large-scale deficits in the social funds at the macro-level.

Dual Labor Markets

A major reason that the payroll tax contributions in China do not meet rising pension obligations is the growing dualism of the labor market. A large and growing part of the labor force is informal, that is, working under ad hoc employment arrangements that leave earnings largely outside payroll taxes and social benefits. In China there are two different sources of informalization. One is the downsizing of workforces at state enterprises, which pushed tens of millions of workers into various forms of off-book labor (in many cases, as in Russia, workers earn wages outside the enterprise while maintaining formal relationships with firms).[19] The other is vast migration of labor from the countryside to the cities: around one-quarter of the urban workforce in China consists of migrants. This is the most important source of pressure on China's social welfare regime, because until recently, rural migrants in the cities were largely excluded from the extensive social benefits provided to workers with urban residence status. Roughly speaking, 35%-40% of the urban workforce in China is informal, compared with about 30% in Russia.[20]

Informality in China is higher than in Russia because of the significant overlap between migrant workers and the informal sector (most informal workers are migrants).[21] Approximately one-quarter of urban workers in China are migrants, but in typical industrial cities the figure is 40%-45%, and in some cities it is as high as 70%-80% of the labor force.[22] Specialists describe the rural migrant workers in cities as "a huge underclass of super-exploitable and low-cost labor."[23] Only in the last few years have they begun to acquire the right to a labor contract, pension income, health care, unemployment, and other social protections. Actual enforcement of these rights has been slow, however, and the rights themselves are limited. For example, rural migrants obtain their health insurance through their place of residence, making benefits difficult to access when they are in the city. Moreover, when migrant workers move to another province or even city, they lose the employer's portion of the contributions.[24] Although there are not recent figures on the extent of the problem, employers often do not pay into the social insurance funds for rural migrants. [25]

There is much evidence indicating that dualism has increased, both in China and Russia. The new labor contract law that came in force in 2008 in China had perverse consequences: it obliged labor recruiting agencies that supply labor to contractors to pay social insurance contributions, letting the enterprises off the hook. As a result, informality increased, as enterprises hired more agency labor and cut back on wages and benefits for their formal workers.[26] In many cases, migrant workers hired by recruiting agencies are contracted out to other agencies who in turn contract them to construction or other firms. Workers lacking an urban hukou are often in a position of dependency, with little recourse in case the employers fail to pay them the full promised wage.[27]

Adding to the pressure on the social welfare system is a worsening demographic situation. Russia's working age population began shrinking several years ago. In China, the decline in the size of the labor force is just beginning.[28] The booming coastal cities have already experienced labor shortages, raising wage costs and leading some firms to move inland in search of cheaper and politically more docile labor.[29] In both countries, the trend puts upward pressure on wages and further increases the incentive for firms to evade social tax obligations.

Rising Inequality

Reforms of social policy have tended to reinforce income inequality in the labor market. As has been widely discussed, China features levels of income inequality comparable to that of both Russia and the United States. The U.S. Census Bureau reported a Gini coefficient for the United States in 2010 of 46.9 and a decile ratio (the 90:10 ratio) of 11.67.[30] Russia's State Statistical Committee reported a Gini index of 42.1 but a decile ratio of 16.5 for 2010. China's Gini index is a matter of dispute. However, in January, the National Bureau of Statistics reported that China's Gini coefficient was 47.4 in 2012 and 49.1 in 2008.

Like the United States, Russia and China also have experienced a concentration of income gains at the top.[31] As in the United States, theories of globalization and skill-biased technological change fail to explain this fact.[32]

Not only are Russia and China similar in their levels of inequality, but they also have higher inequality than their post-Communist peers. Russia's level of inequality is higher than that of any other former Communist country in Eastern Europe or the former Soviet Union, as China's is higher than that of any country in East Asia.[33] Wage decompression and economic restructuring initially widened income disparities in all post-Communist countries in the immediate post-transition period. In Russia and China, however, the inherited institutional features of the Communist system reinforce labor market inequality, whereas in East Central Europe, rising inequality has been checked by democratic political institutions.

In China, as in Russia, the largely non-redistributive system of taxation and social spending, the preservation of categorical rather than targeted benefits (such as the tie of social privileges to residence status), the widespread diversion of public resources into private gain by state officials, and deepening labor market dualism mean that inequality in earnings is translated directly into high post-tax-and-transfer inequality. Thus in some respects, social policy deepens inequality. Gao and Riskin estimate that the net effect of social benefits other than housing is to increase income differentials.[34] China's minimum livelihood subsistence guarantee, the so-called "dibao," is means-tested but extremely low.[35] Neither in intent or effect is it redistributive. The cumulative effect is to compound advantages for those well-off enough to benefit from access to better services. As in liberal market economies such as the United States, the entrenchment of privilege also increases the ability of the rich and powerful to block moves toward more redistributive taxation, spending or toward broader pooling of risks and benefits.

Certainly Chinese leaders have repeatedly expressed concern over the high level of income inequality. In March 2012, seizing on the issue of inequality in a desperate but futile move to save his political career, Bo Xilai warned that "if only a few people are rich, then we are capitalists. We've failed."[36] The next day Bo was expelled from his leadership posts. Two days later, however, Prime Minister Wen Jiabao declared that the government would do more to reduce inequality.[37] In January 2013 the National Bureau of Statistics published Gini index figures for the first time in 12 years. In February, the State Council released a major planning document detailing measures intended to reduce income inequality, particularly by raising the minimum wage. [38]

While the social welfare regimes in Russia and China have been subject to very different pressures, the similar dilemmas outlined above can be traced to their common origins in the Soviet "social contract." The term refers to the intertwined nature of the political regime, economic system, and social structure of the

Soviet-type socialist state: the state maintained control over the economy, trading a certain level of social security for compliance with the terms of the contract. Unenforceable as it was, and extremely inefficient, it nonetheless allowed the state to achieve certain goals, and provided guaranteed employment and social protection to those segments of the population that it covered—above all, the urban industrial sector. As the China Development Research Foundation observed, "a de facto contractual relationship existed among government, employers, and employees that ensured a lifetime job together with related pension and medical benefits to employees."[39] Like "liberal market economies" and "coordinated market economies" in Western capitalist democracies, the Soviet-type social contract integrated political, social, and economic institutions. Reform of one set of institutions (notably the liberalization of economic relations), therefore, inevitably affects the balance of interests and demands in polity and society. Three lingering features of the old regime have particular significance for reform-era social policy outcomes.

State Enterprises as Central Sites of State Welfare Provision

State enterprises were central to the administration of social benefits and controls, and even more so in China than Russia because Chinese enterprises formed their own pools for pension and other funds.[40] The political implications of this are far-reaching. Because of the weakness of other associational means of pooling and representing collective interests, state enterprises became major sources of power. They were powerful both in their relations with local governments, for which they supplied employment security and a wide range of public goods, and vis-a-vis their employees. The leverage possessed by the large state enterprises has persisted well into the post-Communist era.[41]

The power of the SOEs stems in part from the characteristic gigantism of the Stalin-era enterprises. Often an enterprise is the source of employment and social amenities for an entire town. In Russia, there are several hundred "mono-cities," the equivalent of company towns, that depend on a single massive enterprise. An example is Togliatti, in Samara Oblast, home to the giant AvtoVAZ autoworks. At the point when the worldwide recession struck in 2008, one in seven residents of the city worked for AvtoVAZ, and 90% of the city's revenues came from the plant. Like GM and Chrysler, AvtoVAZ was "too big to fail," so the government intervened with a bailout and a restructuring plan that saw it through the immediate crisis. Post-Soviet Russia has hundreds of similar towns.[42] In other cases, of course, SOEs in both countries serve as state champions in international markets (as in the energy and telecommunications sectors).

State enterprises in China have emerged from the drastic downsizing in the 1990s in an even stronger position than before. According to the World Bank report, a quarter of SOEs in China are loss-making. Often they restrict competition in their industries. Because they provide politically crucial public goods, such as employment and social services, and enjoy privileged relations with governments at different levels, they resist restructuring.[43] One of the dilemmas in China has been that richer state enterprises have resisted turning over their social insurance funds to the fund pools of the jurisdiction to which they are administratively attached. Poorer enterprises of course are only too happy to do so.[44]

Extensive In-Kind Benefits

The old social contract made wide use of in-kind benefits, such as subsidized housing, utilities, transportation, pharmaceuticals, food, recreation, cultural services and the like. Additional benefits were available for designated categories of the population, such as officials and war veterans. In both Russia and China, in-kind benefits and social services represented about one third of the total wage bill.45 Generally the in-kind benefits system was regressive in its effects because higher-ranking people enjoyed better benefits. The infrastructure providing in-kind benefits, such as housing, utilities, and transportation, was inadequately financed. Maintenance costs were deferred. Russia and China have handled the conversion of in-kind benefits to new financing mechanisms somewhat differently. China transferred responsibility for providing many social services to "public service units" on contract to local governments. These have often found creative ways to generate private incomes for their employees.[46]

Both countries have found it difficult to put the in-kind benefits onto a fully market-based footing, in part because monopoly providers are able to keep prices high and services poor, and in part because cash incomes remain low. An attempt at marketizing a few benefits in Russia in January 2005 – badly planned and implemented – resulted in nationwide protests, often featuring elderly people deprived of needed medications and transportation in the dead of winter.

Moreover, the system of in-kind benefits linked social privilege to administrative status. After the transition, therefore, the system enabled officials to continue to use their positions to control access to education, health care, housing, child care, and other services.[47] This has fed rent-seeking and corruption in both countries. Officials often prefer holding on to their privileged access to administratively allocated benefits (elite hospitals, housing compounds) rather than to see them placed in a competitive market.

Weak Organized Labor

A third feature of the old social contract was that labor was incorporated into state-run trade unions that enjoyed organizational monopolies but lacked autonomy from the state. Membership in the unions was universal but labor protest was outlawed. Trade union leaders were part of the party nomenklatura. Labor solidarity was undermined by wide differences in individual earnings within enterprises and by the dependence of workers on the enterprise for social benefits.[48] Rather than negotiating for common wage rates and conditions, trade unions collected and administered social benefits. They were also "transmission belts" for political control over the workforce. In practice, they were part of a clientelistic system in which trade union officials enjoyed access to power in return for enforcing worker quiescence. To a large extent, this relationship between unions, workers, employers, and government has continued.[49] In China, there is universal agreement that the official trade unions have been ineffective in representing workers in confrontations with employers despite the fact that labor protest has increased.[50] The passage and implementation of the new Labor Contract Law in 2007, where the All-China Federation of Trade Unions participated in drafting the law, demonstrated, according to Mary Gallagher and Baohua Dong, "the lack of legitimate bargaining bodies" that could represent workers' collective interests.[51] In China, the ACFTU depends on the government to pay its expenses out of the wage fund.[52] Unauthorized labor organizations are repressed.

In Russia there are legal rival unions to the successor organization of the old Soviet trade union federation. However, the Labor Code makes it extremely difficult for rival unions to compete successfully (only one union may bargain collectively for the workers at any given enterprise). Meantime the main union federation avoids any confrontation with the state or private employers, preferring instead to maintain clientelistic relations with local authorities and a subordinate role in bargaining over wages and social benefits.[53]

In both countries, the weakness of organized labor means that business has not had to generate the capacity to bargain with labor over thorny redistributive issues. Studies of advanced Western democracies suggest that the capacity of business to unite around common interests is greater where organized labor's bargaining power is greater.[54] The ability of peak business and labor associations to constrain their own members and enforce agreements depends in part on the degree to which they must unite against their opposite numbers in the labor market. Where business and labor featured higher levels of centralization, they were also able reach agreements that alleviated redistributive conflict, for example by coordinating investment in human capital formation.[55] This helps explain the lower levels of inequality in coordinated market economies than in liberal market economies. The legacy of the authoritarian social contract in China is therefore not only a weak and clientelistic trade union movement, but also a business sector poorly equipped to form a collective will in dealings with the state or to reach agreements with labor over human capital investment. As Kellee Tsai and Bruce Dickson have shown, private entrepreneurs have little desire to exercise political influence in behalf of their common interests.[56]

The enterprise-centered nature of the welfare system, the importance of non-monetary benefits, and weakness of organized labor under the old regime have shaped the course of subsequent reform in both countries. Powerful enterprises resist demands for higher social spending by underreporting the wage bill on which they pay taxes and expanding the use of informal labor. Organized labor is complicit in labor market dualism and patronage relations rather than championing workers' interests. The government's efforts to rebuild the social contract are hampered by the persisting political leverage of the interests that were most advantageously situated in the old regime: enterprise managers and state officials.

Although China exhibits levels of income inequality characteristic of liberal market economies, its levels of social taxes are similar to those of social democratic welfare states—but only in the formal sector and only for middle-income earners. The growth of the informal sector and rising income gains at the top undermine the regime's goals for social policy by leaving social insurance pools starved of contributions. I have argued that this pattern reflects the enduring influence of institutional arrangements inherited from the old social contract. Greater associational capacity on the part of business, labor and other broad social sectors would enable the state to alleviate some of the conflict between growth and redistribution by raising the productivity of labor and investing in skill formation. This is the proposal of both the China 2030 report as well as that of the Strategy 2020 for Russia. Doing so will require overcoming the cooperation dilemma inherent in the relations between economic agents and the state. Firms and workers are more likely to contribute to the public welfare by paying taxes on the full value of their wages to the extent that they believe that the state is providing public goods such as order, legality, and efficient state administration. Strong institutions for coordination between the state, business, and labor might help overcome many of these dilemmas. In turn, cooperation among them could forge the basis for a new social contract.

Notes

[1] World Bank and the People's Republic of China Development Research Center of the State Council (2012). *China 2030: Building a Modern, Harmonious, and Creative High-Income Society.* Washington, DC, The World Bank. (Hereafter China 2030) (accessed April 12, 2012)

[2] *Strategiia-2020: Novaia model' rosta — novaia sotsial'naia politika: Itogovyi doklad o rezul'tatakh ekspertnoi raboty po aktual'nym problemam sotsial'no-ekonomicheskoi strategii Rossiii na period do 2020 g. (Hereafter Strategy 2020) http://2020strategy.ru/data/2012/03/1 4/1214585998/1itog.pdf.*

[3] Dorothy J. Solinger, *States' Gains, Labor's Losses: China, France, and Mexico Choose Global Liaisons, 1980-2000.* (Ithaca, NY: Cornell University Press, 2009); Mary E. Gallagher, *Contagious Capitalism: Globalization and the Politics of Labor in China.* (Princeton: Princeton University Press, 2005); Azizur Rahman Khan and Carl Riskin, *Inequality and Poverty in China in the Age of Globalization.* (New York: Oxford University Press, 2001).

[4] Li Shi, "Economic Growth and Income Distribution: An Empirical Analysis of China's Experiences," in Cai Fang, ed., *Transforming the Chinese Economy* (Leiden, London: Brill, 2010), p. 298.

⁵ Dorothy J. Solinger, *Contesting Citizenship in Urban China: Peasant Migrants, the State, and the Logic of the Market (University of California Press, 1999).*

⁶ Shirk, Susan, *The Political Logic of Economic Reform in China.* (Berkeley, CA, University of California Press, 1993), p. 5; Yang, Dali L., *Remaking the Chinese Leviathan: Market Transition and the Politics of Governance in China.* (Stanford, CA, Stanford University Press, 2004), pp. 297, 207.

⁷ Thomas P. Bernstein, "Introduction: The Complexities of Learning from the Soviet Union. *China Learns from the Soviet Union, 1949-Present,* Thomas P. Bernstein and Hua-Yu Li, Eds. (Lanham, MD, Lexington Books 2010), p. 19.

⁸ Quoted in Ezra F. Vogel, *Deng Xiaoping and the Transformation of China* (Cambridge, MA: Harvard University Press, 2011), p. 243.

⁹ Bernstein, "Introduction." The Soviet Union was also "fanmian jiaocai" in the late 1950s and early 1960s, when Mao rejected Khrushchev's "phony communism."

¹⁰ Gallagher, *Contagious Capitalism,* pp. 27-28.

¹¹ Song, "Pension Systems," p. 10.

¹² China 2030, p. 33; Cai Feng, "Rethinking China's Pension Reform: Relevance of International Experiences," in Cai Feng, ed., *The China Population and Labor Yearbook, vol. 2: The Sustainability of Economic Growth from the Perspective of Human Resources* (Leiden, Boston: Brill, 2010), pp. 139-151.

¹³ Yang Sibin, "One Step Closer to Full Pension Coverage," *Beijing Review,* July 7, 2011; China Development Research Foundation, *Constructing a Social Welfare System for All in China.* (New York: Routledge, 2012), p. xxiii; Shih-Jiunn Shi, "The Contesting Quest for Old-Age Security: Institutional Politics in China's Pension Reforms," *Journal of Asian Public Policy.* 2011, 4: 1, pp. 42-60; . Magnus Young, "China's Fiscal Budget and Pension Reform," *Asian Journal of Public Affairs.* (2010), 3: 2, pp. 36-47.

¹⁴ Cai Feng, "Rethinking China's Pension Reform: Relevance of International Experiences," in Cai Feng, ed., *The China Population and Labor Yearbook, vol. 2: The Sustainability of Economic Growth from the Perspective of Human Resources* (Leiden, Boston: Brill, 2010), pp. 139-151; Cai Fang and Wang Meiyan, "China's Process of Aging Before Getting Rich," in Cai Fang, ed., *China Population and Labor Yearbook, vol 1, p. 56. The authors state that nearly all accumulated pension funds are spent each year on current obligations.

¹⁵ He Na and Chen Xin, "Age-old question raises a retirement dilemma," *China Daily,* June 24, 2012.

¹⁶ Lin, "Tax Reforms in China and Russia;" Hua Xu and Huiyu Cui, "Personal Income Tax Policy in China and the United States: A Comparative Analysis," *Public Administration Review,* December 2009, p. S75; Russian State Tax Service, http://www.nalog.ru/fl/docs/3856626/print/(accessed 5 july 12). http://www.nalog.ru/fl/docs/3856626/print/; In the United States, the personal income tax generates over 40% of federal tax revenues.

¹⁷ Hua Xu and Huiyu Cui, "Personal Income Tax Policy in China and the United States."

¹⁸ A 2005 survey found that only one-third of migrant workers would want to participate in a pension insurance scheme. Andrew Watson, "Social Security for China's Migrant Workers — Providing for Old Age," *Journal of Current Chinese Affairs.* 2009, 38:4, p. 101.

¹⁹ Wiliam Hurst, *The Chinese Worker after Socialism.* (Cambridge: Cambridge University Press, 2009); C. K. Lee, *Against the Law.*

²⁰ For figures on China, see Albert Park and Fang Cai, "The Informalization of the Chinese Labor Market," in Sarosh Kuruvilla, Ching Kwan Lee, and Mary E. Gallagher, eds., *From Iron Rice Bowl to Informalization: Markets, Workers, and the State in a Changing China.* (Ithaca, London: ILR Press/ Cornell University Press, 2011); Kam Wing Chan, "Introduction: Population, Migration, and the Lewis Turning Point," in Cai Feng and Du Yang, eds., *The China Population and Labor Yearbook, Vol. I: The Approaching Lewis Turning Point and Its Policy Implications,* Leiden, Boston: Brill, 2009), p. xviv; C. K. Lee, *Against the Law.* For figures on Russia, see Strategy 2020, p. 215. A July 2012 report analyzing labor market trends in Russia found about 22 million workers employed in the economy but outside the observed and reported sector. These included unregistered self-employed individuals; private farmers; household service workers such as nannies; and family micro-businesses. The share of informal workers has been increasing throughout the 2000s while the number of workers in

   the formal sector is declining.

21 Mary E. Gallagher, Ching Kwan Lee, Sarosh Kuruvilla, "Introduction and Argument," in Sarosh Kuruvilla, Ching Kwan Lee, and Mary E. Gallagher, eds., *From Iron Rice Bowl to Informalization: Markets, Workers, and the State in a Changing China.* (Ithaca, London: ILR Press/ Cornell University Press, 2011).

22 Kam Wing Chan, "Introduction: Population, Migration, and the Lewis Turning Point," in Cai Feng and Du Yang, eds., *The China Population and Labor Yearbook, Vol. I: The Approaching Lewis Turning Point and Its Policy Implications,* Leiden, Boston: Brill, 2009), p. xviv.

23 Kam Wing Chan, "Introduction: Population, Migration, and the Lewis Turning Point," in Cai Feng and Du Yang, eds., *The China Population and Labor Yearbook, Vol. I: The Approaching Lewis Turning Point and Its Policy Implications,"* Leiden, Boston: Brill, 2009), p. xxxv; Dorothy J. Solinger, "The Political Implications of China's Social Future: Complacency, Scorn, and the Forlorn," in *China's Changing Political Landscape: Prospects for Democracy.* Cheng Li, Ed. (Washington, DC, Brookings Institution Press 2008), 251-266.

24 Du Yang, "The Potentials of Labor Supply and Policy Reactions to the Lewis Turning Point," in Cai Fang, ed., *The China Population and Labor Yearbook, vol 1,* p. 191.

25 Park and Cai, "The Informalization of the Chinese Labor Market" in Kuruvilla et al, eds., *From Iron Rice Bowl to Informalization.*

26 Gallagher, Lee, and Kuruvilla, "Introduction and Argument."

27 Pun Ngai and Lu Huilin, "A Culture of Violence: The Labor Subcontracting System and Collective Action by Construction Workers in Post-Socialist China. *The China Journal,* no. 64, 2010. pp. 143-158.

28 *China 2030,* p. 8; Cai Feng, "Rethinking China's Pension Reform: Relevance of International Experiences," in Cai Feng, ed., *The China Population and Labor Yearbook, vol. 2: The Sustainability of Economic Growth from the Perspective of Human Resources* (Leiden, Boston: Brill, 2010), pp. 141.

29 There is some dispute over whether the difficulty coastal firms have had in finding labor stems from the shortage of workers or the shortage of workers willing to accept extremely low wages. There is general agreement that second generation migrant workers are much more demanding than the first generation. Eg see Lu Zhang, "The Paradox of Labor Force Dualism."

30 Carmen DeNavas-Walt, Bernadette D. Proctor, and Jessica C. Smith, Income, Poverty and Health Insurance Coverage in the United States: 2010, P60-239 (Washington, DC: US Census Bureau, Sepember 2011), p. 41.

31 Atkinson, Anthony B., Thomas Piketty and Emmanuel Saez, "Top Incomes in the Long Run of History." *Journal of Economic Literature* 49:1 (2011): 3-71; .

32 Emmanuel Saez, "Striking It Richer: The Evolution of Top Incomes in the United States (Updated with 2011 estimates)," January 23, 2013,

33 Thomas F. Remington, *The Politics of Inequality in Russia* (Cambridge: Cambridge University Press, 2011).

34 Qin and Riskin, "Market versus Social Benefits," 20-36.

35 Dorothy J. Solinger and Yiyang Hu, "Welfare, Wealth and Poverty in Urban China: The Dibao and Its Differential Disbursement," unpublished paper, University of California, Irvine (2011).

36 Wines, "An Ambitious Chinese Party Chief."

37 China to take further steps to address income gap: Wen," *China Daily,* March 14, 2012.

38 http://www.gov.cn/zwgk/2013-02/05/content_2327531.htm

39 CDRF, p. 8.

40 Edward X. Gu, "Beyond the Property Rights Approach: Welfare Policy and the Reform of State-Owned Enterprises in China," Development and Change 32 (2001), pp. 129-150; Andrew G. Walder, Communist Neo-Traditionalism: Work and Authority in Chinese Industry. (Berkeley: University of California Press, 1986); Xiaobo Lü and Elizabeth J. Perry, Eds. (1997). Danwei: The Changing Chinese Workplace in Historical and Comparative Perspective. Armonk, NY; London, M. E. Sharpe; David Bray, Social Space and Governance in Urban China: The Danwei System from Origins to Reform. (Stanford, CA: Stanford University Press, 2005).

41 China 2030, p. 25; Gu, "Beyond the Property Rights Approach"; Dorothy J. Solinger, "The

    Impact of the Floating Population on the Danwei: Shifts in the Patterns of Labor Mobility Control and Entitlement Provision." in Lü and Perry, eds., Danwei, pp. 195-222; Wang, Boundaries and Categories.

[42] *Remington, Politics of Inequality.*

[43] *China 2030, pp. 25-6.*

[44] *Andrew Watson, "Social Security for China's Migrant Workers — Providing for Old Age," Journal of Current Chinese Affairs. 2009, 38:4, pp. 85-115.*

[45] *Simon Commander and Richard Jackman, "Firms and Government in the Provision of Benefits in Russia," Enterprise and Social Benefits after Communism. Ed. Martin Rein, Barry L. Friedman and Andreas Wörgötter. (Cambridge: Cambridge University Press, 1997), p. 95; Zuliu Hu, "Social Protection and Enterprise Reform: The Case of China," p. 288, in same volume.*

[46] *Christine Wong, "Rebuilding Government for the 21st Century: Can China Incrementally Reform the Public Sector?," China Quarterly 200 (2009): 929-952.*

[47] *Chen Infan, "Kak Kitai perestraivaet sistemy sotsobespecheniia," Vedomosti, November 1, 2011. He indicates that in China, state officials and leading party officials receive a pension equal to their highest pay level, retaining their right to obtain free medical care and numerous privileges to buy housing. On the accumulation of privilege by high-status strata and declining equality of opportunity in China, see Yingqiang Zhang and Tor Eriksson, "Inequality of Opportunity and Income Inequality in 9 Chinese Provinces, 1989-2006," China Economic Review 21 (2010): 607-616.*

[48] *Wang, Boundaries and Categories; Stephen Crowley, "Barriers to Collective Action: Steelworkers and Mutual Dependence in the Former Soviet Union," World Politics 46(4) (1994): 589-615; Stephen Crowley, Hot Coal, Cold Steel : Russian and Ukrainian Workers from the End of the Soviet Union to the Post-Communist Transformations. (Ann Arbor, MI: University of Michigan Press, 1997); Simon Clarke, "Market and Institutional Determinants of Wage Differentiation in Russia," Industrial and Labor Relations 55(4) (2002): 628-648; Claudio Morrison and Gregory Schwartz, "Managing the Labour Collective: Wage Systems in the Russian Industrial Enterprises," Europe-Asia Studies 55(4) (2003): 553-574; Donald Filtzer, Soviet Workers and the Collapse of Perestroika: The Soviet Labour Process and Gorbachev's Reforms, 1985-1991. (Cambridge: Cambridge University Press, 1994); Remington, The Politics of Inequality, p. 44.*

[49] *Solinger, Dorothy J., "Labor Discontent in China in Comparative Perspective." Eurasian Geography and Economics 48:4 (2007): 413-438; Sarah Ashwin, Russian Workers: The Anatomy of Patience. (Manchester and New York: Manchester University Press, 1999); Sarah Ashwin and Simon Clarke, Russian Trade Unions and Industrial Relations in Transition. (New York and Houndsmills, Basingstoke, Hampshire, UK: Palgrave Macmillan, 2003); Clarke;*

[50] *Gallagher, Contagious Capitalism; Lee, Ching Kwan, "Is Labor a Political Force in China?," in Grassroots Political Reform in Contemporary China. Elizabeth J. Perry and Merle Goldman, Eds. (Cambridge, MA; London, Harvard University Press 2007), 228-252.*

[51] *Mary E. Gallagher and Baohua Dong, "Legislating Harmony: Labor Law Reform in Contemporary China," in Sarosh Kuruvilla, Ching Kwan Lee, and Mary E. Gallagher, eds., From Iron Rice Bowl to Informalization: Markets, Workers, and the State in a Changing China. (Ithaca, London: ILR Press/ Cornell University Press, 2011).*

[52] *Lee, "Is Labor a Political Force in China?," pp. 228-252.*

[53] *Remington, The Politics of Inequality, ch. 2.*

[54] *Torben Iversen and David Soskice, "Distribution and Redistribution: The Shadow of the Nineteenth Century," World Politics 61(3) (2009): 438-486; Torben Iversen and John D. Stephens, "Partisan Politics, the Welfare State, and Three Worlds of Human Capital Formation," Comparative Political Studies 41(4-5) (2008): 600-637; Isabela Mares, "The Sources of Business Interest in Social Insurance: Sectoral versus National Differences," World Politics (January 2003) 55:2, pp. 229-258.*

[55] *Torben Iversen and David Soskice, "Electoral Institutions and the Politics of Coalitions: Why Some Democracies Redistribute More Than Others," American Political Science Review 100(2) (2006): 165-181; Isabela Mares, "The Economic Consequences of the Welfare State," International Social Security Review 60: 2/3 (2006), pp. 65-81.*

56 Kellee S. Tsai, *Capitalism without Democracy: The Private Sector in Contemporary China.* (Ithaca, NY: Cornell University Press, 2007); Bruce J. Dickson, *Wealth into Power: The Communist Party's Embrace of China's Private Sector. (Cambridge: Cambridge University Press, 2008); Simon Clarke, The Development of Capitalism in Russia. (London: Routledge, 2007).*

Thomas F. Remington is the Goodrich C. White Professor of Political Science at Emory University in Atlanta, Georgia.

The Clash of Historical Memory: The "Century of Humiliation" vs. the "Post-WWII Liberal World Order"

David Blair
Vol.12, No.2
2013

The U.S. and China share many fundamental interests. Their economies are so tightly inter-twined that any disruption would be extremely painful to both sides. There are no substantial, quantifiable disagreements between the two countries — meaning that there are no direct territorial disputes and neither country would gain by directly threatening the other's vital interests. With so little to gain, and so much to lose, one might conclude that the probability of armed conflict between them would be negligible. But, it is not reassuring that the current disputes are not about "real" resources. Arguments about what are ultimately relatively small assets could be settled by economic agreements and compromise. The current disputes between the U.S. and China are more dangerous than they first appear because they are driven by each nation's elite and public core beliefs, which were learned from key national historical experiences.

The most fundamental U.S. strategic beliefs are derived from the successes of the liberal world order established after World War II. The U.S. has repeatedly shown itself willing to go to war or risk war to maintain this system even when its physical survival or major economic interests are not at stake. Similarly, China's core strategic beliefs are derived from its historical experiences of national "humiliation," including foreign occupation of its territory, during the 19th and early 20th centuries.

Unfortunately, each country is now developing military capabilities that directly threaten the other's historical core beliefs. China's new capabilities to destroy U.S. naval assets, plus its claims on what the U.S. sees as international waters and airspace, threaten the freedom of the seas and the alliance system that has been fundamental to the post-World War II system. Similarly, U.S. "Air-Sea Battle" doctrine, which logically implies striking military forces on Chinese territory, will seem to Chinese thinkers to hark back to the "century of humiliation."

I. U.S. Lessons from Strategic Successes after World War II

U.S. strategic thinking and policies have been shaped by the failures of the inter-war (1918-1939) period and the successes of the post-World War II and Cold War periods. In particular, three historical lessons drive U.S. strategic thinking about China (and the rest of the world) to-day: First, the "lessons of Munich" contrast Chamberlain's appeasement of Hitler in 1937-38 with the success of the containment of the Soviet Union. Second and more positively, the benefits of a liberal international system with U.S. leadership are contrasted with U.S. isolationism, international economic collapse, and the failed League of Nations in the inter-war period. Much of this thinking also is shaped by a generally favorable view of the role of the British Empire in the 19th century. Finally, much thinking about military-operational planning is shaped by the Air-Land Battle strategy NATO adopted in the early 1980s to create a credible counter to the Soviets' overwhelming conventional superiority in Europe.

Lessons of Munich: U.S. Secretary of State John Kerry, when arguing for intervention in Syria, famously said, "This is our Munich moment."[1] Kerry, who one might have thought would be more guided by the "lessons of Vietnam," showed that U.S. policy is still informed by events of more than 75 years ago.

One lesson drawn was that failing to stand up to an evildoer early on leads to worse behavior lat-er. Thus, appeasing Hitler over the Rhineland, Austria, and Czechoslovakia led him to conclude that an attack on Poland would not be resisted. Another related lesson is that not appeasing a "bad guy" may well lead to changes in the potential adversary's internal politics. It is widely argued that Hitler might have been overthrown if Britain and France had resisted his aggressive moves in 1936-1938. These lessons of Munich have had a large influence on both the grand strategy and the details of U.S. policy since World War II. They drove both the overall policy of containing the Soviet Union and such otherwise inexplicable decisions as the intervention in Vietnam. Despite problems, policies based on the lessons of Munich are widely seen as leading to the successful conclusion of the Cold War.

Liberal International Order with U.S. Leadership: Lessons drawn from the inter-war period were far from purely military. U.S. grand strategy after World War II focused on creating strong prosperous allies in Western Europe, Japan, and elsewhere, and on establishing international organizations, norms, and rules. Especially in its trade policy, the U.S. was willing to go against its short-term economic interests to implement this strategy. In the U.S.'s eyes, U.S. leadership has largely been about providing international public goods—which are not only good for the U.S., but also for most of the rest of the world.[2]

American strategic thinkers are most familiar with, and influenced by, the history of the British Empire in the 19th century. In particular, the Royal Navy's role is seen not only as promoting British interests, but also in providing an important benefit for the world—"freedom of the seas." In this view, the U.S. Navy has continued this responsibility and therefore provides an international public service that is critical to continuation of a liberal world order.[3]

Air-Land Battle: NATO's primary strategic problem throughout the Cold War was always that the Soviet Union had numerically far superior conventional forces near the "central front" at the inner-German border. Plus, the geography dictated that the Soviets would have a much easier time resupplying or replacing combat forces in the event of war. NATO initially tried to deter the possibility of a Soviet surprise attack on Western Europe by threatening to escalate to the use of nuclear weapons, but such a threat always lacked credibility since it implied subjecting the U.S. homeland to nuclear strikes and entailed tactical nuclear warfare in densely populated Ger-many. By the time the Soviets achieved large nuclear and rocketry capabilities in the mid-1970s, the threat to answer a conventional attack with nuclear escalation lost even more plausibility.

Technology pushed by the Carter administration that came to fruition in the early Reagan administration gave NATO a much more plausible non-nuclear option for stopping a Soviet invasion. Using the combination of vastly improved intelligence (to find Soviet reinforcements), stealthy aircraft and cruise missiles (to penetrate Soviet defenses), and precision-guided weapons (to be able to hit key forces and transportation nodes), NATO would strike Soviet second- and third-wave forces and supplies with purely conventional weapons. This operational plan was known as "follow-on forces attack" or "Air-Land Battle."[4]

It is hard to remember now how credible the threat of a Soviet surprise attack on Western Europe seemed in the early 1980s. Now, the concept of Air-Land Battle is most widely known as a best selling video game. It is plausible that NATO's advanced conventional capabilities led the Soviets to agree to the truly revolutionary 1986 Intermediate Nuclear Forces (INF) treaty and the 1989 Treaty on Conventional Armed Forces in Europe (CFE).[5] By foreclosing the option of a Soviet invasion of Western Europe, these capabilities may have contributed to the rise of Gorbachev and the peaceful end of the Soviet Union. So, in the light of this history, Air-Land Battle can be seen as a stunningly successful solution to NATO's strategic problem.

Despite the fact that the new highly coordinated precision deep-strike capability was developed for dealing with a Soviet attack on Western Europe, the first

Gulf War also demonstrated the value of this operational doctrine in a very different scenario. It's not surprising that U.S. strategists seek similar solutions to today's problems.

II. Chinese Views from the Century of Humiliation

Anglo-Saxon strategic thinkers look at the pros and cons of the British Empire, but the widely used term Pax Brittanica implies that it was, on net, a positive for the world. Americans often see U.S. policies in the world as an even more benign follow-on to the British Empire. Chinese, on the other hand, remember the British Empire as an organized gang of drug traffickers.

China's century-plus of "humiliation" began with the first opium war in 1839, progressing through various military defeats and "unequal" treaties, culminating in the 1937-1945 Japanese War. So the Chinese view of the 19th and early 20th centuries is very different from the generally positive view of Britain or the U.S. It's hardly surprising that Chinese, based on their history, are particularly emphatic about avoiding further humiliation. Of course, the government rein-forces these views both in education and in the media, but average Chinese of all political persuasions are widely believed to share them.[6]

Recent history also looks different from a Chinese perspective. Americans remember 1999 as the year U.S. airpower finally stopped the ethnic murders in the Balkans. Chinese remember that as the year the U.S. bombed their embassy in Belgrade. Americans and Western Europeans are likely to see the fall of the Soviet Union as being good for the Russians and others — essentially they were being invited to join a benevolent liberal world order. Chinese (and Russians) are much more likely to see those events as a defeat for the Russian nation.

III. U.S. Perception of Growing Chinese Area-Denial Capability

As recently as 2006, Philip Saunders, a leading U.S. analyst of the Chinese military could summarize Chinese strategy as seeking to reassure neighbors (partly by downplaying territorial disputes) and seeking "to reassure Washington that China regards the U.S. military presence in Asia as a stabilizing factor and does not seek to push the United States out of Asia."[7] However, in August 2013, the same author argued, "Washington is concerned about China's increasingly muscular military, which is developing anti-access/area-denial capabilities that might challenge the U.S. military's ability to operate in Asia."[8] China's neighbors, meanwhile, are pushing for increased U.S. capability in the region.[9] What changed over those seven years?

On the Chinese side, a decade of double-digit growth in defense budgets (albeit from a low base) has greatly increased the PLA Navy's offshore capability and portends even greater future capability. Much of this capability, especially "carrier killer" anti-ship and anti-aircraft weapons, could deny the U.S. Navy the ability to operate in international waters throughout the region.[10]

Chinese military strategists discuss denying U.S. Navy ability to operate inside the "first island chain" (Japan-Taiwan-the Philippines-Malaysia).[11] This would eliminate "freedom of the seas" in the South China Sea, the East China Sea, and the Yellow Sea — all of which are major ship-ping corridors. Thus, China's new military capabilities, combined with its newly assertive claims on disputed islands,[12] can be seen as a fundamental challenge to the key U.S. strategy of securing a liberal international order. If the U.S. ceased operating in these areas, it would certainly be accepting that it has no leadership role in the region and cannot provide assurance to its allies.

In the words of the Chief of Staff of the U.S. Air Force and the Chief of Naval Operations, "To-day, the development, proliferation, and networking of advanced weapon systems specifically built to circumvent U.S. defenses threaten America's freedom of action and its ability to project military power in strategically significant regions. This development could erode the credibility of U.S. security commitments to partners and allies, and with it their political stability and economic prosperity. Air-Sea Battle responds to this concern."[13]

When President Clinton moved U.S. aircraft carriers into the Taiwan Strait in 1996, he had no fear that those ships might be successfully attacked. The U.S. could achieve its strategic objective by positioning of forces with no realistic possibility of this move resulting in combat between the U.S. and China. In this U.S. view, the decision protected the liberal international order at almost no cost. For Chinese strategists, on the other hand, it was another example of superior Western military capability leading to an outcome similar to those of the century of humiliation.

The growing Chinese sea-strike capabilities mean that this virtually risk-free option is no longer available to the U.S. As a result, a very different strategy, involving strikes against military tar-gets on Chinese territory has been developed. Air-Sea Battle, which was formally directed to be operational doctrine by the Secretary of Defense in 2009, draws on the strategies and capabilities developed for Air-Land Battle in the 1980s. Rather than limiting action to a central battlefield, U.S. forces would strike deep against military capabilities in the adversary's homeland.[14] Following the logic of the "lessons of Munich," U.S. strategists do not necessarily view this as an aggressive plan. Responding to increased Chinese capability, it simply returns us to the status quo ante (circa 1996). Furthermore, like the 1980s Air-Land battle strategy, this plan is seen as reducing the chance of escalation by giving the U.S. a credible capability to defeat an attack that involves only precision strikes against the adversary's conventional forces that are involved in the battle.

Of course, U.S. analysts recognize that an attack against the territory of any nation, especially a major nuclear-armed power such as China is fraught with danger. This is the case even if the U.S. is responding to a Chinese maritime attack. T.X. Hammes argues, for example, that U.S. war planning should be focused on an offshore strategy that does not include any strikes on Chinese territory.[15] Similarly, Amitai Etzioni argues that Air-Sea Battle will lead to an arms race between the U.S. and China, inevitably increasing tensions between the two nations.[16]

Let me be clear that no one is planning an attack on China or a war with China. Air-Sea Battle is seen as a way to deter war. In the unlikely event of a U.S.-China war, Air-Sea Battle is seen by American planners as the best way to eliminate the Chinese forces that threaten U.S. maritime capability and reduce the danger of escalation. How will the Chinese see it? A key conclusion of this paper is that Chinese historical memory makes it more likely that Chinese military and political leaders, and the public at large, would view any strike on Chinese territory, even a precision strike that hits only military forces, as a humiliation and as an existential threat. It is difficult to imagine any Chinese government suing for peace in that scenario.

IV. Current Disputes and Policy Recommendations

As recently as five or six years ago, East Asia (apart from North Korea) seemed to be strategically untroubled. The U.S. mostly welcomed China's economic growth and China appeared to view the U.S. as a fairly welcome balancer in East Asian affairs. Some former flashpoints, most notably Taiwan, appear to be quiet, although not entirely settled. But, the almost daily disputes about the East China Sea and the South China Sea have worsened the atmosphere throughout the region.

The loud disputes between China and Japan about the "fishing"[17] islands are not really about fishing rights or about any possible but unproven petroleum reserves in the area. The U.S. has no real interest in any of these islands, but believes that allowing China to claim them by force or retaliation threatens the credibility of its alliance system and the post-World War II, U.S.-led world order. Chinese, both leaders and the general public, interpret these disputes as vestiges of its humiliation. China's recent imposition of an air defense zone (ADIZ) in the East China Sea has been strongly supported by the Chinese general public because they see it as an anti-Japanese move. For example, during a recent business dinner in Beijing, this author faced many questions about why the U.S. supported Japan. And, the Chinese businessmen at the table talked openly about their support for war with Japan.

Several steps could help reduce the danger of the situation:

(a) American strategy, doctrine, and tactics should explicitly be planned with options that avoid humiliating the Chinese. Historical memory implies that any strike on Chinese territory is much more likely to lead to some type of escalation than to an end to conflict. U.S. military forces should develop doctrine and forces that give the president options that protect U.S. and allied interests without escalating to strikes on Chinese territory. If the U.S. military plans, trains, and exercises using Air-Sea battle strategy, we could be giving ourselves the stark choice between going to large-scale war with China or withdrawing from Asia.

(b) China needs to recognize that military forces that threaten U.S. Navy carriers can be interpreted by the U.S. not as a regional threat but as a challenge to freedom of the seas. Similarly, putting the U.S. in positions where its only choices are to U.S. military force or to ignore treaty commitments turns minor situations into threats to the U.S. global post-World War II strategy. This makes little strategic sense unless China has taken the huge decision to try to overturn the U.S.-led liberal world order. There is no evidence that such a strategic choice has been made at the high levels of the Chinese government. Furthermore, China has gained so much economically from the current world order that it could well be the biggest loser in such a change.

(c) Finally, there is little indication that either government is changing its behavior because it has made a deliberate grand strategic decision. If this is indeed the case, then each side should negotiate accordingly. If each side interprets each dispute as involving its core historical beliefs and strategy, compromise is impossible. It would be a great advancement if we could find a way to put a dollar (or RMB, or Yen) sign on the disputes.

The big danger is that small disputes shape thinking about future strategic options. The extreme Chinese position is that President Obama's "pivot to Asia" is an attempt to build a military cor-don around China with the goal of keeping China down. The extreme U.S. position is that China's actions over the past years are the start of a scheme to expel the U.S. from its interests in Asia. Each side needs to take seriously the historical roots of the other's strategic vision. If we are not careful, a situation will arise in which each side comes to view the other as an adversary.

Notes

1 "Syria: This is our 'Munich Moment'" says John Kerry," *BBC* 7 September 2013. *http://www.bbc. co.uk/news/world-us-canada-24004687*

2 *The literature on liberal internationalism is immense. For a recent article focusing on its success in East Asia, See "Cox, Michael (2012) Indispensable nation?: the United States in East Asia IDEAS reports – special reports, Kitchen, Nicholas, ed SR015. LSE IDEAS, London School of Economics and Political Science, London, UK. Nation: The United States in East Asia," http://www.lse.ac.uk/IDEAS/publications/reports/pdf/SR015/SR015-SEAsia-Cox.pdf*

3 *See Alfred Thayer Mahan, The Influence of Seapower Upon History, 1660-1783, which is one of the foundations of Anglo-American strategic thinking.*

4 *For a good summary of this history, see John L. Romjue, "The Evolution of the Airland Battle*

Concept", Air University Review, May–June 1984.

[5] See, for example, David Blair, "After Lance: U.S. Moves the Wrong Way," The Wall Street Journal, February 14, 1989, p.A14.

[6] An excellent discussions of the century of humiliation is: Wang Zheng, Never Forget National Humiliation: Historical Memory in Chinese Politics and Foreign Relations (Contemporary Asia in the World). Columbia University Press, 2012. See also, Orville Schell and John Delury, Wealth and Power: China's Long March to the Twenty-first Century, Random House, 2013.

[7] Philip C. Saunders, "China's Global Activism: Strategy, Drivers, and Tools," Institute for National Security Studies, National Defense University, occasional paper, October 2006. pp. 14-15.

[8] Philip C. Saunders, ""The US isn't trying to contain China…and China's neighbors don't want it to anyway." Foreign Policy, August 23, 2013. pp. 2-3.

[9] For an excellent overview of increased Chinese assertiveness in the region, see Anthony H. Cordesman, Ashley Hess, Nicholas S. Yarosh, "Chinese Military Modernization and Force Development: A Western Perspective" CSIS July 25, 2013 http://csis.org/files/publication/130725_chinesemilmodern.pdf

[10] See John Reed, "People's Power: Eight ways China's military is catching up to the United States," Foreign Policy, December 20, 2012.

[11] See Global Security.org, "People's Liberation Navy—Offshore Defense," http://www.globalsecurity.org/military/world/china/plan-doctrine-offshore.htm

[12] For a beautifully illustrated discussions of the disputes, see Council of Foreign Relations, "China's Maritime Disputes, A CFR Infoguide," http://www.cfr.org/asia-and-pacific/chinas-maritime-disputes/p31345#!/ . See also, Jim Himmelman, "A Game of Shark and Minnow," New York Times Magazine, October 27, 2013. http://www.nytimes.com/newsgraphics/2013/10/27/south-china-sea/?pagewanted=all

[13] General Norton A. Schwartz, USAF & Admiral Jonathan W. Greener, USN, "Air-Sea Battle," The American Interest Magazine, February 20, 2012.

[14] The best public explanation of Air-Sea Battle is Air-Sea Battle Office, "Air Sea Battle: Service Collaboration to Address anti-Access and Area Denial Challenges," http://www.defense.gov/pubs/ASB-ConceptImplementation-Summary-May-2013.pdf

[15] Hammes, T.X., "Offshore Control: A Proposed Strategy for an Unlikely Conflict," National Defense University, Institute for National Strategic Studies, Strategic Forum, No. 278. June 2012, https://www.google.com/search?q=ndu+offshore+control+hammes&rlz=1C5CHFA_enUS514US514&oq=ndu+offshore+control+hammes&aqs=chrome..69i57.12532j0j4&sourceid=chrome&espv=210&es_sm=119&ie=UTF-8 See also, Jeffrey E. Kline and Wayne P. Hughes, "Between Peace and the Air-Sea Battle: A War at Sea Strategy," Naval War College Review, Autumn 2012, Vol. 65, No.4, pp. 35-42.

[16] Etzioni, Amitai, "Who Authorized Preparations for War with China?" Yale Journal of International Affairs, Summer 2012, pp. 37-51.

[17] Perhaps English speakers can avoid naming arguments just by translating the name of the mail island in dispute. The Chinese name for the island, "Diaoyu," means "fishing" as does its Japanese name, "Uotsori." Senkaku means "pinnacle."

David Blair is a Professor of Economics at the Eisenhower School, National Defense University, Washington, DC.

Found in Translation

John Israel
Vol. 12, No. 2
2013

Editor's note: The following are the author's verbatim notes for a speech he delivered to the Atlanta chapter of the U.S.-China People's Friendship Association in October 2013.

Xinan Lianda – Southwest Associated University – was an amalgam of three institutions that fled Beijing and Tianjin in 1937 at the outset of the Second Sino-Japanese War. These were Peking University, Tsinghua University, and Nankai University. Lianda kept the light of learning burning in Kunming for eight years of war in the face of Japanese bombing, material shortages, devastating inflation, and official oppression that sometimes morphed into terrorism.

When I first heard of Lianda in the early 1970s, I decided to write a book about it. Besides the historical importance of the university, I was attracted to the subject because it was a ripping good story – and I am a rather old-fashioned practitioner of narrative history. But there was another dimension that tied together author and subject – shared values. So much of what I found in Lianda resonated with my own values as a liberal American academic: a vision of liberal education marked by diversity, tolerance, and academic freedom. The people I was writing about were subsequently characterized by my mentor, John King Fairbank, as "Sino-Liberals."

Following a quarter century of research, interviews, writing, rewriting, procrastination, and unanticipated problems, my work was published by the Stanford University Press as Lianda: A Chinese University in War and Revolution.

Friends in China – many of them Lianda alumni – heard about the book.

Some volunteered to translate for a Chinese edition. Knowing that a serious translation depends upon close cooperation among author, translator, and publishing house, they invariably asked me if I would cooperate in such an enterprise. I agreed to do so if they could satisfy three conditions:

They would have to have a high level of proficiency in English. The response here was invariably affirmative.

They would have to write Chinese with stylistic verve. Further smiles and nodding of heads.

The publisher would have to agree not to change a single word for political reasons.

This always elicited a crestfallen expression and nipped our Sino-American joint enterprise in the bud.

There were two reasons for my zero tolerance stand on censorship:

Personal convictions and values. I have been a card-carrying ACLU member for half-a-century.

The nature of my subject. Professors and students at Lianda risked (and sometimes gave) their lives for freedom of expression. It would have been unseemly to sacrifice such a noble legacy to publish a sanitized version of the university's history.

Over time, I became more fully aware of what I was up against. Chinese censorship did not operate from the top down. To be sure, the Communist Party's Propaganda Bureau was charged with guarding against politically incorrect ideas. However, publications were not submitted to some official with a wary eye, a green eyeshade, and the countenance of the Grand Inquisitor. Rather, publishers had to self-censor authors' manuscripts before they were published. If anything slipped through that would rankle higher-ups, the entire publication run could be confiscated and months of hard work and piles of renminbi would be consigned to the dustbin of history.

Given this system of self-censorship, it was inevitable that publishers would err on the side of caution and that self-censorship would, in effect, out-inquisit the Grand Inquisitor.

So I resigned myself to the reality that a billion-plus Chinese would have to survive without access to my magnum opus in its native language.

Fast-forward to November 2007. I was packing up for a trip to China when an email arrived from a certain Rao Jiarong. Mr. Rao identified himself as a recent graduate from the history department of Xiamen University who had taken a job in Beijing. There, a friend of his had lent him a copy of my book. So enamored was he of my work that he finally quit his job to devote full time to writing a translation. After a year's work, he had completed the manuscript, which he attached to the letter.

Would I help him find a publisher? I was awestruck by this intrepid young man who had poured his financial and spiritual resources into this labor of love, the beloved object being my own literary progeny. But I had already said no to more than one ardent suitor, including a good friend, so what could I tell Mr. Rao? Maybe, I pleaded rather lamely, he could find a publisher in Taiwan or Hong Kong, but I had little hope that this unknown recent college graduate would have access to such remote realms.

I had underestimated Mr. Rao. Within a few months, he had a contract from the Zhuanji Wenxue Chuban She (Biographical Literature Publishers) in Taipei. The Taiwan edition appeared in 2010, complete with a preface that lay bare the realities of literary censorship on the other side of the Taiwan Straits. Now my work was available to some 20 million Taiwan Chinese. I took some solace when I found the book advertised on a Mainland website, but I realized that few people in the PRC would go to the trouble of ordering an expensive book from the Unliberated Province, printed in traditional Chinese characters.

Then, in the summer of 2011, I received an email from Mr. Rao. The Jiuzhou Chuban She – Nine Continents Publishers – in Beijing was prepared to produce an uncensored simplified characters edition. We soon had a contract guaranteeing that not a single word would be changed for political reasons.

This seemed too good to be true. And it was. In December 2011, Mr. Rao forwarded from the publisher a list of about a dozen "sensitive passages," as he called them, with suggestions for softening the wording. Would I approve them? I went down the list, wrote "No!" next to each item, and returned it to Mr. Rao. He replied, to my amazement, that, in every instance, the Press had accepted my decision. Then, a couple of weeks later, I got an email from the Press. The fact that they were writing me directly underscored a note of desperation. Three particularly sensitive passages had to be dealt with before publication. We finally agreed to place controversial words in quotation marks, followed by footnotes attributing the quotation marks to the publisher rather than the author. Here is how the passages appear in the translated version:

After seizing power in 1949, the Communists were able to impose unprecedented restraint upon the words and deeds of liberal academics.

Quotation marks around "restraint."

Academic freedom, which reached its apogee in Beijing during the warlord era and in Kunming under the patronage of Long Yun, was challenged by the Guomindang and finally crushed under the Communists.

Quotation marks around the word "crushed."

The frenzied reassertion of political and ideological control following the destruction of the democracy movement in June 1989 is a further reminder of the official strictures that limit political and philosophical discussion.

Quotation marks around "democracy movement."

Here is a poignant example of the inanity (if not insanity) of censorship. The translated version not only retains criticism of the Communists for political and ideological oppression, but actually calls attention to these passages!

So much for my experience with China's system of censorship. Equally intriguing is what I learned about China after the spring of 2012, when the Beijing translation hit the bookstores.

First of all, my history had appeared in the middle of a phenomenon called "Lianda Re" – meaning Lianda Fever. What was going on was the familiar Chinese passion for using history as an oblique way of commenting upon the contemporary scene. There had been a minor tsunami of books, articles, reviews, and commentaries identifying Lianda as a high point in modern Chinese higher education. Such publications, as not even the dullest reader could fail to observe:

Highlighted the inadequacies of Chinese higher education in the 21st century

Provided a Chinese pedigree for ideas, values, and institutions that might otherwise have been dismissed as bourgeois American intrusions

Reminded people, sometimes quite explicitly, that under Chiang Kai-shek's (Jiang Jieshi's) officially reviled Guomindang regime, China's universities had reached a height unequalled under the People's Republic.

Because my subject was so hot, the author also became a hot item. Reviews of my book proliferated; reporters besieged me with requests for interviews. And my history of Lianda, of which the English edition had sold fewer than 500 copies from 1998 to 2013, reached the 20,000 mark less than two years after the publication of its Chinese translation.

Most interesting was my personal experience in talking about my book in universities and book stores in Beijing, Shanghai, Nanjing, Xiamen, and Qingdao. For the first time I came into contact with audiences of educated young Chinese. I quickly had to reassess my preconception of the political mentality of the younger generation, an image left over from the 1990s. I had assumed that these young men and women were chauvinists, supportive of ultra-nationalist rants, hostile to whatever their leaders labeled as foreign interference in the realm of ideas and values, and more receptive of ideologies that bordered on fascism than on anything akin to Jefferson or even Mao.

My moment of truth came at my very first public lecture, at Xiamen University. Following my talk, a gentleman in the back row stood up and asked how an American, whose armed forces ran around the world seeking excuses to interfere in the affairs of inoffensive nations, could stand up in front of an audience and prattle on about liberal values.

My own response to this question is less interesting than the fact that virtually the entire audience sprang to support an old American professor's defense of liberal values against a challenge from this young Chinese critic of U.S. imperialism. Wow!

On a broader level, I realized that I was seeing up close what I already sensed from daily life in China: In striking contrast to a political elite – self-perpetuating, insulated from the people in whose name it ruled, and paranoid in defense of its privileges – sectors of China's civil society were creative, energetic, vibrant, searching fearlessly for answers.

The question remained as to how widespread and how representative was the kind of critical thinking and open discourse in which I had been privileged to participate. But the fact that it existed at all gave reason for hope.

John Israel is Professor Emeritus of History at the University of Virginia.

A Short History of the Party Congresses

Yawei Liu
Vol. 11, No. 2
2012

Over its history of 91 years, the Chinese Communist Party has held 18 national congresses. Seven came before 1949 when the CCP came to power and 11 were convened since then. Only 12 delegates attended the first Congress, representing about 50 members of the Party, whose founding was financed by Moscow. When the 7th Congress was held in Yanan in 1945 before the Chinese Civil War, more than 700 delegates attended, representing 1.2 million members of the Party. In those years, the meetings were often held in secret and were highly irregular. Most decisions since 1936 were made by Mao Zedong, who used the 7th Party Congress to establish his supremacy in leadership and subsequently shelved such meetings.

After Mao's fighters dismounted from their horses in 1949, they took up positions behind desks in a corner of the Forbidden City called Zhongnanhai. But Mao saw himself as a new emperor, and failed to establish a regular pattern for Party congresses. The 8th Congress was not held until September 1955. By this time the Party had grown to more than 10 million in members. The 9th Congress was not held until 1969, a full 14 years after the previous gathering. Liu Shaoqi, one-time anointed successor to Mao, was expelled from the Party at the 12th Plenary Session of the 8th Congress, and died shortly before the 9th Party Congress was convened, which established Lin Biao as Mao's successor.

The 10th Congress was held in August 1973 with 1,249 delegates representing 28 million members. Only four years elapsed between the 9th Congress and the 10th, but many tumultuous events happened in-between. Moscow and Beijing clashed along their countries' border, and Soviet leader Leonid Brezhnev even considered using nuclear weapons against China. Lin Biao died in a fiery crash in Mongolia in 1971. President Nixon visited China in 1972. Mao's health was deteriorating. The Gang of Four, led by Mao's wife, Jiang Qing, was leading the nation into a ditch of economic stagnation, ideological rigidity, and revolutionary fervor. The country was inching toward collapse.

Mao died in September 1976. Barely a month later, the Gang of Four was arrested and the new leader, Hua Guofeng, selected by Mao shortly before he died, vowed to follow Mao's policies and dismissed Deng Xiaoping, who was also brought back by Mao to restore order. Mao's comrades did not like Hua and they maneuvered to bring Deng back. Hua continued as the nominal leader, but decision-making was now in the hands of Deng.

The 11th Congress was held in August 1977. A five-year interval between CCP congresses was finally institutionalized. But transitions of power were yet to be institutionalized. Between December 18 and December 22, the 3rd Plenary Session of 11th Congress met in Beijing. Momentous decisions were made to abandon Mao's legacy. The policy of reform and opening up was introduced. Three days before the meeting, Beijing and Washington decided to normalize relations. China was finally able to climb out of anger and isolation.

Ten years later, in October 1987, the 13th Congress was held. With support from Deng Xiaoping, General Secretary Zhao Ziyang formally announced that the Party would move forward with political reform. On April 15, 1989, Hu Yaobang – Deng Xiaoping's first choice of Party Secretary, who was forced resign by the old guard of the Party – died. Popular mourning for him led to the tragic crackdown on June 4, 1989. Zhao Ziyang was dismissed from the position of General Secretary of the Party and Jiang Zemin, an obscure Party secretary in Shanghai, was abruptly brought in to be the new leader. Zhao was never allowed to appear again publicly, and he died in 2005.

In 2002, Jiang Zemin, who served as the CCP's General Secretary for 13 years, finally stepped down. Hu Jintao, who was chosen by Deng Xiaoping as the fourth general leader and became a member of the Standing Committee of the Politburo in 1992, finally became the General Secretary. He assumed the presidency of the republic in March 2003, but Jiang Zemin did not relinquish his chairmanship of the Central Military Commission. He wanted to "babysit" Hu for a while. Wen Jiabao -who was Zhao Ziyang's chief of staff and accompanied Zhao to Tiananmen Square where he bid farewell to the world – was now in charge of the State Council. Initially, there was euphoria about the new leadership. The Hu-Wen administration's response to the case of Sun Zhigang and its efforts to inject accountability in the wake of the SARS outbreak convinced many in China that they were witnessing a New Deal. Hu and Wen's emphasis on the welfare of the people rather than GDP growth alone also caught the imagination of the reform community. However, the signs of a can-do administration quickly dissipated. Even after Hu assumed the chairmanship of the Central Military Commission in 2005, there was no significant attempt to introduce political reform, despite Wen Jiabao's repeated statements to foreign visitors that the Hu-Wen administration planned to do so.

In October 2007, the 17th Congress was held. Before the meeting, there was a lot of speculation about who would be named to the Standing Committee of the Politburo, and more important, who would be groomed to become top leaders of the fifth CCP generation. It was quite a surprise when Xi Jinping, who was only a member of the Central Committee, catapulted into the Standing Committee and was slated to be the next Party leader. Li Keqiang, who was Hu's protégé and favorite to succeed him as president, was chosen instead to replace Wen Jiabao as premier in 2013. While details of the back room dealings of the personnel arrangement of the 17th Congress are yet to emerge, it is clear that Jiang Zemin was the chief engineer of the sudden shakeup at the top.

Yawei Liu, Ph.D., is Director of the China Program at The Carter Center, Atlanta, Georgia.

The 18th Party Congress:
A Turning Point in Chinese Politics?

Yawei Liu
Vol. 11, No. 2
2012

On November 14, 2012, after a week of listening, discussing and "electing," the 18th National Congress of the Chinese Communist Party (CCP) finally came to an end. The next day, the new Central Committee had its first plenary session to finalize the Politburo and its all-powerful Standing Committee. The media were told a press appearance would happen at 11 a.m. A crowd of domestic and foreign reporters waited patiently in a cavernous room of the Great Hall of the People for Xi Jinping and the other six members of the Standing Committee to emerge. The new leadership was more than an hour late in showing up. But when the "magnificent seven" filed into the room with Xi in the lead, the world got its first look at the men who will run the world's most populous nation for the next several years. No other CCP National Congress in recent history had been so difficult to convene. And at no time since CCP was established in 1921 had the world paid such intense attention to its gathering of more than 2,300 delegates, meetings that were largely ignored or misunderstood in the past outside China. Xi told the reporters that for the CCP to be good and effective in leading China to an even brighter future, Party members had to be responsive, accountable and responsible. With that pledge, the power transition finally began, surviving multiple threats in the months leading up the November 8 meeting.

The Congress clarified at least some things. First, in a year of the shockingly public airing of the Communist Party's dirty laundry in the form of the Bo Xilai and other scandals, the top positions were handed to the men who were long touted to receive them: Xi Jinping and Li Keqiang. Beyond that, the conservative Jiang Zemin faction dominated, and Hu Jintao's power was circumscribed. It is clear that the Xi-Li administration will not waver from the economic reform opened by Deng Xiaoping three decades ago. But there is no roadmap to political reform, despite a great deal of talk about the need to deal with corruption and bureaucracy.

Prelude to the Congress

To understand the political changes unveiled at the Congress, some background is necessary. In the years leading up to the event, China's economy surpassed that of Japan to become the second largest in the world. Beijing awed the world with its successful 2008 Summer Olympic Games. The celebration of the 60th anniversary of the founding of the People's Republic in 2009 also was a smash. The relationship with Taiwan, due to the KMT's success at the polls and Hu Jintao's open-mindedness, was calm and productive. At the same time, social disturbances continued to grow, escalating according to some scholars to about 180,000 in 2010. The expanding gap between the rich and the poor became a rallying cry for the new left, which openly praised Mao Zedong and tried to turn nostalgia into policies.

Hu Jintao signaled that the CCP would promote political reform, but there was no follow through. On July 23, Hu declared in a speech at the Central Party School that the CCP would introduce political reform. Hu said reform must be conducted within the framework of three pillars: the supremacy of the CCP leadership, people being masters of their own destinies, and rule of law. At the time, many observers indicated this speech would establish the tone of political reform in the upcoming political report to be delivered by Hu at the Congress. Judging from the speech, nothing new would be produced at the Congress. Indeed, there was no breakthrough announcement about how the CCP would introduce political reform or what shape it might take. Neither an action plan nor timetable was offered. Hu's political swan song, like all his policy speeches, was boring, listless, and utterly devoid of an implementable plan.

Bo Xilai makes his move

Bo Xilai, a Politburo member who was sent to Chongqing as Party Secretary, executed populist programs in a masterful fashion, at least for a time. Playing on leftist sentiments, he unleashed a populist campaign that inspired many in China who were concerned about the growing gap between the rich and the poor. The campaign also planted fear among many who despised his overbearing leadership style, manipulation of the media, and neglect of the rule of law.

Bo deeply resented his assignment to the southwestern metropolis of more than 30 million people, and his populist initiatives were part of his strategy to get back to Beijing with the goal of being named to the Standing Committee of the Politburo at the 18th Congress. He believed he was qualified to be vice premier, and many top leaders, including Xi Jinping, went to Chongqing to praise his achievements. During a meeting with a few foreign NGO representatives, a top advisor for Bo Xilai boasted that his boss would move into the Standing Committee. The only uncertainties were when and which portfolio Bo would take. The possibilities were the premiership, the propaganda portfolio, or the job overseeing the Party's law enforcement arm.

Bo was playing on neo-Maoism as a solution to corruption, which had become a cancer spreading wide and deep at a time when the leadership seemed stalled. Hu Jintao and Wen Jiabao continued to govern without vision, imagination, and bold measures despite popular sentiment in favor of political reform. At the top, a split seemed apparent. While Wen Jiabao kept talking about China needing political reform and embracing universal values, other top leaders ignored him. When Tunisia, Egypt and Libya were engulfed by the Arab Spring, the top leadership strengthened media controls and the gigantic stability maintenance apparatus was revved into high gear against any sign of a Color Revolution in China. In March 2011, Wu Bangguo, the number two man of the nine-member Standing Committee, declared in his opening speech to the annual session of the National People's Congress that China would adhere to "Five Nos," namely, 1) no multiple party system, 2) no diversity in ideology, 3) no checks and balances and bicameral parliament, 5) no federal system, and 6) no privatization. In July, at the celebration of the 90th anniversary of CCP's founding, Jiang Zemin did not appear, leading to speculation that he had already died. When he did attend the October 10 meeting to commemorate the centennial of the Republican Revolution, Jiang appeared to be frail and weak, creating more uncertainty about behind-the-curtain power arrangements. Meanwhile, the economy was slowing down, the relationship with the United States was on a downward slide because of Washington's pivot to Asia, and decision-making at all levels of the party-state began to slow down in anticipation of the power transition that would take place in the fall of 2012.

At this time of gathering challenges, the CCP needed a smooth 18th Congress to maintain its leadership, political stability, and unity. The usual controls on the official media were in place, and, as usual, the Chinese people themselves had no say in who would be named to leadership posts. But two other things had changed. The international press focus on the upcoming leadership changes would be more intense than ever, and social media inside China had become a new, more potent vehicle for politically helpless citizens to make comments and spread "secrets" about China's byzantine politics. Still, at the beginning of 2012, there was no sign that the power transfer could suffer a meltdown that was unprecedented in the history of CCP.

A series of events changed all that:

On February 6, Wang Lijun, the deputy mayor of Chongqing who had just lost his position as police chief of the city, walked into the U.S. Consulate General in Chengdu and requested political asylum. This shocking incident eventually led to Bo Xilai's dismissal from all leadership positions, his expulsion from the CCP, and his wife's conviction of murdering a British businessman.

On March 18, a Ferrari crashed near the North Fourth Ring Road in Beijing with the driver killed on the spot and two half-naked women severely injured. The driver turned out to be the son of Ling Jihua, who was Hu Jintao's chief of staff and widely expected to be elevated to the Politburo at the 18th Congress. Despite his efforts at cover-up, the facts were "leaked" and shocked Party officials. A few retired Party leaders led by Jiang Zemin intervened, and Ling was transferred to the United Front Work Department.

On June 29, New York-based Bloomberg news service stepped into unchartered political waters in China by reporting on the family wealth of Xi Jinping. According to public documents compiled by Bloomberg, as Xi climbed the Communist Party ranks, his extended family expanded their business interests to include minerals, real estate and mobile phone equipment. Those interests involved investments in companies with total assets of $376 million. They included an 18% indirect stake in a rare earths company with $1.73 billion in assets and a $20.2 million holding in a publicly traded technology company. The report said, "The figures don't account for liabilities, and thus don't reflect the family's net worth."

All eyes were on Xi Jinping and there was speculation that this "foreign intervention" might derail his ascension to the top. But Xi continued to appear in public and behaved like a man ready to take the reins in October. Then in early September, Xi suddenly disappeared. His scheduled meeting with United States Secretary of State Hillary Clinton on September 3 was canceled, and a Chinese Foreign Ministry official told upset American officials that Xi had sustained shoulder injuries. Xi also missed the scheduled meeting with the Danish prime minister on September 10, and no official explanation was given. This set off furious speculation on the Internet that either the physical or political health of the 59-year-old Xi was failing. A Chinese language website hosted in North America even put out an unverified report that there was an assassination attempt on Xi, and that He Guoqiang, a fellow member of the Politburo Standing Committee, also was wounded in a separate incident. The Chinese government kept silent until Xi resurfaced without prior announcement on September 20 when he visited China Agricultural University.

Another bombshell dropped on October 30, 10 days before the 18th Congress was to open in Beijing. The New York Times reported that many relatives of Wen Jiabao, including his mother, son, daughter, younger brother, and brother-in-law, had become extraordinarily wealthy during his tenure in office. A review of corporate and regulatory records indicated that the prime minister's relatives — some of whom, including his wife, had a knack for aggressive deal-making — controlled assets worth at least $2.7 billion. Both the English and Chinese versions of the Times website were shut down in China hours after the report came out. The Chinese Foreign Ministry spokesperson declared that the report was false. Two U.S.-trained lawyers threatened to sue the paper. Overseas Chinese websites began to publish accounts that Wen's family was clean. However, there was no official rebuttal from Wen himself.

The CCP nevertheless muddled through, and the 18th Congress opened and closed without any glitches. On November 15, the new members of the 18th Central Committee met and "elected" the Politburo and Standing Committee. To the surprise of many, neither Li Yuanchao, former Minister of Organization, nor Wang Yang, Party Secretary of Guangdong Province, was placed in the Standing Committee. Both are known to be reform-oriented, and their failure to move into the top tier is indicative of the conservative nature of the new leadership. With the exception of Xi Jinping and Li Keqiang, the other five members of the Standing Committee — Zhang Dejiang (NPC), Yu Zhensheng (Chinese Political Consultative Conference), Liu Yunshan (Secretariat), Wang Qishan (Central Discipline Commission) and Zhang Gaoli (State Council) — all appeared to be handpicked by Jiang Zemin or his allies. A bigger surprise of the first plenary session of the 18th Congress was that Hu Jintao relinquished his chairmanship of the Central Military Commission, and then Xi was "elected" to succeed him. Both Hu Chunhua (who will replace Wang Yang in Guangdong) and Sun Zhengcai (who already became the Party secretary of Chongqing) moved to the Politburo. Barring any unforeseen developments, in a decade, Hu and Sun will become China's top two leaders.

Political writings on the wall

Looking back at the rocky road to the 18th Party Congress, we offer some tentative observations on CCP politics in action. It is worth noting that this is just the second time in CCP history that a power transfer was peaceful and predictable. Despite fierce power struggle and factional rivalry, no attempt was made to challenge the pre-agreed setup that involved Xi becoming CCP general secretary and Li Keqiang being named premier. The next generation of the top leaders is also in the pipeline. It is unclear whether this so-called method of top leader chosen by the retiring leaders once removed (i.e. Hu Jintao chosen by Deng

Xiaoping, Xi Jingping by Jiang Zemin, and Hu Chunhua by Hu Jintao) can be sustained. The best that can be said is that without real intra-Party competition for the top leadership, the current arrangement is a step-forward.

It also is worth nothing that the unseemly convention of geriatric politics continues inside the CCP. Jiang Zemin demonstrated great influence in determining who was elevated to the Standing Committee. Li Peng was probably instrumental in eliminating reformer Li Yuanchao from the race to the top. Other retired leaders might have played roles in removing Ling Jihua, whose son was killed in the Ferrari crash, from contention for the Politburo. Li Changchun could have been the crucial factor in getting Liu Yunshan into the Standing Committee.

That said, the era of political domination by elderly, retired leaders may slowly be coming to an end. Hu Jintao's inability to hang onto the Military Commission chairmanship signaled a repudiation of Jiang Zemin's ability to exercise power once the Congress had finished its work. Just a day after Xi Jinping replaced Jiang as the chairman of the military commission, he praised Hu Jintao as a person of high integrity and moral standards. This is tantamount to criticizing Jiang in a very serious manner because he insisted on retaining the military commission chairmanship when he stepped aside as president and Party general secretary. Despite Hu's inactivity on the political reform front, many hailed his last act — stepping down from the military commission — as the most memorable of his entire political career.

The jockeying for power at the top in the months before the Congress highlights the reality that the CCP is rife with factional disputes and conflicts of interests. The fact that five of seven members of the Standing Committee will have to retire in 2017 is evidence that the final lineup was the result of compromise and concession. Just like any other political party, the CCP has to face the reality of political dissent and allow intra-party competition. Power-sharing and consensus-building through negotiation is the first step toward intra-Party democracy. It is safe to say that the day may come when factional fights within the CCP become a zero-sum game and can no longer be contained, resulting in a break into two or more political parties. Democracy could come to China, not through social movements but by virtue of top-down politics.

The days of non-interference in Chinese politics by foreign countries are gone now. The size of China's economy and its international influence do not permit non-intervention. Second, the increasing tendency by CCP factions to leak sensitive information to further their quests for power and to undercut their rivals has enabled both mainstream Western media outlets and online Chinese-language entities to publish reports that are not available inside China. As a result, Western media and think tanks have fully engaged the Chinese political process, despite the utter opacity and secrecy of the inner workings of the Party. Western reporting and analyses play a role in the final outcome of Chinese politics. I n addition, the growing popularity of weibo in China has magnified the impact of these information channels. On the one hand, the dynamics of Chinese politics has changed because of rapid and omnipotent distribution of information that has put secret holders on the defense. On the other hand, it has created new ways for Chinese citizens to engage in Party politics in a way that was never available to them before.

Popular indifference inside China to official propaganda about the Congress coupled with intense interest in elections abroad also could be impetuses for political change in China. Organized efforts by the CCP to promote the spirit of the 18th Party Congress through publicity tours nationwide have remained a Party affair outside the life of ordinary Chinese citizens. In contrast, many Chinese people, including media outlets, spent a good deal of time reading, watching and thinking about power transfer through elections in countries such as Mexico, France, and the United States. These elections were fascinating and reminded the Chinese people what was lacking in their homeland.

The future of political reform

The need for movement on political reform is clear. For the CCP not to chart a new course in the wake of the Arab Spring, the Bo Xilai and Ling Jihua scandals, and the revelations of obscene amounts of wealth accumulated by the families of the top leader would be shocking to many reform-oriented scholars and political observers. Hu Wei, dean of the School of International Affairs and Public Administration, Shanghai Jiaotong University said China is facing a "three-D" crisis: social decay, social disorder and social divide. Only one "D"— democracy — could overcome the three-D corrosion. Historian Zhang Lifan wrote, if we do not see reform in five years we will see collapse in ten years. Sun Liping, professor of sociology at the Tsinghua University, recently told a gathering of both Chinese and foreign financial workers, "A silent revolution is taking place in China. The biggest force against reform in China is those who do not want to go back nor desire to move forward but to maintain the status quo. Reform and China will be like Taiwan. Without reform, China will be like the Qing dynasty." Li Weidong, former publisher of the China Reform Magazine, said in a "Tweet" that the entire nation is daydreaming now and one of the new dreams is the so-called "three self-confidences." (In his political report, Hu Jintao talked of the CCP's unswerving endeavor to build socialism with Chinese characteristics and urged the Party to have self-confidence in roads chosen, theories adopted, and institutions established.) Li declared, "Not only is this a pipe dream, it may soon engulf China in a nightmare." The most popular weibo nowadays is this: "Introducing reform means seeking death and not introducing reform means waiting to die."

Where does Xi Jinping stand amid hope and frustration, expectation and anger? During his November 15 press appearance, Xi delivered a powerful pledge. He focused his messages on the nation, the people, and the Party. He spoke of the collective but not the individual; he advocated responsibilities but not rights; he called the Party to serve the people and change its work style, but there was little about institutionalizing accountability and transparency. He identified four cardinal problems the Party is facing: corruption, condescending, formalism, and bureaucracy. He said that unless the Party overcomes these challenges, it will not be able to lead the nation in building socialism with Chinese characteristics.

In 2002, shortly after the 16th Party Congress, Hu Jintao took all members of the Standing Committee of the Politburo to Xibaipo in Hebei Province, where Mao and his comrades lived and worked before marching to Beijing and establishing the People's Republic. Hu vowed that the new leadership would call on all Party members to overcome arrogance, maintain integrity, and serve the people well. On November 29, Xi took "the magnificent seven" to the National Museum to see "The Road to Rejuvenation," a Party history exhibition. He repeated everything he mentioned or alluded to in his November 15 speech. He talked about the destiny of the nation and the China Dream. He used three lines from the poems of Mao Zedong and ancient poet Li Bai to highlight China's humiliating past, its glorious opening up and reform, and its bright future. Again, the focus was on a mysterious and historical Chinese collective.

To follow up his two speeches, on December 4, Xi convened a Politburo meeting that adopted a resolution to improve the work style and deepen the ties between the CCP and broad masses. Included were measures to cut Party circulars; reduce domestic inspection trips and foreign visits; prevent the blocking of roads when top leaders travel; eliminate profuse media reports; cut national meetings to only those absolutely necessary; stop publication of speeches; end the practice of traveling the country and writing inscriptions that become memorialized; and stop unnecessary meetings, ceremonies, and groundbreakings. Also in December, Xi made a trip to Guangdong. In Shenzhen, he placed a wreath in front of Deng Xiaoping's statue and vowed not to deviate from the road of reform and opening up, a policy that was put in place by Deng Xiaoping in late 1978.

Xi's performance in the wake of the Congress is impressive, and has made it very clear to both the Chinese people and the outside world that he has no intention to deviate from the road chosen by Deng Xiaoping and his cohorts 34 years ago. What is a bit disappointing is that he has not delineated a clear vision on the issue of political reform. In his political report to the Congress, Hu Jintao solemnly declared that China will not take the old road of xenophobia and lack of innovation, nor will it take the deviant road of implementing any reform that weakens the Party's supremacy. There is no sign at this point that Xi Jinping will break away from this pledge.

However, people still remember what Xi Jinping said in a speech at the Central Party School in 2010: "The Marxist view of power can be summarized in two sentences: 'power comes from the people' and 'power has to be used for the people.' The first sentence highlights the source and foundation of power, and the second informs us of the essence and destiny of the power. The sole mission of the CCP is to serve the people heart and soul. This is the difference between the Marxist view of power and capitalist view of power." The interpretation of this statement is that Xi may move forward with political reform, installing procedures through which the governed will offer their consent to the governing party. Even though Xi has great power because he is fully in charge of the Party and the military, he has not made any reference to his earlier statement that has inspired many in China.

Some suggest waiting for the Third Plenary Session of the 18th Party Congress to see whether the Xi-Li Administration is serious about introducing meaningful political reform. It was during the Third Plenary Session of the 11th Party Congress in December 1978 when Deng Xiaoping finally was able to marshal his political capital and move the Party from the narrow road of rigid ideology to the highway of pragmatic economic growth.

China's growth dividends will expire soon. When they do, the CCP's legitimacy will face daunting challenges and fierce questioning. The extent of corruption, the loss of trust, the increasing unemployment of the young and educated, and the opacity of decision-making may all become the trigger of a Chinese Spring. Will China muddle through and sustain its economic growth without making significant social and political changes? If it does, the model touted in Beijing of sustained economic development and authoritarianism will get a boost and pose a serious challenge to the conventional wisdom that political accountability is necessary for long-term, economic prosperity and social harmony. If not, the entire world will watch as turmoil engulfs China and very possibly shakes up the global power balance and ushers in a period of instability.

Yawei Liu, Ph.D., is Director of the China Program at The Carter Center, Atlanta, Georgia.

China's Push for Urbanization and Its Accompanying Challenges

Qiulin Chen and Li Qi
Vol.12, No.1
2013

Urbanization has been the new buzzword in China ever since the opening of the 18th National Congress of the Communist Party of China (NCCPC) in November 2012. Former President Hu Jintao's report outlined the tremendous growth in China since economic reforms started more than 30 years ago. For example, China now has the second-largest economy in the world. In 2012 its per capita GDP reached USD$6,100.[1]

However, this rapid economic growth has also produced an array of social and economic problems. One of the most serious and acute is the gap between rural and urban development. This gap is reflected not only in personal income. The ratio between urban and rural per capita GDP has risen from 1.85 to 1 at the beginning of the reforms to 3.1 to 1 by 2012 (see Figure 1). The gap is also reflected in the inequity of public services and government-offered benefits such as education, health care, and social security. These

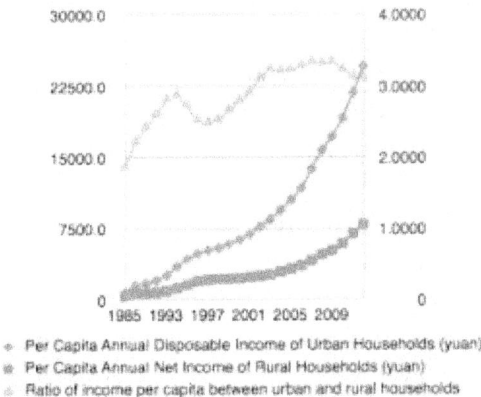

Figure 1. Rural and Urban Income Gap in China
Source: China Statistical Yearbook 2012; Statistical Communique on the 2012 National Economic and Social Development.

inequalities have negatively influenced household consumption.[2] Even though more rural residents migrated to cities for higher-paying jobs, this vast population of migrant workers still has significant barriers in accessing urban public services, which do not typically accommodate rural workers without the official urban "hukou" (city residence permit).

The 18th NCCPC recognized the importance of improving the livelihood of all Chinese people and adopted urbanization as its main strategy for achieving this goal. Urbanization was not a new term for the NCCPC. However, in the past it mainly referred to a means to coordinate and balance regional developments. The new report of the 18th NCCPC reframed urbanization and emphasized the term – together with industrialization and agricultural modernization – as key factors for adjusting China's economic structure and developmental model. This initiative stirred both optimistic support as well as strong opposition.

Proponents[3] believe urbanization will do the following:

1) Transfer surplus rural labor to the cities. China faces an aging population and potentially a less-than-adequate labor supply for future economic growth. As Meng notes, since the late 1970s the government has included rural-to-urban migration in its set of tools to combat high rural unemployment.[4] Currently about half of China's population lives in urban areas,[5] though not all of this population actually has official permission to live there. Both of these numbers are far below those of developed countries. More urbanization will thus transfer rural surplus labor to urban areas, providing a supply for labor-intensive industries.

2) Increase consumption and investment. Urbanization will promote the construction of basic infrastructure, such as housing and public facilities, thus supporting demand-driven growth while lowering China's reliance on exports. A recent report by the Academy of Macroeconomic Research of the National Development and Reform Commission shows that each new urban resident will lead to an average increase of 100,000 Yuan (about USD$16,200) in government investment for public facilities, including water, electricity, roads, housing, heating, health care, education, employment, and social security. Similarly, each rural resident is expected to bring an increase of 10,000 Yuan (about USD$1,600) per year in consumption in the urbanization process.[6]

3) Promote economic structural adjustment. Urbanization, and the accompanying higher population densities, will accelerate the process of transitioning from a secondary-industry-based economy to one that relies more on tertiary (service) one, increasing the industry's part in the national GDP. In addition, an increasingly well-educated population will promote the development of new technologies, benefiting manufacturing.

These enthusiastic views are challenged by skeptics, who voice the following concerns:

1) Many people believe this process will most certainly damage the interests of rural farmers, both those who choose to stay in the countryside and those who choose to venture into the cities.[7] For those who choose to stay, the challenge shall lie in the new waves of urban construction, which will occupy a great deal of rural land and reduce the space available for farmers and agriculture.[8] For those who choose to migrate to the cities, the challenge is finding employment, housing, and educational opportunities for their children, while trying to secure social security benefits. In addition, most current migrant workers are not enrolled in urban medical insurance, unemployment insurance, or workers' injury insurance (ibid).

2) There is a real possibility of over-investment. Many local governments are rushing to start new construction and other development projects in hopes of stimulating rapid economic growth. Recent National Bureau of Statistics (NBS) data shows that in January and February 2013, investment in real estate reached 667 billion Yuan (USD$106 billion), a 22.8 percent increase compared to the same period last year (2013). Some are concerned that this investment-driven growth is a high-risk strategy that can form a dangerous circle of investment-debt-credit growth.

3) Local government-led urbanization tends to not be very efficient. The use of large areas of land will no doubt lead to larger cities. But if resources are not used prudently, many worry that the rush to build bigger towns will simply result in operational inefficiencies that will produce more traffic jams and air pollution, which does not benefit anyone.

Generally speaking, the biggest concern for urbanization is the potential waste of investments and resources as local governments rush to build new cities but fail to truly improve the living standards of rural migrants. People fear that urbanization is a mere relocation of farmers to urban areas, without enough planning and policy consideration for the lives of these new migrants.

Premier Li Keqiang outlined the principles of this new urbanization strategy with Chinese characteristics in an opinion he wrote in the China Daily (2012). He pointed out that China used to focus on urbanizing the land by simply taking it and using it to geographically expand the cities. But now China needs to focus on urbanizing the people. This new round of urbanization aims to create more urban employment opportunities and provide public services to all new and existing urban residents, through the following:

1) Combine urbanization with industrialization to provide stable employment for new migrants.

2) Combine urbanization with modernization of agriculture to improve the

efficiencies of economies of scale so that rural residents who stay behind can also increase their income.

3) Provide equal public services and benefits to both rural and urban residents. Ultimately Chinese people should enjoy the same level of government-offered benefits whether they live in rural or urban areas. The Chinese government has set 2020 as the target year to realize equality of basic public services including education, social security, employment, health care, and housing. The 12th Five-Year Plan of China outlined a fiscal investment plan to reach this goal, especially the plan to invest more in western provinces and poor areas. In fact, China has already increased its fiscal support to these regions with an annual growth rate of 26.3 percent.[9] Such momentum is expected to continue as China bridges the gap between rich and poor areas.

Premier Li's suggestions addressed the major concerns about the new urbanization strategy. However, it is undeniable that this new initiative still faces significant challenges, especially the anticipated huge fiscal expenditure.

Equalization of public services is not the only factor straining the government's budget. The aging population in China is estimated to require double the current fiscal expenditure on social security and to increase health care expenses by 50 percent by 2030.[10] With concurrent plans to increase expenditures for public services, China's fiscal pressure will no doubt escalate.

Furthermore, these big increases in fiscal burdens coincide with a rapid decrease in fiscal income due to both internal and external factors. It is not likely that China can maintain the high fiscal income growth of previous years under such pressures. Figure 2 shows that the growth of fiscal income has experienced sharp drops.

China is now entering a new era of economic modernization in which Beijing is shifting its focus from mere rapid income growth to equality and social justice. The road to urbanization will not be smooth, but the un-

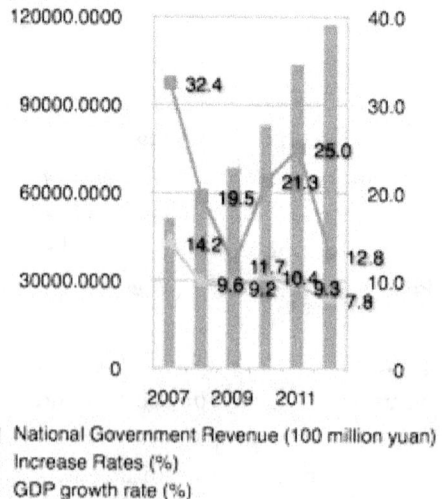

Figure 2: China's GDP and Fiscal Income Growth Source: China Statistical Yearbook 2012; Statistical Communique on the 2012 National Economic and Social Development.

derlying transition of structural change and social adjustment is a crucial step that all modern economies must take.

Notes

¹ *National Bureau of Statistics 2012*
² *Qi and Prime 2009*
³ *e.g., Li, 2013; Zhang, 2013; Yang, 2013*
⁴ *2012, p. 76*
⁵ *Bloomberg, 2012*
⁶ *Huo, 2013*
⁷ *Banyuetan, 2013*
⁸ *Chen, Liu, & Tao 2013, p. 32*
⁹ *Zhang, 2012*
¹⁰ *World Bank 2012*

References

Banyuetan 2013, "专家吁防城镇化快而不优 拆除农民市民化政策屏障", Banyuetan 6 January. Available from: <http://www.bloomberg.com/news/2012-01-17/china-urban-population-exceeds-rural.html> [8 June 2013].

Chen, M; Liu W; Tao, X 2013, "Evolution and assessment on China's urbanization 1960–2010: Under-urbanization or over-urbanization?", Habitat International, vol. 38, pp.25–33. Available from: ScienceDirect [8 June 2013].

Li, K 2013, "Releasing Growth Potential", China Daily 20 February. Available from: <http://www.chinadaily.com.cn/opinion/2012-02/20/content_14643432.htm>. [9 June 2013]

Li, Y 2013, "城镇化既是发展转型又是体制转型", Nanfang Daily 4 March. Available from: <http://news.xinhuanet.com/fortune/2013-03/04/c_124411984.htm>. [9 June 2013].

Huo, K 2013, "马晓河：城镇化与经济新动力", Caixin Online 8 January. Available from: <http://special.caixin.com/2013-01-08/100480516.html>. [9 June 2013].

Meng, X 2012, "Labor Market Outcomes and Reforms in China", Journal of Economic Perspectives, vol. 26, Number 4, pp.75–102. Available from: KSU SuperSearch [8 June 2013].

National Bureau of Statistics, 2012, Statistical Communique on the 2012 National Economic and Social Development, China Statistics Press, Beijing

National Bureau of Statistics, 2013, National Real Estate Development and Sales in the First Two Months of 2013, available at http://www.stats.gov.cn/english/pressrelease/t20130311_402878958.htm

Qi, L. and Penelope B. Prime, Market Reforms and Consumption Puzzles in China, China Economic Review, Vol. 20, pp. 338-401, Sep. 2009

World Bank, 2012, China 2030 Building a Modern, Harmonious, and Creative High-Income Society.

Yang, Y 2013, "城镇化绝对是方向 提升工资有点纠结", People's Daily 7 June. Available from: <http://tech.ifeng.com/it/detail_2013_06/07/26223913_0.shtml>. [9 June 2013].

Zhang, L 2013, "提高城镇化质量 释放中国发展潜力", People's Daily 29 May. Available from: <http://gx.people.com.cn/n/2013/0529/c352269-18761880.html>. [9 June 2013].

Zhang P 2012 "2007-2011年公共服务财政支出12.7万亿", The 18th National Congress of the Communist Party of China Press Center 10 November. Available from: <http://cpc.people.com.cn/n/2012/1110/c350000-19538713.html>. [9 June 2013]

Qiulin CHEN is Assistant Professor of Economics at the Institute of Population and Labor Economics of the Chinese Academy of Social Sciences in Beijing, China.

Li Qi is an associate professor of economics at Agnes Scott College.

Economy

The China Standards Engine

Michael Murphree
Vol. 12, No. 2
2013

China's accomplishments in economic modernization, urbanization, industrialization, and science and technology are legion. The question to which China watchers, as well as the Chinese state, have now turned is how will China spur and sustain its future economic development? Research and media reports have shown that the low-wage, capital-intensive, and export-oriented strategies using China as a final assembly platform are providing diminishing returns. Future growth will be both slower and more difficult. China must therefore find new engines for economic progress.

China's reckoning with its growth model has been long in coming. Indeed, the seeds of change in China have been visible since the mid-2000s. China's output of high technology goods for export, mostly IT hardware, has soared, growing consistently at more than 10% per year (NSBPRC 2001-2013). Despite these achievements, other high technology statistics suggest existing incentive policies and business strategies are yielding diminishing returns. To provide one example, in the decade beginning in 1994, China's share of high technology exports in its total export mix grew exponentially. Since 2005, however, this share has leveled off at roughly 30% of total exports.[1] The inability to continue to increase the share of high technology goods in the overall export mix means the low-hanging fruit of high technology industrial development has now been picked, but new means of driving rapid innovation have not yet been found.

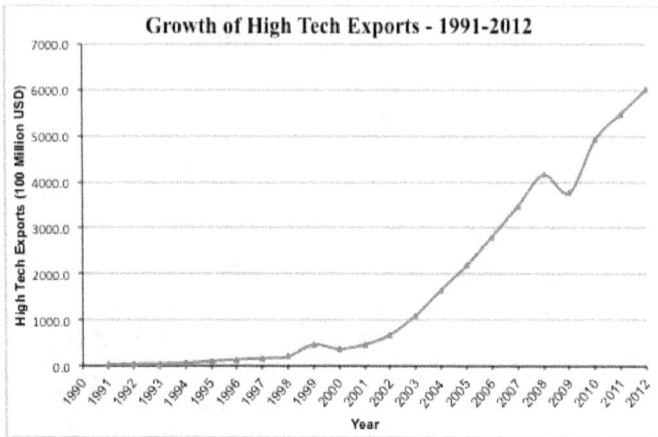

Figure I: Growth of High Technology Exports – 1991-2012 (Source: National Statistics Bureau of China)

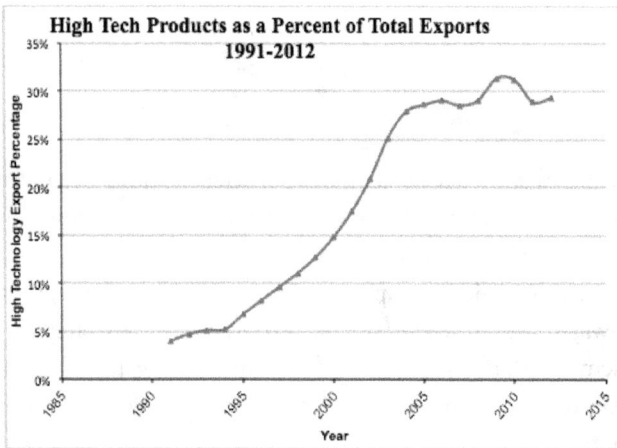

Figure II: High Tech Exports as a Percent of Total Exports – 1991-2012 (Source: National Statistics Bureau of China)

The universal prescription for resolving China's economic challenges is mastery of "innovation." However, the exact definition of innovation varies within the Chinese state and economy. Some adopt a Schumpeterian perspective and argue that innovation is the application of knowledge to improve the development, sale, or production of goods and services. Others take a harder approach, saying that innovation is synonymous with invention and that only the creation of wholly new and wholly Chinese-owned technologies will yield sustained competitive advantage and economic growth. These competing perspectives have influenced the raft of policies adopted by China's central, provincial and local governments to encourage technological upgrades by firms and greater technology independence.

Policies for Technology Upgrading and Innovation

Despite competing visions about the nature of innovation, the Chinese government at various levels has pushed incentive policies since the late 1980s and increasingly through the 1990s and 2000s intended to encourage firms to move up the value chain, become more innovative, and increase their investment in R&D. These promotional policies include major national plans such as the 15-year Medium-to-Long Range Plan for Science and Technology (MLP), the 863 and Torch programs, and the most recent Five Year Plans. Investment rules and joint-venture agreements in the 1990s and early 2000s often made the sharing or transfer of advanced foreign technology a prerequisite for investment permits. National incentive policies are complemented by a host of provincially and locally administered promotional policies such as R&D tax breaks, export promotion, duty-free imports of certain goods, and human resource policies granting legal residency (hukou) to new residents in different cities such as highly desirable Beijing and Shanghai.[2]

These policies appear to have been largely ineffective in encouraging Chinese firms to move "up" the value chain and become independently innovative. Many of the recipients of state incentives and investment have used the funds to expand productive capacity or diversify rather than make concerted efforts at R&D and technological upgrading. Requirements to transfer technology have not resulted in transfers of the most advanced technology and foreign firms remain reticent to move their most advanced production or research activities to their Chinese subsidiaries or partners. Seeing the limited efficacy of these long-running programs, the government has more recently pushed for an alternative innovation strategy: development of technology standards.

Since the early 2000s, China's central government – most notably the ministries of Industry and Information Technology (MIIT) and Science and Technology (MoST) – has actively pushed the development of technology standards in order to upgrade and increase profitability of Chinese firms[3]. Often couched in the language of "technology independence," the broad goal of the standardization policy is to enable Chinese firms to produce goods with global demand and markets without having to pay licensing fees to foreign IP holders. Apart from this goal, pursuing the development of unique standards also has the potential to upgrade China's overall innovation capacity as standardization requires sophisticated R&D, technology transfer and management capabilities – all skills China needs as it seeks to upgrade its economy.

To accomplish this, Chinese firms are developing alternative or wholly new technology standards-essential patents, often licensed at free or nominal rates.

Preliminary research suggests that driving down the costs of intellectual property through this method, just as China has driven down the costs for other inputs, will make Chinese-manufactured goods even more competitive. Increased profitability for Chinese manufacturers should also provide resources for further investment in new technologies, enabling China to produce ever better and cheaper high technology goods for domestic consumption and export.

Concerning Technology Standards

Technology standards are agreed upon protocols that enable goods and services, regardless of supplier or country of origin, to work together. To illustrate, the Universal Serial Bus (USB) enables computers and peripheral hardware to work together regardless of operating system, computer brand or peripheral manufacturer. This facilitates consumer choice, enhances competition, and – according to many scholars – provides a platform for faster innovation. Without common standards, markets are fragmented, consumer choice is constrained, and the pace of innovation arguably is slowed down.

Standards are developed through either formal or market processes. Formal standardization is bureaucratically managed through established national, regional, or international standardization bodies such as the China Electronics Standardization Institute (CESI), the European Telecommunications Standards Institute or the International Electrotechnical Commission. In formal standardization, specific protocols for a standard are developed in working groups composed of experts in the technology or industry in question. Working group members debate proposals and competing technologies before sending their recommendations to technical committees under the formal organization for more debate, comment and adoption – usually by consensus. In formal standards, intellectual property holders declare potentially relevant IP and the terms under which they are willing to license the technology. Most frequently, incorporated technologies are licensed on the Reasonable and Non-Discriminatory (RAND) principle: firms agree to charge reasonable licensing rates and not restrict which firms or countries may license their technology in order to produce standards-compliant goods.

Market standards are produced by single firms or ad hoc industry consortia. These are not formally adopted by standardization bodies and become "standards" through their dominance of the market for their respective goods or services. The IBM PC became the standard for personal computers after achieving "critical mass" in the market for computers in 1984. Thereafter, computer firms either conformed to the IBM standard or else were relegated to niche status (as in Apple). China is using both the formal and market approaches to set new standards. Given the nature of China's standardization system, however, even market approaches often include significant state support and influence.

Technology Standardization in China: Justification and Challenges

How can standardization benefit Chinese firms? Standards represent the means of completely changing China's position in global production networks. Currently, Chinese firms generally operate at the lowest value-added level in many industries, particularly IT hardware. Chinese firms tend to specialize in the final assembly of imported high-value components or in the production of low-value commodity components such as plastic or metal cases. Indeed, the low value-added by Chinese manufacturers in such prize exports as Apple iPhones has been long recorded and reported in the media.[4] While many IT hardware components are increasingly produced in China – notably in Dongguan and Shenzhen – the highest value components – logic chips, digital signal processing chips, and software – are designed and manufactured overseas and imported by Chinese assemblers. Chinese firms have come to specialize in the integration of components from a highly disparate production chain consisting of hundreds of supplier firms. This is not to downplay the accomplishment or innovation characteristics of contract manufacturers and assemblers. Their skills and upgrading capabilities remain among the best in the world – making it difficult to find partners as capable when foreign firms show interest in diversifying away from Chinese manufacturing.[5] Nonetheless, the overall contribution of China to the wholesale price of products is usually only a few percentage points.

Stan Shih of Taiwan's Acer Computer once described the difficulty facing firms that specialize in final assembly. He argued that the profits that accrue to different firms in a production chain form a "smiling curve" where the definers of product architecture and after-sales service or branding firms reap the highest profits. Assemblers and contract manufacturers are at the bottom of the "smile." Shih argued that firms had to move away from low value-added manufacturing in order to survive. In China today, many companies find themselves at the bottom of the "smile."

In electronics and information technology hardware, however, moving up from this low value-added position is difficult as the technologies being produced are subject to established and clearly defined technology standards. Having not contributed to the development of the standards currently in force in many sectors, Chinese firms are "standards takers." In order to compete in these technology sectors, Chinese firms must accept internationally determined standards for various products and produce goods according to the terms of the standard. Producing goods such as mobile phones requires manufacturers to pay licensing fees for the raft of patents that establish transmission standards for the phone (such as CDMA). These license payments reduce the already low profits for Chinese manufacturers. Finally, standards define the basic features of large categories of products, leaving little room for innovation or improvements as the protocols of the most basic level have already been defined.

Were China to successfully develop new technology standards and have them adopted internationally, this situation could change. Chinese firms would be able to earn royalties and potentially limit the access of competitors to key essential technologies (as Motorola did with its restrictive licensing of patents for the GSM mobile telephony standard). China would thus be able to control the structure of an industry by determining which firms are allowed to participate. Chinese manufacturers would also owe less in licensing fees. Firms and research institutions would gain valuable experience conducting collaborative in-depth and sustained research toward a common industrial goal.

Since the mid-1990s, China's research institutions and firms have developed dozens of unique information technology standards. Despite their promise, none has been internationally successful.[6] China's standardization system continues to face several problems:

Lack of coordination: While many Western observers continue to view China through the lens of a centrally coordinated "China Inc," there is significant complexity and lack of coordination. While the Ministry of Industry and Information Technology and the Ministry of Science and Technology remain the most active government ministries in standardization, and formal national standards remain the sole responsibility of the Standardization Administration of China, recent standards efforts have been fragmented. In electric vehicles, for example, different cities have established their own regional standards for charging stations, thus making equipment from different regions incompatible. Standards created by organizations under one government ministry – such as MIIT – may face challenges from standards created by groups under other bodies. At the same time, industry has become increasingly active in standardization and frequently seeks to adopt international standards rather than push for unique Chinese standards that are unlikely to be adopted internationally. These conflicting interests and proposals make for a confused standardization environment. A common result is that many firms in China take a "wait and see" attitude toward standardization, preferring to let the situation resolve itself rather than getting actively involved.

Lack of core innovation: Technology standards codify the state of the art in technology at a given point in time. They ideally embody the most sophisticated, basic and essential technologies necessary for a given system to work as a platform for other products and services. To create technology standards, a country or firm needs to have strong core innovation capabilities. To date, many of China's leading indigenous standards efforts have relied heavily on foreign core technology. Using foreign technology is a pragmatic means of addressing weaknesses in China's innovation system as well as enabling new standards to be released quickly. However, use of core foreign technology undermines the potential benefits of lower licensing fees since expensive foreign technology remains at the core of the standard.

Strong role for government in standards: like all areas of the Chinese economy and society, there is a major role for the state in the standardization process. This role is mandated through the 1989 Standardization Law of China, which gives the state sole responsibility for setting the agenda and legitimizing standardization efforts. On the one hand, the state is able to marshal resources and direct industry to invest in standards development, perhaps where it hitherto had been disinclined. On the other, the state has historically been such a strong force in the economy that many firms are hesitant to standardize without first receiving a direct order or clear signal from the state that a new standard is desired. This makes the state responsible for initiating standardization, a difficult process to master, as it requires intimate familiarity with technology and technology trends in order to start processes when opportunity presents itself. State leadership in standards is generally considered inferior to industry leadership,[7] yet it remains the norm in China.

Potential Benefit from Technology Standardization

Despite these challenges, China's approach to standardization has yielded benefits for Chinese firms and may become internationally influential. Unlike American and European firms, which emphasize the monetization of intellectual property as a core business strategy, Chinese firms generally see intellectual property as a means to improving the value of manufactured goods and not primarily as an opportunity for monetization. For technology standards, this is highly significant. In most internationally accepted standards today, there are thousands of "standard essential patents" (SEP). U.S. and European firms frequently seek to maximize their returns from SEPs by setting "reasonable" licensing fees as high as possible. Alternately, firms with major SEP patent portfolios enter technology-sharing agreements with other major contributors, lowering mutual licensing rates. Chinese firms have to date contributed relatively little to major international standards (the contributions of Huawei and ZTE to 4G LTE are an important exception) and thus must license technologies to produce standards-compliant goods while also being excluded from technology-sharing agreements.

In China's indigenously developed technology standards, there is a movement toward the demonetization of intellectual property. In the Chinese model, intellectual property is just another factor input in the production of goods and services. Like all components and resources, it is in the interest of firms to reduce the costs of this input. For indigenous standards, Chinese firms increasingly have made the intellectual property they contribute available at extremely low rates. Ideally, Chinese enterprises will license their standard essential patents on a free or nominal price basis. For Chinese firms interested in selling more goods, offering intellectual property for free is a means of helping to widely disseminate their technology while keeping costs low and thus encouraging adoption of their products. China's standards-making bodies have begun establishing patent pools for core standards-essential patents that will make one-stop licenses available at a nominal basis.

In Chinese standards for home networking (IGRS) and audio-video encoding (AVS), the standardization consortia have set low or nominal rates for technologies licenses. Firms seeking to produce compliant goods thus reduce their production costs, increasing profitability while maintaining low final consumer costs. China's Electronics Standardization Institute (CESI) has begun discussing how to make low-cost patent pools standard procedure.

While it remains to be seen whether this approach will successfully change global approaches to intellectual property and its economic value, China's inexpensive IP model has already had some successes in forcing foreign holders of standards-essential IP to lower their licensing fees.[8] In several cases, low-priced Chinese standards have been created and adopted by China's standardization authorities. Shortly thereafter, the licensing rates charged by foreign IP holders to Chinese manufacturers have decreased. This occurred for DVD, Blu-ray, MPEG and 3G mobile. While China may not yet change the world's perspective on IP, its economic and industrial power is already sufficient to force the rest of the world to pay attention to China's moves in this area and perhaps act to preempt them. Again, this lowers the costs for Chinese manufacturers, making them more profitable and able to further drive down global costs for desired technologies.

Concluding Thoughts

China faces real challenges to its economic development model as it seeks to upgrade its technological capabilities and find new sources of sustained competitive advantage. The Chinese leadership has targeted development of technology standards as a means of improving the competitive position of Chinese firms and developing all-around technology innovation capabilities. Many of the standardization efforts to date have been unsuccessful, as they remain underutilized – or even wholly ignored – within Chinese or global markets. At the same time, China has realized two important benefits from its standardization activities. First, China may be changing the global perspective on intellectual property. Just as China's scale and incremental innovation capabilities have redefined global manufacturing and sourcing of goods, China may also be able to significantly lower the cost of intellectual property for manufacturers. It may do so either through creation of low-priced alternative technologies or through pressuring foreign IP holders to lower the licensing fees for standards-essential patents. In either case, China's firms improve their profitability while also remaining focused on their core capabilities in manufacturing. It is likely that China will continue its development of technology standards, meaning we should anticipate even great price and normative influence from China in the coming years.

Notes

1 *MoST 2012, NSBPRC 2001-2013*
2 *see, for example: Breznitz and Murphree 2011*
3 *Wang et al 2009, Linden 2004, Kennedy et al 2008, Suttmeier and Su 2004*
4 *Batson 2010*
5 *Zhang et al 2013, Yao 2012*
6 *Kennedy et al 2008, Kennedy 2006, Breznitz and Murphree 2013*
7 *Funk and Methe 2001*
8 *Breznitz and Murphree 2013*

References

Batson, Andrew. "Not Really 'Made in China'." *The Wall Street Journal* (2010). Web. November 8, 2013.

Breznitz, Dan, and Michael Murphree. *Run of the Red Queen: Government, Innovation, Globalization, and Economic Growth in China.* New Haven, CN: Yale University Press, 2011.

Breznitz, Dan, and Michael Murphree. *The Rise of China in Technology Standards: New Norms in Old Institutions.* Washington, DC: US-China Economic and Security Review Commission, 2013.

Funk, Jeffrey L., and David T. Methe. "Market- and Community-Based Mechanisms in the Creation and Diffusion of Global Industry Standards: The Case of Mobile Communication." *Research Policy* 30.4 (2001): 589-610.

Kennedy, Scott. "Between Bureaucrats and Markets: China's Frustrating Involvement in Standards Wars." *Annual Meeting of the Midwest Political Science Association.* 2006.

Kennedy, Scott, Richard P. Suttmeier, and Jun Su. *Standards, Stakeholders, and Innovation.* Seattle, WA: National Bureau of Asian Research, 2008.

Linden, Greg. "China Standard Time: A Study in Strategic Industrial Policy." *Business and Politics* 6.3 (2004).

MOST. "2011 Nian Woguo Gaojishuchanpin Guoji Maoyi Zhuangkuang Fenxi." Ed. Technology, Ministry of Science and. Beijing: STS.org.cn, 2012.

NSBPRC. "2000-2012 Nian Guo Min Jing Ji He She Hui Fa Zhan Tong Ji Gong Bao (2000-2012 Citizens' Economic and Social Development Statistics Reports) (in Chinese)." Beijing: National Statistics Bureau of China, 2001-2013.

Suttmeier, Richard P., and Xiangkui Yao. *China's Post-WTO Technology Policy: Standards, Software, and the Changing Nature of Techno-Nationalism.* Seattle, WA: National Bureau of Asian Research, 2004.

Suttmeier, Richard P., Xiangkui Yao, and Alex Zixiang Tan. *Standards of Power? Technology, Institutions, and Politics in the Development of China's National Standards Strategy.* Seattle, WA: The National Bureau of Asian Research, 2006.

Wang, Ping, Yiyi Wang, and John Hill. "Zhongguo De Biaozhun Zhanlue – Chengjiu Yu Tiaozhan." CS09. National Bureau of Asian Research, 2009.

Yao, Kevin. "Analysis: Investors Make $100 Billion Bet on China's Drive up Value Chain." *Reuters* (2012). Web. November 8, 2013.

Zhang, Yajun, et al. "China Loses Edge as World's Factory Floor." *The Wall Street Journal* (2013). Web. November 8, 2013.

Michael Murphree earned his Ph.D. in international affairs at Georgia In-

stitute of Technology, Atlanta, Georgia.

Negotiating the Trans-Pacific Partnership: Possible Effects on the U.S.-China Relationship in Asia

Amitendu Palit
Vol.12, No.1,
2013

The Trans-Pacific Partnership (TPP) being currently negotiated by eleven economies from both sides of the Pacific is an exceptional trade agreement in its ambitious coverage of issues and the emphasis on new regulations.[1] However, the agreement could reorganize the regional trade architecture of the Asia-Pacific area by engineering a strategic economic division between the U.S. and China. This paper examines the U.S. and China contexts to argue that a division is not inevitable, but is increasingly likely.

'WTO Plus' and 'Behind-the-Border' Issues

The TPP is discussing not only 'WTO plus' issues, that is issues involving further scaling-up on commitments already made by countries at the WTO, but also 'WTO extra' subjects that are beyond the WTO's current mandate.[2] The 'WTO plus' matters being discussed include wider and deeper elimination of tariff barriers between negotiating members, removal of technical barriers to trade (TBT), deeper commitments in cross-border trade in services, framing new intellectual property (IP) rules and rules of origin for determining value addition, market access in textiles and apparel, and trade remedies for addressing rights and obligations of members. Environment and labor standards, government procurement, competition policy, customs laws, e-commerce, and financial services are the 'extra' issues. The TPP is also aiming to achieve regulatory convergence among members. The convergence is expected to facilitate seamless movement of goods and services among the members by minimizing obstructions created by differences in domestic regulations that are 'behind the border' factors adding to trade costs and affecting competitiveness of exporters and their market access prospects.

Proactive U.S. Role

The TPP's ambitious and expansive scope has much to do with the strong U.S. commitment to the framework. The commitment is being driven by several factors. The TPP provides the U.S. the template for a regional economic and trade framework that can be the benchmark for other future regional agreements involving the U.S. These agreements, like the TPP, can accommodate more 'WTO plus' issues, as in several U.S. PTAs, in line with the comparative advantages of the U.S. A TPP negotiated successfully on these lines will help the U.S. in digging a deeper foothold in the Asia-Pacific in areas of its specific comparative advantages, such as trade in digital and entertainment products, and contribute to revitalization of its domestic economy by increasing exports and creating new jobs. The TPP can also help the U.S. in increasing its economic presence in an Asia-Pacific that is heavily interconnected through a dense network of bilateral PTAs, most of which do not feature the U.S., and are dominated by ASEAN, China and Japan.

The Chinese Perspective and Counter-Response

Various implications of the agreement are also becoming critical for China. From a larger geostrategic perspective, the TPP can arguably be perceived as a U.S. effort to 'ring-fence' China. The perception stems from the negotiating members including U.S. political, military, and strategic allies such as Australia, Canada, Japan, Mexico, and Singapore. Vietnam's presence in the TPP is a further irritant for China. China's discomfort with the agreement is also due to its emphasis on the 'WTO plus' issues on which many of its views are radically different from the U.S. and other OECD economies. China's domestic regulations on IP and government procurement, for example, hardly come close to those likely to be adopted by the TPP.

These hostile impressions on the TPP in China coexist with alternate pragmatic views arguing that entering the TPP can be economically beneficial for China by blocking the potential diversion in trade and investment following the formation of the TPP. China's joining the TPP in the long run, however improbable it might appear now, is at least a hypothetical possibility given that the TPP is likely to have an open annexation clause allowing other APEC economies to join.

The TPP has provoked responses from the Asia-Pacific by activating parallel regional integration efforts. These efforts in the Asia-Pacific are typically distinguishable between Trans-Pacific efforts involving the U.S. and Asian efforts excluding the U.S. Both tracks have proceeded independently with the Asian track, or the Asia-centric approach to integration, aiming to combine regional economies through initiatives such as the East Asian Summit (EAS) and ASEAN+3. The Asian track assumes the centrality of ASEAN in a hub-and-spoke model of integration. The latest effort in the Asian track is the Regional Comprehensive Economic Partnership (RCEP) announced in November 2012, for bringing together all Asian economies with whom ASEAN has bilateral free trade agreements (FTAs) into a composite framework. Comprising ASEAN, Australia, China, India, Japan, New Zealand and South Korea, the RCEP has been enthusiastically endorsed by China.

China and RCEP

China, most probably, views the RCEP as an opportunity for balancing some of the strategic and economic losses inflicted on it by the TPP. The RCEP has a significant economic size and presence in global trade. Its share in global GDP measured in purchasing power parity (PPP) terms is 33.6 percent, which is larger than the corresponding share of 26.1 percent for the current 11-member TPP group. The TPP's share will increase to 34.4 percent of global GDP (PPP) with the inclusion of Japan, South Korea, and Thailand. On the other hand, the TPP currently accounts for 20.7 percent and 20.9 percent of global merchandise and commercial services trades respectively. While these shares will also increase substantially with the joining of Japan, South Korea, and Thailand, at this point in time, the RCEP has a larger presence in global trade with shares of 27.7 percent and 22.5 percent in global merchandise and commercial services trades.

China will be comfortable negotiating the RCEP since the agreement is expected to evolve by imbibing key features of the Asian-track negotiations that China is familiar with. Unlike the TPP, the negotiations are expected to be non-binding and voluntary. The TPP and the RCEP are also likely to differ in structural characteristics, which would reflect features distinguishing the bilateral FTAs of the U.S. from those of ASEAN. As noted earlier, U.S. FTAs have relatively greater focus on 'WTO plus' issues such as NTBs, e-commerce, government procurement, investment, services, labor, and environment. ASEAN FTAs have much less focus on these issues and are more 'accommodating' toward members by granting special and differential (S&D) provisions allowing greater flexibilities in phased tariff reductions. China (as well as India, the other major regional economy figuring in the RCEP, but not in the TPP) is more comfortable with not only less emphasis on 'WTO plus' issues, but also the flexible, non-binding approach of the Asian track. In this respect, it is happy to accept the centrality of ASEAN in the RCEP negotiations. Along with the RCEP, it is also participating actively in other Asian-track integration efforts such as the trilateral FTA with Japan and South Korea for maintaining its strategic presence and market access in the Asia-Pacific.

New Trade Architecture and Strategic Division

The progress on the TPP negotiations, and the counter-response produced by the TPP through the RCEP, are reorganizing the trade architecture of the Asia-Pacific into distinct blocs based on specific negotiating templates. These blocs are also reflecting the strategic economic interests of the U.S. and China.

With the RCEP negotiations under way, progress on both the TPP and the RCEP might be influenced by each other. Overlap of issues at both negotiations is unavoidable, given the presence of the common members (Australia, Brunei, Japan, Malaysia, New Zealand, Singapore, Vietnam, and possibly South Korea and Thailand in the future). The roles of these members will be crucial in determining whether the two frameworks will converge in the future or remain separate and irreconcilable. The common parties might visualize both as different means for achieving the same end of a pan-regional Asia-Pacific free trade pact.[3] The eventual progress on the TPP and the RCEP, depending on whether it follows a mutually inclusive or exclusive course, will also determine whether the Asian and Trans-Pacific tracks can assimilate to produce a common path for economic integration in the Asia-Pacific.

At present, though, the possibility of such convergence appears limited. This is not only due to different templates of the two agreements and the TPP's greater emphasis on 'WTO plus' issues and regulatory coherence. The low possibility of convergence is also due to the contrasting geostrategic perceptions of the TPP and the RCEP. These perceptions are coloring them as alliances that can be strategically manipulated by the U.S. and China. If these perceptions become stronger, the Asia-Pacific might witness more intense trade-driven strategic competition between the U.S. and China to mold the TPP and RCEP into templates accommodating their specific economic interests and comparative advantages.

The TPP is already experiencing the U.S. influence not only through coverage of 'WTO plus' issues, but also the emphasis on cementing regulations strengthening and sustaining its comparative advantages, through measures such as stronger protection for IP and greater market access in government procurement processes of member countries. Similar dominant influence exerted by China on the RCEP (if any) will become known only over time as the negotiations are still at an early stage.

Unlike the U.S., which as the world's largest exporter of commercial services is keen on entrenching its comparative advantages in the TPP accordingly, China is expected to focus on consolidating its comparative advantage in manufacturing through the RCEP. China's economic relationship with several ASEAN members as well as with other major RCEP economies such as Japan and South Korea is unique in that it imports large quantities of intermediates, parts and components from these countries, which are processed and assembled in the mainland, and exported to third country markets such as the U.S. and Europe. These regional supply chains have been vital for the Chinese economy. It is imperative for China to utilize the RCEP for sustaining these supply chains given that the TPP is likely to create a different trade space in the Asia-Pacific with new trade regulations and exclude China.

It is evident that the TPP will substantively influence the trade architecture in the Asia-Pacific through its regulations and geo strategic implications. The possibilities of new trade templates such as the TPP and the RCEP, and their rules, becoming major sources of strategic antagonism between the U.S. and China in the economic turf of the Asia-Pacific is not a foregone conclusion but can hardly be ruled out.

Notes

1. *The negotiating members are Australia, Brunei, Canada, Chile, Malaysia, Mexico, New Zealand, Peru, Singapore, United States of America and Vietnam. Japan has decided to join negotiations. South Korea and Thailand have also expressed interest.*
2. *Horn et al (2009) categories policies into 'WTO plus' and 'WTO extra' groups in their comparative study of such features across PTAs signed by the US and EU with various trade partners. There are overlaps between the groups, though, such as in IP or government procurement.*
3. *The Australian Prime Minister Julia Gillard has opined that the two are 'paths to the same destination'. See; http://csis.org/publication/asean-and-partners-launch-regional-comprehensive-economic-partnership (Accessed on 9 March 2013)*

References

Murray Hiebert and Liam Hanlon (2012), 'ASEAN and Partners Launch Regional Comprehensive Economic Partnership', *Centre for Strategic and International Studies (CSIS)*, 7 December; http://csis.org/publication/asean-and-partners-launch-regional-comprehensive-economic-partnership (Accessed on 15 April 2013)

Henrik Horn, Petros C Mavroidis, and Andre Sapir (2009), 'Beyond the WTO: An anatomy of EU and US preferential trade agreements', *Bruegel Blueprint 7, Bruegel Blueprint Series, Volume VII*, Bruegel, Brussels, Belgium; http://www.bruegel.org (Accessed on 15 April 2013)

Peter A. Petri, Michael G. Plummer and Fan, Zhai (2011), 'The Trans-Pacific Partnership and Asia-Pacific Integration: A Quantitative Assessment', *East West Center Working Papers, Economic Series, No.119*, October 24; http://www.usitc.gov/research_and_analysis/documents/petri-plummer-zhai%20EWC%20TPP%20WP%20oct11.pdf (Accessed on 15 April 2013)

Amitendu Palit is Senior Research Fellow and Head (Partnership & Programme) at the Institute of South Asian Studies in the National University of Singapore.

Economy

China's Currency Reforms from a Banker's Perspective

Penelope B. Prime
Vol. 13, No. 1
2014

China's Currency Reforms from a Banker's Perspective: A Conversation with Henry Yu, Managing Director of Fifth Third Bank, Atlanta, Georgia.

Introduction

As China's economy moves ever closer to surpassing the U.S. in terms of purchasing power GDP, China's currency system seems incompatible with its global economic status. China's new leadership led by President Xi Jinping is pushing to modernize and marketize the currency system along with necessary concurrent reforms. The 2008 financial crisis was a wake-up call for many countries, demonstrating the heavy dependence of the global economy on the U.S. dollar. The vulnerability of the U.S. economy became everyone's challenge. Reform of the Renminbi (RMB) became a priority in order to establish the Chinese currency as a global player and lessen China's reliance on the U.S. dollar. Aside from the fall-out from the financial crisis, the sheer size of China's cross-border trade is creating demand for far more depth and flexibility in the currency markets.

On April 28, 2014, China Research Center Director Penelope Prime talked with Henry Yu, Managing Director of Fifth Third Bank in Atlanta, Georgia, via telephone about China's current currency reforms. This commentary is based largely on that conversation.

Based on his observations of China's most recent moves towards currency reform and from talking with bank officials and other experts in China about the on-going policy discussions, Henry Yu expects major changes to occur within three to five years, with the lifting of all capital restrictions a few years later.

Yu believes that the process of establishing the RMB as an international currency will involve merging offshore and onshore currency markets. This merger will require deepening the sophistication and depth of China's financial institutions in order to integrate China's system with global markets. If China's currency is to become a major player, whether as a managed or a free floating currency, many steps need to be taken throughout the economy. Multinational corporations today manage cash on a global basis, and the RMB is acting as a constraint in this process. As has been the norm in China during the reform era, China's leaders are taking measured steps, one baby step at a time, to achieve these goals, but Yu sees definite movement forward.

Historical Context

In the early days of economic reform and opening, China established Foreign Exchange Certificates as a parallel currency to the domestic Renminbi, or "people's currency." Yu remembers this as an awkward system, especially as cross-border trade increased, but it served the purpose of controlling access to foreign currency by domestic business and consumers to shield the economy from global markets. This was a political imperative at the time.

By the early 1990s, the Chinese National Yuan (CNY) was introduced as part of comprehensive banking and financial reform, and Foreign Exchange Certificates were retired. Soon after this the Asian financial crisis revealed that freeing capital flows without a sophisticated financial system could lead to serious trouble. One could surmise that China's leaders took this lesson to heart and decided to delay more currency reform until after successful banking reform. The next decade saw measures to lower China's banks' bad debt, to create and strengthen the supervision of the banking, securities and insurance sectors, and to prepare for and successfully carry out initial public offerings of the four major state banks in the global market place.

Yu emphasizes the importance of Hong Kong in China's currency reform process. From the beginning of China's reforms, Hong Kong played a major role in both the shift of manufacturing from the territory to southern China and the financial logistics and support behind it. By the early 2000s, Beijing tapped Hong Kong to play a key role in the next steps of currency reform. Hong Kong was designated as a test location where banks could facilitate individuals' retail conversion of Hong Kong Dollars to RMB with a small daily conversion limit imposed, but companies were not yet allowed to do so. This was the first offshore currency trading in RMB, and was distinguished from onshore RMB (or CNY) as CNH.

As Yu put it, "The way I look at it, the leadership is creating a new currency outside of China using Hong Kong as a window."

The Yuan Offshore Market

The movement of onshore and offshore RMB became possible as part of China's cross-border trade transactions rules. Over the last decade the yuan offshore currency market has steadily developed, propelled by China's entry into the World Trade Organization in 2001. The currency has been freely convertible for trading purposes since 2009, and growing offshore access facilitates these transactions. The currency is not deliverable outside of China except in offshore centers, which now include Singapore, London, and Taipei. At this time the offshore circulation is quite small, estimated at less than 1 percent of the onshore circulation. However, about 15 percent of China's cross-border trade is settled in domestic currency, which means that many traders have access to RMB either onshore or off. As a result, then, there is a rising demand to hold RMB outside of China, creating an even greater need for offshore markets.

China's Vice Premier Li Keqiang visited Hong Kong on August 19, 2011 to reaffirm China's Central Government's commitment to develop the territory as the offshore RMB Center. The People's Bank of China designated the Bank of China as the clearing institution for CNH in Hong Kong. An offshore link to China's domestic national advance payments system (CNAPS) is needed for the free flow of fund, Yu says. Ideally there would be a one-to-one correspondence between the value of the CNH and CNY. This is evolving, with CNH commanding a premium for now.

With an estimated $140 billion worth of RMB now in Hong Kong, a balance of RMB assets and liabilities and broader investment options are needed for offshore RMB to expand its reach, value, liquidity, and acceptance to investors and traders, Yu says. Right now, RMB can be held in Bank of China accounts, with some options to buy bonds (known as Dim Sum bonds) or derivatives offered by Hong Kong banks tied to the stock exchange. The latest option is lending offshore CNH back to onshore Chinese or foreign companies. This is being tried on a very limited basis with large companies in special zones such as the Qianhai zone in the West Shenzhen (announced in 2012) district and the new Shanghai Free Trade Zone (announced in September of 2013). Both the Qianhai Free Trade Area and Shanghai Pilot FTZ broadened the usage of RMB and for the first time allowed companies within the zone to borrow offshore RMB for operating needs on a limited basis, as well as pooling of onshore and offshore RMB. One of the major benefits is that companies can borrow at lower costs offshore, which will also eventually lower the onshore interest rates. In addition, the new practices create a limited testing ground for free movements of onshore and offshore RMB.

According to Yu, on the official level, China has negotiated bilateral currency swaps worth over $400 billion with 20-plus countries, with approximately half of these countries in the Asia-Pacific region. These have two purposes. One is that in the case of distress, the two countries can have access to each others' currency. Second, it opens a currency channel between the two central banks, allowing liquidity to be shared.

The Capital Account Opens

A key aspect of moving the RMB toward serving as an international currency is the continued loosening of restrictions on inward and outward flows of capital. New moves are expected with respect to allowing Chinese tourists to convert more RMB into foreign currency, allowing some investors to begin buying foreign equities and eventually increasing the amount of capital that can be used outside of China for investment purposes (Davies 2014). Ultimately private outflows of capital would lessen the need for official purchases of government bonds, assuming China continues to experience trade surpluses. Outward flows would also serve as a counter-balance to the inward flows aimed at capturing an ever rising value of the RMB.

What to Expect Next

The strategy of "taking baby and calculated steps" is expected to continue, Yu says. Chinese policymakers will not want to introduce currency value volatility or encourage "hot money" flows, especially when they still need time to create currency instruments, extend banking sector experience, and improve the debt and equity markets to handle the new stage of financial deepening. But eventually, according to Yu, there will be few if any restrictions on offshore RMB flowing back into China. The ultimate goal is to increase the circulation of offshore RMB and eventually merge the offshore and onshore markets into one currency system with one value. Yu feels strongly that the new leadership team of President Xi and Premier Li is serious about increased market reforms, and financial reform in particular, to allow the market to be the force in driving the economy and to further reduce government intervention. Yu cites as one example an official at the People's Bank of China indicated that if a transaction can be done in dollars it should also be able to be done in RMB.

As China's economy grows and with cross-border trade expected to surpass $10 trillion by 2020, the sheer quantity of currency transactions will require more options and flexibility. All indications are that China's policy makers are responding to this growing global demand for RMB.

References

Davies, Gavyn (2014). "China's changing exchange rate policy," *The Wall Street Journal*, May 4th. http:/blogs.ft.com/gavyndavies. Accessed May 6, 2014.

Penelope B. Prime, Ph.D., is Professor of international business at Georgia State University and the director of the China Research Center.

In Due Time: China's business environment makes the case for due diligence

Katherine Peavy
Vol. 13, No. 1
2014

The South China Morning Post headline jumped out at me: Steel Princess's trading company in liquidation. I leaned a little closer to my neighbor on Hong Kong's Star Ferry to read over his shoulder. The article claimed that liquidators were looking for about US$500 million that the company should have had in the bank. "Yes!" I mentally fist-pumped. Some people might view a missing half-a-billion as a failure, for me the headline meant success. I had investigated the CEO of Pioneer Iron and Steel, dubbed the "Steel Princess" by the press, on behalf of a client.

Fortunately, occasions when front-page headlines support the analysis in a due diligence report remain rare. On this occasion, the bankruptcy of Pioneer Iron and Steel leading to transfers of company assets from the trading company to other entities owned by the Pioneer Metals Group fulfilled the worst-case risk scenario in a due diligence report I'd given to a client a few years before. The largest risk, depending on what business the client planned to do with Pioneer, was that the corporate structure allowed for undocumented asset transfers. I never expected to see the exact risk we'd documented on the front page of a newspaper.

I noticed the client's name was not on the list of creditors, so it was likely they had put measures in place to protect their company from the financial losses and potential reputation issues that headlines about deals gone bad can bring.

For most companies, due diligence focuses on protecting a company's reputation and finances through understanding business partners better. To highlight the importance of due diligence on investment partners or supply chain partners in China, let me provide examples of successes and failures companies have experienced in their China business and show how robust – or superficial – due diligence affected the outcome.

Deals go bad all over the world and in one's own backyard. Yet, it is often the lure of China, the promise of increasing revenues, the exciting focus on guanxi (networking and relationships), and the mystique of the potential in this huge market that make executives overlook risks they might not ignore in a domestic market or one without as much perceived upside potential. I've been involved in numerous situations in which executives with the stars of market potential in their eyes ignored the necessity of deep due diligence on a pre-transaction project. The dealmakers stuck to a fig leaf compliance approach, wanting to cover up the full picture of a risky investment. They would check a compliance box to satisfy a board prior to pushing through a lightly vetted deal. The investment team may have received their bonuses that year, but down the road the fig leaf would fall and companies would often suffer financial and reputation losses. Those types of clients are the best for consultants, public relations firms, and lawyers because we know that these types of deals will probably result in lucrative investigations once the deal goes bad.

A basic principle of any partnership is understanding the identity and experience of a partner. Most people wouldn't get married without knowing their future spouse's background, but companies regularly don't take the time to learn about the companies and executives they do business with, paying them millions of dollars and often losing millions.

The first step of any due diligence is to verify the company's registration details with China's Administration for Industry and Commerce (AIC) or Hong Kong's company registrar. In this case, the AIC records showed the Steel Princess set up a network of companies, ultimately owned by her and her mother, through which she held shares in iron and steel producers in China. The parent company also had holdings and links to Hong Kong companies that in turn had interests in entities in the British Virgin Islands, providing an easy route for transferring money out of China or Hong Kong and causing large risks to investors.

Either the Steel Princess or her mother were the legal representatives of each of the companies in the Pioneer Group. In China, the AIC registration file shows the name of the company's legal representative, the person responsible for any of the company's legal obligations such as paying bills or transferring funds. The legal representative is the ultimate controller of the company. The legal representative must sign any contract a company in China enters into. The Steel Princess set up her companies well. She was clearly the boss. By contrast, we often come across scenarios where clients are negotiating with people who are not the company's legal representatives. Deals are not valid until the legal representative signs off.

The CEO of Pioneer Metals, called by China's press the Steel Princess because her grandfather was the Minister of Metallurgy in the 1970s, did have connections in the metals industry in the country as a princeling, a child or grandchild of government or party official in China. However, during our research for the client's due diligence report, we interviewed industry insiders and did not find any history of the Steel Princess having worked in government steel producers or in the Ministry of Metallurgy. The structure of her company and cash infusions appeared to be her main contribution to the industry.

Another risk I pointed out to the client was that the CEO's grandfather was a policymaker more than 30 years ago. As such, it was unlikely she or her family had any influence with current policymakers. For the client, the risk could be that they were paying a person for a pedigree without any evidence the person had practical skills to get the job done. If the client wanted her to lobby for or against regulations or gain connections in the current government, they might find her connections dated and irrelevant. If they were looking for practical industry knowledge, they might consider someone with different experience.

Restrictions in the metals industry required multinationals to deal with domestic Chinese companies, and Pioneer Metals had a high profile. The CEO was one of the richest women in China, according to various annually published lists. The Forbes or Hurun "rich lists" often attract investors or business partners for those on the lists on the assumption that connections with perceived money and power will help them do business in China. But in our experience, a spot on the rich list is often short-lived. Many former rich list stars have experienced meteor-like falls from grace as a result of high-profile investigations by China's Economic Crime Bureau. By 2010, China's richest man in 2006, Huang Guangyu, CEO of Gome Electrical Appliances, was serving a 14-year prison sentence on a fraud and corruption conviction. Another 2006 rich list rising star, Wu Ying of Bense Group, later received a commuted death sentence for the allegedly fraudulent activity that got her onto the rich list.

A quick Internet search will identify high-profile individuals such as the Steel Princess or Huang Guangyu, but a few times, clients provided only the English name of a Chinese person they saw as the key to success of their China business based on a dinner or business meeting. That's how one due diligence report started on a Shanghai-based gentleman applying for a high net worth account with a multinational bank in New York. The client sent us the individual's English name and China bank account number. First, like most countries, privacy laws protect bank accounts in China. Second, a Chinese bank account must be registered with the individual's Chinese name as it appears on his or her Chinese identity card or passport. Obviously, the English name could have been made up. We asked the client for better identifying information, such as a Chinese name and copy of a passport. Fortunately, they sent a business card and passport copy the next day, so we had a proper Chinese name and a company name and address.

The AIC records showed that the gentleman in question was indeed the legal representative of the investment firm he claimed to own, but a visit to the offices in Shanghai's Pudong district found an office with a locked door. The management of the high-end office building was not familiar with the company or the legal representative, but confirmed the company did rent the office space and pay its bills. Media searches found no record of the investment firm or the firm's CEO. Industry contacts had never heard of the firm, which according to the client had about US$300 million in assets.

With most companies or individuals in China, it is possible to research and find information on track records within an industry and trace a CEO's "first bucket of gold," as many rags to riches stories of Chinese entrepreneurs are documented in profiles of executives for business magazines, known by industry insiders or by current and former employers. But the assets and seed money of our client's potential client were untraceable. It was as if he had created the money out of thin air.

We had to issue a report stating that we couldn't find the source of funds or any business profile for the executive and concluded that any transaction with him would be high risk. Fortunately, anti-money laundering regulations require banks to prove the source of their clients' funds. A few months later, the executive's name was all over China's front pages, but not connected to our client. The executive and his investment firm reportedly were the cover for a corrupt government official attempting to siphon off millions of dollars from the Shanghai municipal pension fund and hide the money abroad.

Another scenario where due diligence plays an important role involves compliance with laws in the client's home country. The U.S. and U.K. both have anti-corruption statutes that apply to multinationals in their home markets as well as international markets. In the U.S., they are the Foreign Corrupt Practices Act and Sarbanes-Oxley acts. In the U.K., it is the Anti-Bribery Act. Companies must have transparent programs in place to show they understand the identities of their suppliers, vendors, and distributors.

Consider cases in which companies applied a fig leaf compliance approach, determining only whether the company is registered with the AIC, for example, rather than verifying any government connections or reputation issues:

By 2010, Siemens AG paid more than US$ 1 billion in fines to U.S. and German government agencies for overlooking the fact that subsidiaries in foreign countries, including China, used consultants or marketing firms to pay bribes to government officials to obtain contracts. Most of the consulting firms were owned by friends and relatives of government officials.[1]

Also in 2010, telecommunications company Alcatel-Lucent paid US$135 million to the Securities and Exchange Commission for similar payments to government officials made via consultants acting as agents for telecommunications bids.[2]

And British pharmaceutical giant GlaxoSmithKline has been involved for the past year in a corruption scandal that began in China where sales and marketing vendors are said to have paid bribes in the forms of airplane tickets, vacations, and cash to doctors to get the company's drugs in Chinese hospitals, which are state-owned and thus government entities for purposes of the U.K. Anti-Bribery Act and U.S. Foreign Corrupt Practices Act. It should be noted that while fines have not been set, a number of GlaxoSmithKline executives and business partners in China have been imprisoned as the case came about through investigation by China's Ministry of Public Security.[3]

For industries such as telecommunications, pharmaceuticals, and real estate, government restrictions on participation by foreign companies, project bidding, and a high level of government ownership in domestic China assets creates risk for many forms of corruption in the downstream supply chain.

One telecommunications multinational wanted to get ahead of the game and start a due diligence program for its existing sales and marketing vendors. These vendors were assigned to participate in bids for government projects, and their task was to understand the technical requirements, outline technical specifications for the client, and manage the bid process. They thought that by keeping this kind of arm's-length approach, they would protect themselves from any situations in which their staff would be in a position to bribe government officials during the bid.

We were assigned to conduct due diligence on hundreds of these agents. The client maintained a few agents in every province in China. The main objective was to determine whether any of the agents were linked to government officials.

We initially identified a few agents either linked to government officials or entities, or linked to the client's own employees. Unfortunately, the client put its employees in a difficult position requiring sales staff to find the agents, brief them, and sign contracts with them. They had no front-end due diligence process in place to check agents prior to signing contracts. In other words, they had no substantial controls in place. The sales team was, of course, under pressure to win bids and make money. Without any initial controls, the sales team found whomever they thought could win the bid, which included companies with close government connections.

The client also had a substantial base of agents with a track record for working on telecommunications bids and no obvious government connections, so they were not in danger of losing too many of their agents.

The vice president of sales in charge of our project, who reported findings to corporate legal counsel, came to me one day with a report that raised red flags about an agent. The AIC records showed the agent's company had a connection to an employee and a government official as a minor shareholder. He said, "Are you sure about the findings on this company?"I explained to him that the AIC records were very clear. "But this is my top agent and my top salesperson here. What am I going to do?"

The vice president of sales did not flinch when it came to cutting out a few of the initial agents with unwanted connections, but he balked in this instance. Taking action against this agent could hit sales figures. Shortly thereafter, the system I had set up to compare agent company AIC filings to sales staff names and known government official names was taken back for the sales and marketing team to handle.

It is not uncommon for companies like this one to find themselves a few years down the road caught between over-reliance on guanxi and the vagaries of fig leaf compliance. Executives are often fearful of dropping the fig leaf because of what might be revealed.

From a slightly different perspective, the real estate industry in China has been the source of the most exciting and scandalous due diligence reports and fraud investigations I've been involved in. The combination of government ownership of land and skyrocketing land and housing prices over the last 15 years has created interesting bedfellows and motivations.

A U.S. based multinational investment bank requested a due diligence report on a Chinese-owned real estate development company that approached them for funding of a five-star hotel in a prime location of a major Chinese city.

The client felt comfortable with the Chinese real estate company through the CEO, a man born in China who had immigrated to a European country in his 20s after making his first "bucket of gold." A few years after returning from abroad, the CEO had a thriving real estate development company and planned to list it on the Hong Kong stock exchange. It was not surprising when the investment bankers and the legal counsel requested a conference call to discuss the findings of our report.

With many companies and people involved in the hot real estate market, industry insiders were easy to track down. They led us to other industry insiders and even family members of the CEO. We discovered that the CEO made his first "bucket of gold"through working with the Triads (Chinese mafia) in southern China, and sometimes still used them to threaten business partners. Additionally, the CEO had close connections with the Communist Party secretary of the city involved in granting the land use rights for the hotel, and in the past the developer had received some deals that simply could not have happened without under-the-table government support.

On the phone, the client said, "I just can't believe these findings. This sounds like a mafia organization, but when we go to their office everyone speaks fluent English. They're very professional. I mean, the staff are all wearing khakis and Polo shirts."

To which his colleague (the legal counsel, I presume) replied, "The 9/11 terrorists were also wearing khakis."

I explained to the investment team that the findings were definitely unusual, and because of that we made sure that we corroborated the most serious allegations with three or more sources that included former and current employees, business partners and even a family member. The client did not go through with the deal, but the developer found other investors. When I'm in China, I go to the bar of the luxury hotel the developer built and wonder whether the story will ever hit the headlines.

For me, China is still one of the most interesting markets for due diligence because of the competition between a market potentially teeming with deals and profits and a very opaque business and legal environment. In that context, many companies have gotten burned financially or their reputations have taken a beating merely due to not taking the time or spending the money to understand their business partners.

Notes

[1] See https://www.sec.gov/news/press/2008/2008-294.htm for a full article.

[2] See www.sec.gov for plenty of examples of similar cases

[3] For a thorough article on this case see: http://www.nytimes.com/2013/07/16/business/global/glaxo-used-travel-firms-in-bribery-china-says.html.

Katherine Peavy spent 15 years in China working in the risk management field on hundreds of due diligence cases and fraud investigations. She is a founding partner of the consulting firm Cross Pacific Partner (www.crosspacificpartner.com).

What's Up with U.S. Big-Box Retailers in China? The Cases of The Home Depot and Best Buy

Jing Betty Feng
Vol.12, No.2
2013

China, with a rapidly increasing middle class, has drawn tremendous attention from foreign retailers and become one of the hottest markets in today's global economy. By some measures foreign retailers have done well, even though Chinese retailers dominate the market. The number of foreign retail stores in the Top 100 increased faster than their Chinese counterparts in 2010, even though foreign retailers had slower sales growth compared with Chinese retailers (18 percent for foreign firms compared with 25 percent for Chinese retailers, according to a Deloitte report). Six major foreign supermarkets opened 135 new stores in 2010, up 22 percent over the previous year, and seven foreign retailers increased the number of their stores by more than 20 percent in 2010.

But what seemed like fertile ground for two of the largest and most prominent U.S. big-box retailers proved anything but. Best Buy and The Home Depot announced their retreats from China within a month of each other in early 2011. Electronics retailer Best Buy closed its nine branded stores around the country and its Shanghai headquarters after three years of preparation for market entry and five years of expansion in China.[1] In September 2012, The Home Depot decided to close the last of its seven stores in China after years of losses. The media was flooded with experts' opinions that Western retailers are not acclimated to Chinese culture, referring to a common Chinese idiom, "not adapting to the water and soil."

What made these two companies withdraw from this hot market after less than six years of operation? The general perception of their failures is lack of adaptation to Chinese consumer culture. Are other reasons contributing to the failure of The Home Depot and Best Buy in China? The following discussion provides a deeper understanding of the factors challenging these companies to perform in China's market.

The U.S. Big-Box Retailers

The experience of these two companies contrasts with other U.S. firms doing business in China. KFC and General Motors reported record sales in China at the same time and have higher profits in China than they have back home. Another U.S. retail giant, Walmart, also has seen growth in its China sales. It operated 380 stores on the mainland by early 2013, becoming No. 2 in market share in China.[2] With the rapidly increasing middle class and a housing boom, it should have been a very good time for The Home Depot and Best Buy to establish themselves in China, like other global brands.

The majority of U.S. retailers are big-box stores, which means they provide a wide variety of products in a large physical space. A big-box retailer often uses a low price strategy to drive sales volume. The big-box retailer also has many stores across the country. Examples of famous U.S. big-box retailers are Walmart, Target, and Sears, as well as Best Buy and The Home Depot.

The Home Depot is the world's largest retailer of home improvement and construction products and services, headquartered in Atlanta, Georgia. Founded in 1978, The Home Depot created the "do-it-yourself" concept and changed consumers' perspectives about how they could care for and improve their homes. Today, The Home Depot serves three primary customer groups: do-it-yourself ("DIY") customers, do-it-for-me ("DIFM") customers, and professional customers. The Home Depot has opened more than 2,200 locations throughout the United States (including Puerto Rico and the Virgin Islands), Canada, China, and Mexico. Stores average 105,000 square feet with approximately 23,000 additional square feet of outside garden area. Each store sells as many as 40,000 different kinds of building materials, home improvement supplies, appliances, and lawn and garden products for all kinds of projects (www.homedepot.com). Its primary rival, Lowe's, currently has less than half of its market size.

Headquartered in Richfield, Minnesota, Best Buy Co. incorporated in 1996 and specializes in consumer electronics. Today, Best Buy operates 1,150 stores around the world. Besides its big-box retail stores, the company also manages more than 100 Best Buy Express automated retail stores or "Zoom Shops," operated by Zoom Systems, in airports and malls around the United States. Best Buy markets itself as having superior customer service provided by knowledgeable sales associates. Best Buy had its glory era: it was named "Company of the Year" by Forbes magazine in 2004, listed in the Top 10 of "America's Most Generous

Corporations" by Forbes magazine in 2005, and made Fortune magazine's list of "Most Admired Companies" in 2006. After its rival Circuit City went bankrupt in March 2009, Best Buy became the largest electronics retailer in the eastern United States. For years, Best Buy has been reducing store space allotted for music CDs because of the surge of digital music access via Internet download. Today, online retailers, particularly Amazon.com, are seriously challenging Best Buy. E-retailers do not have the fixed costs of store space and employees, and therefore can often provide the same products for lower prices. Many customers often go to Best Buy stores to find products they like, but purchase them from online stores. In 2011, revenue and profits of Best Buy declined. In 2012, Best Buy announced a""transformation strategy" to close 50 stores in the U.S. In early 2013, Best Buy announced a partnership with Samsung Electronics for a store-within-a-store concept to better utilize floor space. A strong 2012 Christmas sales season and the mini-mall strategy apparently gave investors confidence as Best Buy's stock more than doubled in 2013.[3]

The Retail Industry in China

As a result of successful economic development over the last three decades, China has become the most attractive and rapidly growing market for multinational companies. The size of the middle class, which has an appetite for spending, has been increasing rapidly. Meanwhile, China's retail market is very fragmented with many small and medium-sized retailers. Cross-provincial retail stores are still rare because of local-access barriers that limit such growth. In 2008, the sector was composed of 549,000 small and medium-sized retailers, each with an average of 15 employees.[4] For global big-box retailers, China appears to be easy territory to conquer with its abundant capital resources and global brand reputation. However, the retail industry in China has proven more complex than expected. Foreign retailers face various challenges from distinctive local consumer cultures to different industry practices in terms of the business model, marketing and sales practices, and supplier relationships.

Store-Based Retailing Business Model

The Chinese retail industry has its own distinctive business model, which provides Chinese retailers cost advantages over their global competitors in their home market. Instead of running the retail business as a buyer and reseller as American retailers do, Chinese retailers are more like commercial property management companies. They own or rent the buildings, design the buildings as department stores or super markets, and rent out shelf space to individual manufacturers. Chinese retailers charge manufacturers space rent and commission from sales revenue. Manufacturers in the retail stores manage their own promotions, inventory, and operation to make sure they cover those costs, and make profits. Under such a business model, Chinese retailers do not worry about investment for inventory, operational costs to manage the products, or payroll to sales associates.

However, foreign retailers are running their businesses in a completely different way. The foreign retailers are resellers. They decide the "best" product offerings for customers, select and purchase the products for resell, or contract suppliers to manufacture the products under their own brands. The foreign retailers not only commit large capital investments on inventory, but also carry the burdens of administration, marketing, sales, and service costs. The reselling model works in the U.S. because large retailers benefit from purchasing large quantities of products, managing retail prices to ensure their profit margins, and controlling the product quality level. However, this model causes challenges in China. The majority of retailers do not have the financial capability to hold a large inventory, nor do they have a mature retailing management system. Thus a "consignment" model gives them more flexibility to minimize burdens of holding inventories and managing products.

Marketing & Sales Practices

Along with managing their own products for Chinese retailers, the manufacturers also arrange their own sales associates to manage sales in the retail stores. Trained by manufacturers and motivated by sales commissions, sales associates of Chinese retailers are more aggressive in promoting their represented brands and products. Unlike their Chinese competitors, the Western retailers hire their own sales associates, who often are not paid through sales commissions. Therefore, they might be less knowledgeable about the products and less motivated to interact with customers to drive sales.

In the case of household products, Chinese retailers display products by brands. Each brand owns its own section in the store. For example, when a customer goes to the section of Hai'er, the most famous Chinese brand for home appliances, he or she will find all of the products offered by Hai'er in the same area. However, American retailers display products by product categories. It is common for American consumers to go to the same product category and compare products across brands. But for Chinese consumers, the depth of a product category offering can better represent the competitiveness of a brand. Displaying by brands is also preferred by suppliers as they can better present their brands by controlling the setup, more effectively run their sales promotions, and use fewer associates to manage the concentrated area. The typical marketing strategy also gives Chinese retailers advantages over Western retailers. Chinese retailers spend millions on advertising; however, the expenses are mainly paid by suppliers to promote their own brands and products. Western retailers focus on promoting their store brands and have to pay the majority of the advertising costs themselves. With a lower level of spending on advertising in general, Western retailers have trouble effectively leveraging their brand names in China.

Supplier Relationships

Suppliers to Chinese retailers have complete autonomy to manage their own products. Even though they carry the inventory cost, they do not carry the burden of late payment from retailers. Suppliers have more control over their promotions and prices. As long as they can pay the space rental and commissions to the retailers, it is a harmonious partnership.

On the other hand, the Western retailers procure products from their suppliers and often decide the retail prices based on demand. Suppliers need to keep up all clauses of service agreements to guarantee order fulfillment, on-time delivery, and sales performance. Failure to meet service standards will result in financial penalties or loss of shelf space. Late payment is common, causing financial pressure on suppliers. Procurement management is not yet mature in China, thus communication between buyers and suppliers focuses on operational transactions with less emphasis on product development or marketing strategies. Suppliers are not able to effectively learn the needs of consumers through buyers for further product improvement. In order to improve sales performance, Western retailers often require suppliers to lower their prices to drive sales volume, and thus squeeze profits out of their suppliers. For suppliers, the required deep discounts ultimately make the retail stores the place to get rid of outdated and obsolete products. Bribing buyers also becomes part of the game so that suppliers can get a bigger volume or better shelf space. For all of these reasons, the relationship between suppliers and Western retailers is a challenging one. Because of the increased costs of doing business with the Western retailers, many small and medium-size suppliers choose to terminate the supplier relationship. Consequently, there are fewer brand selections in Western retail stores.

There are significant differences between Western and Chinese structure and practices in the retail industry (See Table 1). The differences seem to give Chinese retailers competitive advantages while challenging foreign retailers to penetrate the Chinese market effectively. In addition, the unique Chinese consumption culture poses extra barriers for foreign retailers. The following sections will discuss these issues as they apply to The Home Depot and Best Buy.

The Home Depot in China

In the last decade, the housing market in China has experienced annual double-digit growth. Unlike in the West, most new homes are sold in China as empty

Table 1: Business Practices in the Retail Industry: A Comparison of the U.S. and China

Retail Industry Business Practices	China	U.S.
Business Models	Acting as property management and rent out space to manufacturers	Acting as buyer and reseller
Marketing & Sales	• Manufacturers hire and train sales associates; • Sales associates are commission based; • Products are displayed by brands to show the product variety of brands; • Manufacturers hire fewer associates to service the concentrated area and brand promotion is easier.	• Retailers hire and train sales associates; • In some cases, sales associates are not commission-based; • Products are displayed by product category to show the broad selection of brands.
Supplier Relationships	• Suppliers rent the space and manage their own inventories, promotion, and revenue; • Suppliers benefit from cash flow and have full autonomy to manage their products and prices.	• Retailers decide the items to sell in their stores; • Requires constant price reductions; • Suppliers often experience late payments from retailers, are penalized by late deliveries or inventory issues.

frameworks with only concrete walls. Homeowners need to invest significantly to finish the home, from flooring, ceiling, windows, bathroom fixtures, kitchen cabinets, to doorbells. Very often the homeowners will select the design and materials they like and hire contractors to do the work. The new homeowners or the contractors will visit the traditional home improvement markets, which are often located in giant warehouses close to expressways. In these markets, dozens of manufacturers show their products for each category, such as tiles, toilets, bathtubs, etc. Customers can bargain over prices with the sellers and cut deals. After the transactions, sellers are responsible for delivering the goods.

The home improvement business in China is still underdeveloped. With millions of new homes sold every year, China should be the best investment destination for The Home Depot with its expertise in home construction/improvement and high quality installation services. When Chuck Elias, The Home Depot's China head, started investigating the market opportunity in China in 2005, he visited 25 cities, scouting competitors' outlets and traditional markets. As he observed, "China is an incredibly exciting opportunity." China became the top priority for The Home Depot to grow its business and to increase its stock price.[5]

The Home Depot started its journey in China in December 2006 through an acquisition of the Chinese home improvement retailer The Home Way. The Home Depot was able to establish its presentence in China quickly with 12 stores in six cities. However, the performance of the stores did not meet expectations, even amid China's housing boom. By April 2011, The Home Depot had closed its last Beijing store, the fifth one in China, which left seven stores in Tianjin, Xi'an, and Zhenzhou. The Home Depot shook up its strategy by focusing on specialty stores in Tianjin to cater to specific needs and shopping preferences of Chinese consumers. It opened one paint and flooring store and one home decorations outlet, and planned to launch online operations with a Chinese partner. Later, in September 2012, The Home Depot decided to close all remaining big-box stores in China.

There are various reasons for The Home Depot's unsatisfactory performance, including the change in company presidents three times in four years, a dispute with a commercial property landlord, and poor supplier relationships. But the most common criticism focuses on the unique DIY business model. Many believe the failure of The Home Depot in China is mainly because Chinese consumers do not have the same "do-it-yourself" attitude as people in the U.S. Hiring home improvement contractors is very convenient and inexpensive. Chinese consumers do not have time or know-how to improve their homes on their own. The Home Depot admitted it misread China's appetite for do-it-yourself products. With its announcement of the stores closing in China, a Home Depot spokeswoman said: "The market trend says this is more of a do-it-for-me culture."[6] Another interesting cultural issue is the signature orange apron worn by The Home Depot sales associates. In the U.S., the apron signals expertise and knowledge of home improvement. In China, a man wearing an apron is often looked down upon as someone who lacks authority. Therefore, customers in China did not feel they should ask for suggestions from people wearing aprons.

In the U.S., The Home Depot is proud of its services and the knowledge of its sales associates who provide guidance to customers for home improvement projects. The company also provides installation services in the U.S., fulfilled by third-party service providers. In fact, many American families prefer to use installation services for complex projects such as flooring and roofing, rather than trying to do it themselves.

So the "do-it-yourself" model might not be the only factor in The Home Depot's failure in China. The product offerings suggest another problem. Products were perceived to be too cheap and simple. A longtime Chinese tile saleswoman says, "It's mainly for poor people."[7] Chinese families like to decorate their new homes with high quality products. Chinese consumers are used to finding bargains from hundreds of suppliers at traditional home improvement markets, so shopping in a home improvement retailer is a new concept. The Home Depot was not successful in promoting and leveraging its global brand as the world's largest retailer of home improvement. Many Chinese consumers are not even aware of the brand.

Meanwhile, The Home Depot's major competitor in China, B&Q, a subsidiary of Europe's do-it-yourself giant Kingfisher, set the example of adaptation to local consumer culture. In Shanghai since 1999, B&Q stumbled through some rocky first steps, and then developed strong brand awareness through offering innovative services for customers. B&Q provides customers full design and decorating services from floor to ceiling to help customers transform their new houses from empty concrete shells into stylish homes at a reasonable cost. With this full-service strategy B&Q is the market leader in China with 39 stores, and is one of the largest Western retailers in the country as of 2013.

Best Buy in China

In 2003, Best Buy dipped its toes in the Chinese marketplace by establishing its office in Shanghai. In 2006, after three years of research, Best Buy acquired a majority interest in China's fourth-largest appliance chain, Jiangsu Five Star Appliance Co., Ltd., obtaining 136 stores in eight of China's 24 provinces.[8] In January 2007, Best Buy opened its first flagship store in Shanghai with great fanfare. However, Best Buy also faced tremendous challenges. In the first five years of market entry, Best Buy expanded very slowly. By 2011, when Best Buy announced its store closings in China, only nine stores had been opened, six of them in Shanghai.

With the increased disposable income among Chinese consumers, Best Buy should have appealed to the high-end middle class consumers. According to retail analyst Paul French of the Shanghai-based firm Access Asia, Best Buy offered "a concept ahead of the consumer." Unlike their top Chinese competitors, Gome and Suning, which used the warehouse style of Chinese electronic chains, Best Buy moved the U.S. business model completely to China and built large, high-end flagship stores. These stores did not use glass cases. Instead, customers could touch and examine products without having to ask permission from staff. Products were displayed by different quality standards: "good, better, best." Instead of aggressive and pushy vendors' representatives, well-trained sales associates who did not earn sales commissions helped customers when they needed it. The associates were there to provide expert introduction to the products so customers could make their own purchasing decisions. Best Buy provided a much nicer shopping environment at prices no higher than its competitors.[9]

However, Best Buy apparently fell well short of its goals and did not flourish with this "customer-focused" business model in China. With only one percent market share after six years of operation in China, Best Buy decided to close its nine stores at the end of 2011. Many reasons are suggested for the failure of Best Buy. One of the most commonly heard is that Chinese consumers are "too cheap" to buy expensive products or to care about service, and prefer bargaining for discounts rather than choosing from set prices in these stores.[10]

Compared with its Chinese competitors, Best Buy spent more on store decoration and employee benefits, and had only a few stores. As a result, Best Buy had a much higher cost structure compared to its competitors, which may have led to higher prices for some products. In addition, except for a few Chinese brands, the majority of products in Best Buy were foreign brands, leaving consumers with fewer options. Although many enjoyed the shopping environment in Best Buy, consumers were also disappointed to see very few discounts in the stores, compared to the ubiquitous promotions in Chinese electronic chains. With few choices and not many special deals, Best Buy was perceived to be more expensive to Chinese consumers. While Best Buy selected the best of every product for their customers, Chinese consumers preferred to choose for themselves from hundreds of options. Kal Patel, head of Best Buy's Asia operations, stated: "What we learned, very crucially, is that in China you cannot make revolutionary change. You have to work at the pace of the Chinese consumer."[11]

Emphasizing large flagship stores could be another mistake Best Buy made. The four-story store in the Xu Jia Hui area of Shanghai's premier shopping district is the largest Best Buy in the world. However, unlike American consumers who often drive to shop at the big-box stores, most Chinese consumers prefer to shop closer to home. With its slow pace of store expansion, Best Buy was unlikely to stand against fierce competition from Gome and Suning, both of which owned more than 1,000 stores nationwide.[12]

Ironically, the "cheap" consumers and flagship stores were not completely to blame either. Gome and Sunning did not hesitate to duplicate Best Buy's business model, operation and marketing strategies, and even store decoration. Gome used blue as its store color, which some consumers confused with the blue logos of Best Buy. Gome also adopted the sales strategy to provide fixed prices and non-commissioned salespeople in some stores in 2010. As a result, sales soared because wealthier consumers were afraid of over-paying and prefer not to waste time negotiating.[13]

The Home Depot and Best Buy try new strategies in China

Both The Home Depot and Best Buy closed their big-box retail stores in China suddenly with no advance notice. Consumers and employees found announcements of permanent closure and locked doors when they came to the stores to shop or work. The sudden closures left many angry customers who had bought products with warranties and services, frustrated employees who received no sign of losing their jobs and worried suppliers who were still waiting for payments. All they could do was to work with support centers to deal with any refunds or payments. Actually, neither The Home Depot nor Best Buy planned to completely leave the Chinese market. Both companies planned to shape up their strategies in China by focusing on specialty stores and online sales. As previously mentioned, The Home Depot opened several paint and flooring stores and one home decorations outlet in the northern port city of Tianjin. Best Buy has continued to work with its Chinese subsidiary, Jiangsu Five Star Ltd., to open more electronic stores and is testing a Best Buy mobile store-within-a-store concept in some Five Star stores.[14] Both companies are trying to cater to specific needs and shopping preferences of Chinese consumers.

While U.S. big-box retailers prepare to shrink to smaller stores and focus on special products in China, one of their Chinese counterparts, Suning Appliance, China's largest appliance retailer, plans to create superstores over the next three years, adding daily necessities and books to 400 existing outlets.[15] Clearly, The Home Depot and Best Buy will continue to face challenges from local and global competitors, and will need to be creative to respond to the different Chinese retailing practices and consumer culture.

Conclusion

What can we learn from the cases of The Home Depot and Best Buy in China? The retail market in China is complex. Both these companies took cautious steps when they entered China. (See table 2 for a summary of the comparisons.) They conducted detailed market research, but apparently still failed to customize their business models to fit the market. They entered the market through acquiring previously successful Chinese stores, but were not able to fully leverage the acquired knowledge and experience. Both retailers faced tremendous challenges as a result of the different consumer culture, from major ones such as the consumption habits to minor ones such as the different perception of The Home Depot's signature orange apron.[16] In addition, Chinese retailers are more flexible and cost-effective than foreign competitors with their unique practices. Both The Home Depot and Best Buy failed to provide an education about premium Western brands. Neither retailer provided consumers superior value from a price advantage or sufficient product differentiation. The Home Depot's products were too cheap and simple, while Best Buy's offerings were too limited. As foreign brands are not very familiar to Chinese consumers, The Home Depot and Best Buy also faced tremendous challenges from distinctive industry practices that were not compatible with the norms for these companies. Nonetheless, with strong corporate leadership and a vision of long-term development in China, these challenges could be overcome.

Table 2: Experiences of The Home Depot and Best Buy in China

	The Home Depot	Best Buy
Length of market research	1 year	3 years
Entry mode	Acquired 12 stores from the Home Way in 2006	Acquired 136 stores from Jiangsu Five Star Appliance in 2006 and opened first flagship store in 2007
Years by the final store closing	6 years	5 years
Total number of new big-box stores	0	9
Major consumer cultural issue	The Home Depot has a do-it-yourself model while Chinese consumers prefer "do-it-for-me."	Consumers prefer to choose from thousand of items on their own and negotiate a discount.
Consumer perception issue	Products are for poor people.	Price is higher than other local electronic stores.
Product issue	Products are too cheap and simple.	There are limited varieties and most of them are foreign brands.
New strategy in China	Opening paint and flooring stores and one home decorations outlet.	Working with its Chinese subsidiary, Jiangsu Five Star Ltd., to sell appliances, and is opening mobile phone specialty stores.
Competitors status	B&G from UK provides customer a full design and decoration service and has opened 39 stores.	Gome and Suning each has 1,000 stores nationwide and opened flagship stores with Best Buy model.

Notes
[1] *Ni, 2011*
[2] *Burkitt, 2013*
[3] *Eule, 2013*
[4] *Lu, 2010*
[5] *Businessweek, 2006*
[6] *Burkitt, 2012*
[7] *Grgurich, 2012*
[8] *Jiang, 2006*
[9] *MacLeod, 2011*
[10] *Rein, 2011*
[11] *Roane, 2011*
[12] *Ni, 2011*
[13] *Rein, 2011*
[14] *Lee, 2013*
[15] *Burkitt, 2012*
[16] *Mei, 2013*

References

Burkitt, L. (2012). *Home Depot Learns Chinese Prefer 'Do-It-for-Me'*. http://online.wsj.com/article/SB10000872396390444433504577651072911154602.html.

Burkitt, L. (2013). *Wal-Mart Says China Growth Is on Target*. http://online.wsj.com/article/SB10001424127887324883604578396090449466504.html.

Businessweek. (2006). *Home Depot: One Foot in China*. http://www.businessweek.com/stories/2006-04-30/home-depot-one-foot-in-china.

Deloitte. (2011). *China power of retailing*.

Eule, A. (2013). *All of a Sudden, Investors Love Best Buy. But Do Shoppers?* http://online.barrons.com/article/SB50001424052748704235404578404641758715174.html – articleTabs_article%3D1.

Grgurich, J. (2012). *Why China Doesn't Like Barbie, Best Buy or DIY*. http://www.dailyfinance.com/2012/06/20/why-china-doesnt-like-barbie-best-buy-or-diy/.

Jiang, J. (2006). *Best Buy Acquires China's Five Star for $180 Mln*. http://www.bloomberg.com/apps/news?pid=newsarchive&sid=aXdoCwlUZ2R8&refer=asia.

Lee, T. (2013). *Best Buy Hires New CEO for its China Business*. http://www.startribune.com/business/206772421.html.

Lu, S. (2010). *Understanding China's Retail Market*. http://www.chinabusinessreview.com/understanding-chinas-retail-market/.

MacLeod, C. (2011). *Best Buy, Home Depot Find China Market a Tough Sell*. http://usatoday30.usatoday.com/money/industries/retail/2011-02-23-bestbuy23_ST_N.htm.

Mei, G. (2013). *Culture Determines Business Model: Analyzing Home Depot's Failure Case in China for International Retailers from a Communication Perspective*. Thunderbird International Business Review, 55(2), 173-191.

Ni, V. (2011). *Best Buy's Withdrawal: American Morals Fail to Transcend Chinese Consumer Market*. http://www.china-briefing.com/news/2011/03/02/best-buys-withdrawal-american-morals-fail-to-transcend-chinese-consumer-market.html – sthash.48ndz7g4.dpuf.

Rein, S. (2011). *Why Best Buy Failed in China*. http://www.cnbc.com/id/41882157/Why_Best_Buy_Failed_in_China.

Roane, K. R. (2011). *Best Buy's Lesson from China: Cluttered Beats Curated*. http://money.cnn.com/2011/02/10/news/international/bestbuy_china_fivestar.fortune/index.htm. \

Jing Betty Feng earned her Ph.D. in international business at Georgia State University, Atlanta, Georgia.

Business

An International Equity Exchange for China? Considering the Options

Vijaya Subrahmanyam
Vol.11, No.2
2012

Introduction

Chinese policymakers are considering reforms to open China's equity markets to foreign capital. A proposed International Board would allow both foreign firms and China's domestic private firms to list on the new Shanghai exchange. With China's increasing role in the global economy, it appears logical for China to open its markets further to foreign capital. However, this proposal has yet to be implemented, indicating there are both potential benefits and possible hidden costs, at least to some of the players involved. This article analyzes the pros and cons of launching an International Board in China, both for China's economy and for Chinese and foreign firms. The conclusion is that having an International Board is an essential step in the development of China's financial markets.

China's stock market development

China began to reform its economy in 1978 when Deng Xiaoping rose to power. Notwithstanding such reforms, firms continued to be largely owned and operated as state-owned enterprises (SOEs), and their lackluster performance implied the necessity of the discipline of a stock market. The government believed that adopting a Western market model, with its diversified ownership and strong regulations, would lead SOEs to become more efficient and competitive in the global marketplace. The Shanghai Stock Exchange was established in 1990. A large amount of investment in technology and infrastructure followed, to develop the exchange. However, while the investment in modern technology was intended to bring the Chinese equity markets up to par with the Western world, the resemblance was minimal at best. In part, this may be a result of trying to fit a U.S.-style stock market into a Chinese-type command-economy, wherein much of the equity market is run and owned by SOEs which, in turn, also regulate the markets. To correct these deficiencies, China has made efforts to be more financially inclusive, and China's regulatory body, the China Securities Regulation Commission (CSRC), is playing a critical role in changing the composition of market participants.

Chinese firms typically are classified by ownership type as state-owned enterprises, domestic privately-owned enterprises or foreign-funded enterprises. SOEs are either wholly owned by the government or have majority shares belonging to the government (state-holding enterprises). Privately-owned firms by definition are not state-owned but are private limited liability corporations and private sole and partnership enterprises. Foreign-funded enterprises include firms that are registered as joint ventures, cooperatives, sole-proprietorships or LLCs that are funded with foreign funds, including funds from Hong Kong, Macao or Taiwan.[1]

The government increasingly has been making provisions to attract foreign firms and their investments. Given these efforts, the Chinese stock markets have grown substantially, in both wholesale and retail investment sectors. Financial markets in China offer different types of shares. The most prominent are A-shares and B-shares, which are issued by companies incorporated in mainland China. The main difference between A-shares and B-shares is who is allowed to trade them. A-shares, the largest class of shares in China, are renminbi (RMB) denominated shares, which can be traded only by Chinese nationals and foreign institutional investors classified and authorized as Qualified Foreign Institutional Investors (QFII). B-shares are denominated in foreign currency, USD or HKD. They were originally designed solely for foreign investors, but since March 2001, they also include domestic retail investors with access to foreign currency.[2]

In 2002, institutional investors made inroads into China's markets. By 2011 they accounted for only two percent of the total stock market value, but their depth and impact on the Chinese markets was substantial, because of the composition of the participants in the program. Eighty percent of the 192 QFIIs approved since 2002 are long-term investors, including asset management companies, insurers and pension funds. Further, in April of 2012, the CSRC raised the investment ceiling for QFIIs to $80 billion from $30 billion, and in July China eased its investment controls on QFIIS allowing them to enter the interbank bond market. These moves will increase the importance of QFII investors in China. On the flip side, China also has begun to allow domestic institutional investors to invest abroad via the Qualified Domestic Investors (QDII) program, allowing them to diversify risk and reduce excess liquidity.

China's equity markets also have witnessed innovations. For example, ChiNext in Shenzhen lists companies in high growth sectors, and there is now a futures stock exchange. Mini-QFII recently was introduced, which allows qualified Hong Kong subsidiaries of China's securities and fund management companies to channel RMB deposits in Hong Kong into the mainland financial markets via investment products. With a high savings rate, and few investment options because of limited product offerings, when the government and regulators offer new financial products, the market in China responds quickly.

The Chinese markets have grown tremendously, and in June 2012, based on domestic equity market capitalization, both Shanghai and Shenzhen exchanges in mainland China were listed among the top 10 largest exchanges in the world with market capitalizations of 2,411 billion and 1,149 billion USD respectively.[3] By the end of fiscal year 2012, the Shanghai exchange had 944 companies listed with A-shares and 54 with B-shares.

The latest development is the expected rollout of the Shanghai Stock Exchange's International Board allowing foreign companies access to the Chinese markets and domestic investors to share in the returns achieved by international companies. While in theory this seems like a logical next step, market analysts in China have not been completely on board with the idea. Many argue that while the International Board may successfully put China on the global financial map, the ride may be very bumpy because of possible effects on the existing system. The recent global economic downturn has increased funding pressures in the A-shares market, and some market experts voice concerns about the proposed International Board creating pressure to sell existing shares to raise cash to buy stocks on the new exchange. Further, the financial crisis largely has halted the B-shares market, and analysts argue that the introduction of the International Board may result in redundancy with B-shares. Market experts also have pointed out potential problems in share price evaluation, erratic capital flow and supervisory issues that remain unresolved.

Before launching the International Board, China's regulators need to spell out listing requirements, reporting regulations and disclosures. So far, information has gotten out through news reports. These indicate that the Board will require a company seeking a listing to have a market capitalization of more than 30 billion yuan ($5.5 billion) and a combined three-year net income of more than 3 billion yuan.[4] In addition, proceeds of an initial public offering may only be used abroad.[5] These are reasonable stipulations by international standards. However, there are concerns around financial disclosures including issues surrounding the use of Chinese accounting standards for non-Chinese companies trading in China, and the type of reconciliation approaches that may be required. Details, if any, are very nebulous on how Chinese regulators would enforce the International

Financial Reporting Standards, or the role of auditing and disclosure requirements for non-Chinese firms who list on the International Board. Criteria for non-Chinese accounting firms to audit non-Chinese firms listing in mainland China need clarity, and so far there seems to be little documentation regarding this issue. Critics strongly urge postponing the launch of the Board until some or all the aforementioned issues have been addressed. Hence, while the Chinese government expressed the possibility launching the International Board to allow foreign firms and domestic private firms to list back in 2009, this has not yet materialized.

Benefits to Chinese firms

Research suggests that the fundamental reason for countries to have a stock market is to provide financing and liquidity for corporations.[6] Because of the political environment within China that favors state-owned firms and investments, private firms in particular have an uphill battle finding financing for projects or expansion abroad. A large number of foreign firms and private domestic firms have expressed interest in the development of an equity market to be able to gain access to available liquidity. Additionally, since the 1980s, as part of the reform process, China has implemented a policy of zhengqi fenkai, which translates as "separating government functions from business operations." In the process, China's SOEs were increasingly privatized. However, this trend has exposed the weaknesses of many of these state-owned companies laden with legacy assets, including obsolete equipment and technology, and expensive social policies that include health care and worker pensions. The potential spillover effect of know-how from foreign firms that may list in the Chinese market is thus considered as a benefit to firms in China. Hence skepticism regarding the opening of the International Board may be only temporary.

While China disallowed non-state-owned companies from the stock markets if they listed elsewhere, it also increasingly made SOEs "public" by issuing shares while continuing to hold majority control. The IPO (initial public offering) process in China is largely mythical since it often is funded by loans from a state-controlled bank and not outside investors. For instance, the Agricultural Bank IPO in 2010 was largely funded by other SOEs. In addition, only a small number of Chinese companies that are not state-owned can trade in the Shanghai markets. The more practical issue is that this leaves no room for non-state companies to raise outside capital, and for listed firms to be correctly valued via trading. Opening the markets to foreign firms should help create liquidity, visibility, depth and better market pricing for firms. To truly reform the Chinese markets, however, the state must exit the equity markets.

As the line between state-owned and privately and/or publicly owned firms blurs, the challenges that confront them would not be dissimilar. Chinese multi-nationals have sought growth, requiring additional capital and visibility (branding) that the larger markets abroad more easily offer. Many of these multinational firms have listed abroad because the CSRC does not allow them to list on the Shanghai or Shenzhen exchanges once they incorporate outside of the PRC. As Chinese companies move from an export orientation to an outward FDI strategy, many companies find themselves ill-prepared to compete in the global markets. The lack of qualified manpower and adequate technology, and limited experience and knowledge of strategy and business processes, puts both private- and public-sector firms equally at a disadvantage in the global arena. Liquidity needs and expansion of products and markets are significant factors regardless of ownership type.

In order to gain ground in the global markets, these companies go abroad to seek talent, tap new markets, search for raw materials and acquire new technologies. China's direct outward investment was only around $20 billion in 2006, but reached around $365 billion by 2011. In addition, while expanding geographically, concentrating largely on developing nations, resource-rich Australia and Canada, since the early 2000s investors have moved more toward Europe and North America.[7] While expanding Chinese companies have had to learn to be apolitical and deal with regulatory policies with regards to governance, disclosures, financial reporting and intellectual property rights, thus forcing them to face a steep learning curve upon expansion.

Further, with capital controls still imposed by the State, large firms that list and trade abroad currently are unable to repatriate profits. If foreign firms are allowed to list in Shanghai, they will be able to more easily retain profits within China, which will create greater liquidity in the domestic markets. Thus, by trading both domestically and in foreign markets where they are listed, they could create more depth in the Shanghai market, and their fundamentals would more accurately reflect their true value. In addition, Cavoli, McIver and Nowland's (2011) study of a sample of Asian markets suggests that higher trade openness, higher output growth and lower inflation may be associated with a greater proportion of foreign listings. They note that the extent of foreign listings on domestic stock exchanges (cross-listings) may serve as one measure of financial and economic integration among nations.

The Chinese investor would then have a potpourri of investment options, including both blue chips and red chips, thus integrating China into the global equity markets. If capital controls were relaxed concurrently with the launching of the International Board, Beijing could allow for cross-border transactions in yuan, thus letting its value be determined in the financial markets via trading. With increasing discussions in the country of making RMB an international currency, this would be an important step toward that goal.

More recently, some Chinese companies have been permitted to settle trade transactions in yuan via Hong Kong banks, and the yuan is being used more frequently in trade conducted between China and its trading partners. In a mere three years, the share of China's international trade settled in yuan increased from zero to eight percent in 2011. Increasingly, yuan-denominated securities are available for investors, such as the "dim sum" bonds traded in Hong Kong. As China's economic might continues to grow, the influence of its currency will inevitably increase with it. Consistent with this internationalization, and with plans to make Shanghai a global financial hub, the new Board will list shares by foreign companies denominated in yuan.[8]

Benefits to firms listing in China

Two reasons largely predominate with regard to why foreign firms list in China. One is to seek capital and the other is to diversify risk. With China's high growth and savings rate, foreign firms can gain access to new sources of capital and expand their investor base to include those who previously had limited investment options. Reese and Weisbach (2002), Karolyi (2006), Hail and Luez (2009) and others have noted financial benefits for firms that cross-list including increased opportunities to raise capital, higher liquidity, greater visibility, and lowered costs of capital.

With growing consumer sophistication in China, there is a large untapped market for foreign firms to sell their goods and services. For well-positioned foreign firms, the opening of Chinese financial markets may create an investment boom, especially in this post-financial crisis period in the U.S. and Europe. Chinese buyers are likely to be a great market for diversifying products and services offered by these firms. In addition, if Chinese multinationals aim at growing via acquisitions of firms in the developed nations, foreign firms may be able to divest of assets/divisions more easily and it may be a win-win for both. In addition, firms in U.S. and Europe in post-crisis mode may welcome joint ventures and partnership alliances in China to diversify their risks as well as gain new revenues. As China is closely connected to the East Asian Tigers and Japan through fairly well-developed production networks (Prime, Subrahmanyam and Lin, 2012), access to those markets may be available via a listing in China, thus making it more attractive for the long run.

The scarcity of resources and human capital, caused by Chinese multinationals also vying for the same resources and workforce as the foreign multinationals, could be a hindrance. On the other hand, because employment opportunities are being limited in Europe and the U.S. for trained professionals in the post-crisis era, Chinese firms or foreign firms in China may offer employment opportunities, thus positively impacting global unemployment. Hence there are numerous positive outcomes that could result from establishing an International Board in China.

Many Chinese companies have been successful and today appear in the Fortune 500. However, restrictions are still imposed by Chinese regulations on domestic firms listing on the Shanghai exchange if they have listed abroad. As the Chinese government contemplates the introduction of the International Board, transparency of information, corporate governance, price discovery and economic development are all necessary for efficient functioning of a public stock market. These are areas in which the Chinese government needs to invest time and effort so China can compete internationally to attract domestic and foreign firms to list in China. This would also greatly benefit Chinese firms, as they would learn to respond to policy structures and changes domestically before expanding globally.

While it is not clear as to when the Chinese government will launch the International Board, for China to be a major player in the global markets, this is a necessary step. China's financial markets have witnessed a major transformation in the past couple of decades, but the global financial crisis of 2008 seems to have dampened that process somewhat. Recent media reports indicate, however, that the government in China is focusing on the technical details with regard to listing, leadership of the Board, and related policies, and may have more definite plans concerning the opening of the Board possibly in the coming year. Reports indicate that more than 300 international companies have contacted the CSRC expressing interest in listing with the Board.[9] For the country's growth and development to continue, the Chinese government should launch the International Board allowing foreign firms and all private domestic firms to list in the Shanghai markets. The focus going forward should be on creating and sustaining an efficient, diversified, liquid and stable financial market.

Notes

[1] *Details of ownership types are provided in, "An Analysis of State-owned Enterprises and State Capitalism in China," by Andrew Szamosszegi and Cole Kyle (page 8, Table III-1); Prepared by Capital Trade Corporation for the U.S.-China Economic and Security Review Commission, October 26, 2011*

[2] *In addition, there are H-shares that can be traded by companies incorporated in the PRC and are traded in HK and denominated in HKD; N-shares that are denominated in USD and include companies incorporated in the PRC and listed and traded on the NYSE; L-shares include companies incorporated in the PRC and listed and traded on the LSE; Red chips are Chinese companies incorporated outside PRC and listed in HK, and are often state-owned or state-controlled companies; and S-shares are like H-shares but are traded in Singapore.*

[3] *World Federation of Exchanges 2012 http://www.world-exchanges.org/files/files/1st%20half%20%202012%20WFE%20market%20highlights%20with%20comments.pdf*

[4] *Compared to NYSE and NASDAQ, these requirements appear reasonable. See details in, http://www.venturelawcorp.com/listing_requirement_chart.htm*

5 *http://www.chinadaily.com.cn/bizchina/2011-05/09/content_12468936.htm*

6 *Mitchell, Lawrence E., Who Needs the Stock Market? Part I: The Empirical Evidence (October 30, 2008). Available at SSRN: http://ssrn.com/abstract=1292403 or http://dx.doi.org/10.2139/ssrn.1292403;*

7 *Daniel H. Rosen and Thilo Hanemann, "The Rise in Chinese Overseas Investment and What It Means for American Businesses," China Business Review, July-September 2012.*

8 *http://blogs.wsj.com/deals/2012/09/17/foreign-firms-line-up-to-list-in-china/*

9 *http://blogs.wsj.com/deals/2012/09/17/foreign-firms-line-up-to-list-in-china/*

Vijaya Subrahmanyam, Ph.D., is Professor of Finance at the Stetson School of Business, Mercer University-Atlanta, Georgia.

Language Services Go Global:
An Interview with Bernie Colacicco at KeyLingo

Penelope B. Prime
Vol. 12, No. 1
2013

Editor's Note: Keylingo, founded in 2004, is a global translations services company with many locations throughout the U.S. and Canada and is one of the China Research Center's corporate sponsors. Center Director Penelope Prime asked Bernie Colacicco, Keylingo Georgia Managing Director, to share some insights into the changing translation services market with a particular focus on Chinese language translation challenges and opportunities.

Q: Many trends in the economy point to growing internationalization of business, such as growing exports, more foreign investment, growing tourism, etc. Does the growth in your industry track these trends closely?

A: Yes, there is a very close parallel to the internationalization growth of business and the continued growth and high demand experienced in the language services industry, not only in North America, but worldwide. In fact, in 2013 the language translation services industry in North America alone is expected to grow from U.S.$11.7 billion to U.S.$13.1 billion or 12%. Looking forward, the language translation industry in North America is projected to grow to U.S.$16.5 billion in 2015 and to U.S.$47.3 billion worldwide.

Q: Did the financial crisis of 2008-09 stall this growth? And if so, has it recovered?

A: Prior to the 2008-2009 recession, the industry had been experiencing growth of approximately 20% annually, but during the 2008-2009 financial crisis, the growth never really stalled or receded, instead it decelerated to very respectable and sustainable annual growth numbers of approximately 10%. I am not so sure the industry will get back to the level of 20% annual growth, but based on the five-year projections that I have seen, the industry is expected to continue growing at a very healthy rate of 12%.

Q: Is there a rising need for translation into, or from, Chinese?

A: While we don't specifically track growth metrics for each client-requested target language, I can tell you that the demand for translation from English to Chinese remains very strong, and Chinese translation requests remain in the top five to six of our most requested languages.

Q: Where do you find your talent for Chinese translation

A: We have a Vendor Management team that works very closely with our Chinese linguists. The Chinese linguist teams that we select must pass a very rigorous vetting process that includes certification from an association belonging to the International Federation of Translators, a degree in translation from a recognized institution of higher learning, years of experience (our linguists average over ten years of experience), previous project references, and sample translations. In addition, there are ongoing proficiency tests each linguist must pass on an annual basis.

Q: What are the most sought-after services in your sector? How much of your work is written translation as opposed to oral translation?

A: The greatest demand for services in the industry is in the form of written content, which is either printed material or digital content for websites. Approximately 10% of the services we provide fall into the oral category, which can either be simultaneous or consecutive interpretation or what is known as OPI (over the phone translation). Conducting a deeper dive, the manufacturing vertical represents the biggest share of where the need for language translation services exists, and this vertical represents about one third of all of the market for outsourced language services.

Q: If a conference needed your services to provide simultaneous translation in Mandarin, how would the process of a bid and delivery work?

A: The most important pieces of information needed in order to successfully fulfill a Mandarin simultaneous interpretation request are: subject matter, duration of the event, number of attendees, venue location, date(s), and whether or not equipment is needed. Once we know these components we can prepare a firm project estimate for the client and secure the services of the appropriate linguists. Of all of the components involved with the scope of the project, the subject matter is the most critical piece. Linguists are very specialized, and if the subject matter is biosciences-related, then an interpreter with translation experience in the biosciences field would need to be used.

Q: How has the delivery of translation changed over time? How does technology facilitate the delivery of your services now?

A: Technology has certainly played a vital role in the development of the industry. One of the biggest technological tools is something called Translation Memory or "TM." TM is a client and client language specific database that stores every translation completed for that client. TM ensures accuracy and consistency of translations by keeping track of what was previously translated and then allowing the linguist to incorporate those translations into future translation projects, when the identical source words or "fuzzy matches" of sentences appear in the source text that is in need of translating. In addition to a cost savings for the client, TM helps improve the speed of translations. Two important items to emphasize are that a separate TM file by target language is kept for each client, and the TM is the client's intellectual property and is treated as such.

Q: How did you become involved in the translation services sector?

A: I was in the midst of a career transition and I was looking for an opportunity in a growth industry. In addition, I felt very strongly about Keylingo's business model and their client centric approach. As I investigated the industry it became clear that the demand for language translation services would be strong for many years to come and that Keylingo was positioned very well to meet this demand.

Business

Commentary: The U.S. House Intelligence Committee Scapegoats Huawei

William Abbott Foster
Vol.11, No.2
2012

On October 8, 2012, the U.S. House Select Committee on Intelligence issued a report warning all American companies against using equipment from the Chinese telecom manufacturers Huawei and ZTE.[1]

The report argues that Huawei and ZTE's' ability to out-compete U.S. and European telecom providers was due to financial support from the Chinese government. The Committee said that this support gave the Chinese People's Liberation Army (PLA) and the Ministry of State Security the ability to force Huawei and ZTE to put "trap doors" in equipment that they sell to American companies and the U.S. government. Electronic trap doors would open a channel for transmission of information, presumably to the Chinese security apparatus. The report makes the claim that if American critical infrastructure is built with Chinese equipment, it cannot be considered secure.

The reality is that U.S. government agencies, hi-tech firms, and universities have already been penetrated by Chinese hackers working at cross-purposes with Huawei and LTE. It is important to point out that there is no evidence that Huawei has had anything to do with these breaches. Instead of dealing with the role of China's hackers and their Chinese People's Liberation Army sponsors, the U.S. House Intelligence Committee has made Huawei the scapegoat for the American government's inability to protect American companies from real threats.

The House Intelligence Committee report claims that Huawei and ZTE were not responsive to questions the Committee's researchers asked when visiting Shenzhen, China, and when called before the Committee during Congressional hearings. According to a source familiar with the visit to China, Huawei gave the researchers access to a wide assortment of decision-makers who did their best to explain a company and a culture which is very different from most in America. The report makes much of the fact that Huawei has a "Communist Party cell" on its premises. The report does not mention the fact that many multinationals in China have "Communist Party cells." It likewise does not cite academic research on the role of such cells.

The Committee also tried to show that Huawei's success was due to "special financing" from the Chinese Development Bank. What the Committee did not point out was how the Chinese Development Bank funding has gone not to Huawei but to many African countries that have begun to move from abject poverty to the possibility of prosperity. Loans from the Development Bank funded purchases of Huawei equipment to build cell phone telecommunications systems in these countries. It can be argued that Huawei's efforts in Africa have had a bigger impact on the continent than any U.S. aid effort.

Given the realities of current U.S. politics, the inability of the Congress to pass cyber-security legislation that could address the growing problem of Chinese cyber-espionage against U.S. hi-tech firms, and the pressure to protect domestic industries such as the U.S. communications giant Cisco, one must wonder whether the Committee went fishing for any sign that could be used as evidence that Huawei was controlled by the Chinese government and could not be trusted to supply infrastructure in the United States.

The Committee report digs up issues that have been brought up over and over, such as Huawei's work with an Iranian telecommunications company, an intellectual property lawsuit with Cisco and a suit regarding a couple of its associated employees working at Motorola. These are difficult accusations for Huawei to respond to under oath. My recommendation to Huawei is to admit that its governance structure has matured as it has become a global company. It has learned from mistakes and has resolved these issues in court. It has now created a company that adheres to all U.S. government rules and regulations and can be trusted by its competitors, suppliers and clients.

Though the Intelligence Committee report raises all sorts of questions about Huawei and ZTE's inability to explain their relationship with the Chinese government, after a year of investigation the Committee and the U.S. intelligence community have not been able to find one instance of Huawei or ZTE putting a back door in equipment they installed for a U.S. customer.

The report never touches on why Huawei has been so successful. It is a well-known fact that Huawei has a fanatical commitment to its customers. It has a well-earned reputation for integrating its customers' legacy systems into Huawei's existing systems, no matter how difficult and complex the integration effort. The basic fact is that U.S. companies such as Motorola and Cisco just cannot compete with Huawei in terms of offering such custom solutions because of the high price of their programmers.

The case can be made that Huawei is so powerful in Chinese society that the PLA simply does not have the clout to make Huawei do something that would run counter to the company's intense loyalty to its customers. Though much is made of Huawei President Ren Zhengfei's work as a PLA engineer and his immense "guanxi," or personal relations with power brokers in China, the U.S. Intelligence Committee report does not explore Huawei's claim that President Ren has deep Confucian morals and would not do anything, such as violating his relationships with his customers, that would be inconsistent with those values. Also Huawei's Chinese employees have most of their salaries tied to corporate profit-sharing, and most have hopes of becoming rich through stock ownership. They do not want to jeopardize their material dreams by doing anything that would lead to the discovery that Huawei had installed trapdoors for the People's Liberation Army into Western telecom equipment.

The House Intelligence Committee Report does not explore the intensely competitive environment of telecom in China in 1998, and how Huawei built its success by providing legacy solutions that incorporate emerging technologies that are perfect for the African, Asian and East European telecom markets. Huawei's "multi-mode" solution allows telecom companies to switch CDMA, WCDMA, GSM, WiMAX and LTE out of one box. Competitors such as Ericsson sell their customers separate boxes for each protocol. Huawei developed a business model based on being able to integrate any legacy system and provide a pathway to the latest technologies.

Sprint, for example, was desperate for Huawei's multi-mode solution, which even supported the Nextel-Integrated Enhanced Network (iDEN) protocol, a technology that Sprint needed to support because of a merger. Huawei bid $6 billion to upgrade the Sprint network while Ericsson bid $8 billion. The U.S. government opposed the Huawei-Sprint deal and then Secretary of Commerce Gary Locke intervened to make sure that Sprint went with Ericsson. The stock market did not react favorably to the forced Ericsson deal, and Sprint's stock value went down by 25% the quarter the deal happened.

Where does this leave Huawei? It was on track to becoming a $100 billion, highly profitable employee-owned company. These plans have been dashed as countries such as Australia have started to follow the U.S. in blacklisting Huawei as a national threat. Huawei has responded by focusing on making low-margin smart phones and tablets, and has become less profitable as a company.

It can be argued that a couple of years ago, Huawei had the opportunity to convince both the U.S. National Security Agency and the Chinese Communist

Party that it was the ideal partner to provide secure technology for the global cloud.

The irony is that Huawei's technology could have been employed to protect the U.S. against real Chinese and other threats. Tony Rutkowski, one of the world's leading techno-diplomats, points out that the capability that the House Intelligence Committee attributes to Huawei is just what Huawei needs to address the new kinds of computer threats that we face. In Rutkowski's eyes, Huawei needs to be able to simultaneously update all firmware and software in its communication equipment worldwide in response to identified threats. This capability should be seen as an asset that makes Huawei a critical partner in the implementation of the U.S. government's STIX automated threat- sharing system.

What few realize is how difficult it will now be to build a resilient global cloud, now that America has poisoned its relationship with the world's major telecom manufacturer.

Note

[1] *The Committee report is available at: http://intelligence.house.gov/sites/intelligence.house.gov/files/ documents/Huawei-ZTE%20Investigative%20Report%20%28FINAL%29.pdf*

Disclaimer

William Foster reports that he has received no funding from Huawei, the U.S. government, or any private entity for his research on Huawei apart from a $5,000 grant from International Data Corporation (IDC) four years ago for a study of Huawei's development of a communications protocol called IMS (IP Multimedia Subsystem). The study was published by IDC.

Growth and Corruption in China

Andrew Wedeman
Vol. 11, No. 2
2012

After the beginning of the post-Mao reform period in 1978-79, China experienced a marked worsening of corruption. The pre-reform period was not free from corruption, but a series of large-scale mass campaigns during the 1950s and 1960s had largely driven corruption underground. Bribes most often were paid not in cash but in kind, with cigarettes, liquor, and meat the common mediums. In the post-Mao period, the scale of corruption increased exponentially as officials cashed in on their ability to manipulate the allocation of valuable resources, including land and capital, in return for bribes valued at hundreds-of-thousands of Chinese renminbi. And whereas much of the corruption during the Maoist period happened at "street level," involving relatively low-ranking officials, in recent years government ministers, senior bureaucrats, members of the provincial government and party apparatus, and even members of ruling Politburo have been prosecuted for corruption. Outside observers were so struck by the rapid spread of corruption during the 1980s and early '90s, in 1995 Transparency International (TI) ranked China the fourth most corrupt country in its Corruption Perceptions Index.

Stunning though the spread of corruption after the adoption of economic reforms may be, it is only half the story. At the same time corruption was increasing, China's economy also grew rapidly. Between 1980 and 2010, Gross Domestic Product (GDP) per capita increased thirteen- fold, according to the International Monetary Fund. China, in fact, had the second-largest gain in per capita GDP globally during this period, two times more than the next-best performer (South Korea) and almost eight times more than the United States, where per capita GDP increased only 65% in these three decades. Equatorial Guinea, which was the only country to outperform China, grew not as a result of sustained economic expansion, but because it struck oil and went almost overnight from abject poverty to vast wealth – wealth that was being swiftly stripped away by a government far more corrupt than China's. China thus not only experienced rising corruption as it moved from a command economy toward a market economy, it also experienced rapid growth, a combination that economists suggest is unlikely, if not impossible.

The worsening of corruption during the reform period thus confronts students of contemporary China's political economy with a series of questions. First, why did corruption worsen? Second, what forms did this new corruption take? Third, why has worsening corruption not slowed or even retarded China's economic growth?

In the pages that follow, I will address these questions to explain why China was able to experience concurrent rising corruption and rapid economic growth.

Rising Corruption

After seizing power in 1949, the CCP cracked down on corruption in a series of major campaigns. In late 1951, the party launched the Three Antis Campaign against corruption, waste, and bureaucratism. In January 1952, the Five Antis Campaign targeted bribery, tax evasion, theft of state property, bid rigging, and the theft of state economic information. The following year, the New Five Antis Campaign struck at bureacratism, commandism, and other violations of law and disciplinary regulations by state officials and party cadres. Subsequent campaigns, including the Socialist Education Movement (1963-66) and the One Strike, Three Antis Campaign (1970-72) attacked other forms of official malfeasance. By the late Maoist period, these repeated attacks on corruption and the political environment ushered in by the Cultural Revolution had largely eradicated most visible manifestations of corruption.

Corruption was, however, far from eliminated. On the contrary, during the 1960s and 1970s a new culture emerged in which individuals sought to cultivate personal relationships (guanxi) that would allow them to slip "through the backdoor" (zou huomen) to obtain scare commodities, get admission to schools, find work, and seek favors from bureaucrats and officials. At the time, money was of secondary importance because it alone could not buy rationed goods or access. More often, people seeking to build relationships and get favors relied on "gifts" of cigarettes, liquor, meat, and other hard-to-find commodities. Officials often peddled equally mundane goods – ration cards or a "chop" on a document. There were, of course, more egregious cases of corruption, including that of Wang Shouxin, a mid-level official whose position as head of a local coal supply unit enabled her to spin a web of illegal deals that netted her and her confederates the then-princely sum of Y500,000 (US$320,000).

In the early and mid-1980s, petty corruption flourished. Many goods remained in short supply and would-be buyers found that they still had to present officials with a carton of cigarettes and a couple of bottles of Chinese liquor (baijiu) to obtain ration cards. Would-be entrepreneurs and private businessmen seeking to establish new enterprises also found the only way to navigate the thickets of red tape was to use personal connections and, increasingly, cash. In the mid-1980s, the party decided to put off comprehensive price reform in favor of a hybrid system wherein commodity prices were fixed by the state based on whether they were being sold within the state-planned economy or in emerging markets. Because ongoing scarcity ensured that market prices were generally much higher than in-plan prices, officials found they could earn quick profits by diverting goods out of the planned sector and onto the market. Arbitraging between the two sectors created by the so-called "two track" price system, and fueled a wave of "official profiteering" (guandao) during the late 1980s. By the later 1980s, official profiteering had become so widespread and visible that the perception that corruption was enabling officials reap the lion's share of gains from reform became a major factor intensifying support for the anti-government demonstrations that swept China in the spring of 1989.

Faced with rising corruption and evidence that corruption was undermining its legitimacy, the CCP cracked down, first in 1982, then again in 1986, and a third time in July 1989. In each campaign, the government announced it had substantially increased the number of officials charged with corruption, made a show of putting the "big tigers" it had caught on trial, and, in some cases, publicly executing corrupt officials. Despite these repeated crackdowns, the best available evidence suggests that corruption increased substantially during the 1980s. The Procuratorate "filed" 9,000 corruption-related cases in 1980, the 1989 anti-corruption campaign yielded some 77,400 cases. Thereafter, the average number of cases hovered around 60,000 from 1991 to 1997. Revision of the criminal code in 1997 resulted in the decriminalization of a range of lesser offenses, and dropped the average number of cases filed to approximately 32,000.

In the early 1990s, after a second round of reforms, corruption intensified. By the mid-'90s more senior-level officials had become corrupt; they were now "auctioning off" control rights for enterprises and real estate and receiving much larger illicit payoffs in return. In 1995, for example, the Party Secretary of Beijing, Chen Xitong, who was also a member of the party's core leadership, was caught raking in millions of dollars in "commissions" from real estate developers. The number of cases involving senior officials (defined in Chinese law as those holding leadership positions at or above the county level) shot up from a dozen a year in the mid-1980s to an annual average of 2,500. The amount of money reportedly recovered per case jumped from Y4,000 (US$1,700) in 1984 to Y42,000 (US$4,900) a decade later. Four years later in 1998, the amount exceed Y121,000 (US$14,600), and in 2007 the Procuratorate reported it recovered funds averaging more than Y273,000 (US$35,800). Meanwhile, the party's Discipline Inspection Commission, which has responsibility for maintain intra-party discipline, was sanctioning around 150,000 party members a year, one-third of them for corruption-related infractions.

As corruption got worse, the party fought back. But the effectiveness of China's anti-corruption effort has been questioned. Official statistics, however, show that about 10,000 officials are sent to prison each year on corruption charges and an additional 20,000 receive lesser punishments. Among those sentenced to prison, roughly 5,000 received sentences ranging from five years to life. Almost 400 individuals are known to have been sentenced to death; an additional 240 got "suspended death sentences." To date, there is no hard or convincing evidence the war on corruption has had a significant effect. Some evidence, however, suggests that corruption actually has worsened over the past decade. So it would appear the war on corruption has succeeded in the sense that it has brought corruption under control.

Assessments by outside experts also suggest some degree of improvement. According to Transparency International's index (using a scale of 1 to 10, with 10 as the most corrupt), corruption in China dropped from a high of 7.57 in 1995 to either 6.4 or 6.5 between 2007 and 2011. In 2011 China ranked overall a middling 75th out of 182. A recent poll of Chinese citizens found that only 9% reported having had either firsthand experience with corruption or had known somebody who had paid a bribe in the preceding year. At that level, direct experience with corruption in China was actually the same as reported by citizens of Singapore, which was one of the five least corrupt countries, according to TI. More surprisingly perhaps, 5% of Americans surveyed reported that they had paid a bribe.

In sum, it is clear that China experienced a significant surge in the incidence of corruption during the 1980s and that in qualitative terms corruption "intensified" in the 1990s. Since then, evidence suggests that corruption has remained at about the same levels and hence has been brought under control in the sense that China's "war on corruption" has prevented it from spiraling further out of control. Rising corruption, however, failed to retard economic growth. On the contrary, according to the IMF, GDP per capita grew at an average rate of almost 8% between 1980 and 1991, then shot up to an average of 12% between 1992 and 1995, and falling to a still torrid 8% between 1996 and 2004. Thereafter average growth rates jumped back up to greater than 11% during 2005-07 before settling back to 9% after the advent of the global recession in the summer of 2008. Since then, growth has slowed, but at 7.5% remains strong by global standards. Growth rates have thus remained robust even after corruption worsened and intensified.

Corruption with Chinese Characteristics

If worsening and intensifying corruption didn't inhibit China's economic boom, is there something "special" about corruption in China? In the 1970s, a number of scholars argued that given gross inefficiency in the allocation of resources by the state, bribery might allow would-be entrepreneurs to "buy" these resources and use them more efficiently. Others argued that bribes were often given to poorly paid government officials with the goal of getting them to cut through red tape. "Speed money," some claimed, might not only lubricate the creaky machinery of government, but also might even give bureaucrats a profit-based motive to perform their duties more efficiently. Some have argued that corruption in China differed from that found elsewhere because it often involved "profit-sharing." Businessmen cut officials in on their profits when officials helped them earn money. In some areas, local governments were said to have transformed themselves into entrepreneurial "local developmental states" by entering into partnerships with businesses and facilitating their operations in return for ad hoc taxes and other forms of illicit profit-sharing.

Although it does not appear that corruption in post-Mao China was qualitatively different, the nature of China's economic reform did create conditions in which some corruption (not all) was compatible with rapid growth. In abstract terms, economic reform involved large-scale transfers of potential value from the state to the market. In the early stages of reform, for instance, the de-collectivization of the agricultural sector transferred control over production to individual households. Because they stood to reap substantial windfall profits from land transfers, farmers had incentives to pay bribes to secure particularly productive plots and control rights for "sideline" production. Local cadres were also often in a position to leverage "considerations" in return for providing farmers with access to state subsidized inputs such as fertilizer, pesticides, and diesel fuel.

As reform deepened in the 1990s and the state began to lease out land for industrial, commercial, and real estate development, would-be industrialists, businessmen, and developers stood to earn quick windfall profits. A plot of unused land attached to a state-owned factory, for example, could generate a very substantial windfall if it were redeveloped into high-priced condominiums, shopping malls, or luxury hotels. Quick profits could, in fact, be made by simply flipping a piece of land leased cheaply from the state and then selling the lease rights to others.

Rapid growth also created a high demand for capital. Because China lacked a developed capital market when the economy moved into high gear, government agencies were often important sources of investment loans. Most government agencies either controlled stocks of capital or had accumulated substantial slush funds (known in Chinese as xiao jinku – literally small golden treasuries) \ they could use to make under-the-table loans with interest rates above those for regular bank loans. Even if they lacked their own capital, government agencies and state-owned enterprises enjoyed better access to the state-controlled banking system and could profit from arbitrage borrowing and re-lending to private entrepreneurs who could not obtain bank loans. The windfall profits generated by reform and the demand for capital thus created a series of new opportunities for officials to cash in.

The reform period also witnessed a major expansion in infrastructure. Since the 1980s, the Chinese government has spent vast sums – upward of Y6 trillion (US$874 billion) from the state budget alone as of 2009 – building new highways, railroads, airports, ports, and urban infrastructure. Public works contracting is a notorious source of corruption worldwide and China has been no exception. The development of China's much-touted high-speed rail system, on which the government will have reportedly spent Y3.5 trillion (US$532 billion) by 2015, has resulted in unprecedented cases of corruption. China's Minister of Railways Liu Zhijun allegedly conspired with middlemen and major state-owned companies to skim about Y800 million (US$122 million) (BBC 2011). Zhang Shuguang, the deputy chief engineer for the project, was said to have stashed Y18 billion (US$2.8 billion) in overseas bank accounts.

China's surge in corruption can be attributed to other factors as well. During the Cultural Revolution, China's law enforcement institutions had been "pulverized." Branded as bastions of "revisionism" and "counter-revolution," the Procuratorate and the party's Control Commission ceased to function or were taken over by the military. In 1979, these institutions were only in the early stages of reconstitution, and it was not until that year that China's first criminal code was enacted. On a very fundamental level, therefore, China entered the reform era with a very rudimentary institutional capability to fight corruption.

The lack of a functioning judicial system staffed by trained investigators, prosecutors, and judges was a major impediment to fighting corruption because, unlike a street mugging in which you have an obvious victim, corruption is a hidden and "victimless" crime to which the actual victim – the public – is not a direct party. Corruption most often involves two offenders – an official who accepts bribes and a private party who pays them – both of whom stand to profit from their transaction. More critically, "properly" done, corruption is a subtle "art," a careful "dance" wherein the parties never directly discuss exchanges of favors for bribes, use multiple subterfuges to hide payments, and conduct all transactions in cash to leave the most minimal trail. Corrupt relationships are best framed not in terms of quid pro quo "deals," but rather as exchanges involving "diffuse reciprocity" wherein financial "considerations" are repaid indirectly and seemingly in the "normal course" of business. For example, an official might discuss a contract with a building contractor who might then engage the official's son as a "consultant" for other "unrelated" matters or donate money to an "educational foundation," which just happens to be funding the official's daughter's doctoral studies at an American university. High-level corruption of the sort that became increasingly common in the mid-1990s is, moreover, apt to be much harder to detect than street-level corruption. Street-level corruption is apt to take place in open view and create aggrieved victims willing to report unjust demands. But high-level corruption is more likely to take place behind closed doors and be mutually profitable for both parties, neither of whom are apt to report their illegal deals to the authorities. In addition, powerful officials can take advantage of their authority to create conspiratorial "protective umbrellas" that enable them to stonewall and even suborn investigators.

China's emerging business culture also has contributed to China's surge in corruption. All of the business fortunes in contemporary China were built in a rough and tumble environment in which new businesses frequently rested on questionable foundations, by bending the rules, very often by paying bribes, providing kickbacks, giving lavish gifts, and participating in a culture of "banqueting" involving not only expensive dishes and fine liquors but often the provision of prostitutes and other "favors." In this environment, corruption only becomes a problem for those willing to pay when officials bought with bribes fail to "stay" bought or cannot deliver the benefits supposedly secured with under-the-table money. Otherwise, bribes can become nothing more than a quick means to obtain inflated profits and remove unwanted government impediments. And as corruption spread, many officials came to view it as "normal" and essentially an official perk enjoyed by "everybody." A "culture of corruption" thus emerged in which embezzlement and bribery were not deemed sins, per se, but more of a fact of life.

Anti-corruption work in China thus faced considerable challenges from the beginning. In fact, what is perhaps most surprising is that corruption did not reach even greater levels and come to the point at which so many officials were engaged in corruption that the state's emerging anti-corruption capabilities were simply overwhelmed.

Rising Corruption and Rapid Growth

If China experienced a significant worsening of corruption and corruption is negatively correlated with growth, why did the Chinese economy to manage grow so rapidly, even as corruption was worsening? Three factors help explain why this was possible. First, corruption was not a serious barrier to the initial acceleration of growth. Second, the most intense period of corruption coincided with large-scale transfers of value from the state to the emerging market economy. Third, despite a somewhat halting start and less than decisive results, China's anti-corruption efforts managed to bring corruption under control by the early 2000s, albeit without significantly affecting its overall severity. The first two factors combined to create a situation wherein corruption fed off growth rather than stifled it. Even though corruption became much worse than it had been in the pre-reform period, it was kept at levels that are not necessarily extraordinary for a developing economy.

At an abstract level, corruption can be broken down into two major forms: "plunder" and "transactive" corruption. In the case of plunder, officials prey on the state, stealing tax monies, looting the treasury, privately selling off state property, and so on. Officials engaged in plunder often target the private sector, ex-propriating profitable businesses and real estate, extorting money from wealthy individuals, or even demanding cash at the point of a gun. Transactive corruption, on the other hand, involves exchanges of money and favors. Neither form of corruption is benign. Transactive corruption may, in fact, involve extortionary bribery that borders on plunder. Nevertheless, plunder is apt to have a much more debilitating effect than transactive corruption because while transactive corruption often involves exchanges that are mutually beneficial to those directly involved, plunder attacks the economy's vitals by rendering property rights insecure and encouraging capital flight. Plunder wreaks economic destruction in much the same way that roving bandits destroy rural communities by driving off farmers' cattle, destroying their crops, stealing their goods and savings, and burning their homes. In its most extreme form, anarchic plunder by official "bandits" can morph into "kleptocracy." Best defined as a form of political system in which the state becomes an instrument for the extraction of plunder by the kleptocrat-in-chief and his inner circle of henchmen and cronies, kleptocracy generally results in a wholesale assault on an economy's core structures and the systematic destruction of the formal economy.

As noted earlier, during the Maoist era, petty bribery predominated. Officials and workers in state-owned enterprises also pilfered state property, stealing goods either for their own consumption or sale on underground black markets. Large-scale bribery was uncommon because so long as the state monopolized the economy, there were few private parties in a position to use illicit means to influence officials. Reform fundamentally changed the dynamics of corruption by creating a set of actors, including not only private businessmen but also the managers of state- owned enterprises, who could leverage financial advantage by bribing officials. As the economy took off, this "demand side" for corruption grew quickly. Not only did the incidence of bribery increase, but it also began to displace plunder as the modal form of corruption. A growing economy and thus increasing profits and incomes caused the size of bribes to grow as the "returns" from bribery grew.

When the state began letting out many more valuable assets, including land, the amounts paid in bribes increased exponentially. More senior officials became involved because they, not street-level bureaucrats, were in a position to "auction off" assets that would yield entrepreneurs and developers large windfall profits in the form of sizable gaps between the state's nominal valuation of assets and their actual market value. Rising corruption was an endogenous byproduct of economic reform; it was this reform, and the rapid economic growth it created, that fed rising corruption. Much of the "new corruption" that emerged during the mid-1990s can thus be linked to transactions involving the transfer of value-bearing assets from the state to the market. Because these transfers also spurred rapid growth, the result was a concurrent worsening of corruption and an acceleration of growth. This is not to say that corruption had a positive effect on growth. Instead, rising corruption imposed real costs. Inefficiency and misallocation, however, were what economists call "marginal costs" because they siphoned off a share of the total gains that might have been realized from investment.

The regime's much-maligned anti-corruption campaign also played a role. As noted earlier, corruption becomes most destructive when it morphs into kleptocracy and state institutions are converted into instruments for corrupt gain. The fact that the regime fought back and brought to justice at least some of those who turned corrupt prevented such a transformation of the Chinese state. Thus, even though individual officials and agencies may have succumbed to the "silver bullets" of corruption, the state as a whole did not degenerate into a kleptocracy. This is not to deny that some localities became "mafia states" where corrupt officials freely and even openly connived with unscrupulous businessmen and even criminals. Nor is it to say that very senior officials, their wives, children, relatives, and cronies were not deeply involved in corruption. The result was a dynamic wherein corruption was "controlled" in the sense that the regime's anti-corruption efforts were minimally sufficient to keep the aggregated level of corruption below the vaguely defined boundary that separates serious corruption and outright kleptocracy.

Conclusion

To some, economic reform in China is a miracle. To others, reform is a tale of ever-worsening corruption. There is no question that the latter version is true. Each new major corruption scandal seems to make those that came before pale in comparison. What was a "shocking" amount in the early 1980s was nothing compared to the corrupt monies being reported in the 1990s, and chump change by today's standards. Today, a case such as that of the Wang Shouxin ring and its Y500,000 (US$320,000) take would hardly raise the eyebrow of a public that has witnessed the 1999 Yuanhua case wherein a ring of smugglers colluded with local, provincial, and central officials to run an estimated Y53 billion (US$6.4 billion) worth of goods through the port of Xiamen in Fujian province in broad daylight, or read reports on the wealth of Premier Wen Jiabao's family, or heard to tales of corruption and murder involving Chongqing Party Secretary Bo Xilai and his wife Gu Kailai.

China's experience with rising corruption and rapid growth does not necessarily contradict the existing economic orthodoxy that corruption is negatively correlated with growth and hence rising corruption causes growth rates to fall. As argued herein, rising corruption in China was actually the result of rapid growth. If China stands out, it is not because it is exceptionally corrupt, but rather because its growth rate has been exceptionally high. There is also nothing about corruption in China that somehow distinguishes it from corruption elsewhere. If anything, "corruption with Chinese characteristics" more closely resembles the sorts of corruption found in much of the developing world than the "structural corruption" found in nations such as Japan, South Korea, and Taiwan.

That China has managed to maintain high growth rates despite rising corruption also does not mean that corruption might not cause greater economic damage in the future. As argued herein, rising corruption was a function of the transition from the planned to market economy. Completing that transition and consolidating a functioning market economy requires that the Chinese government begin to make substantial gains in its fight against corruption. Ultimately, the regime has to implement administrative and political reforms that would increase transparency and accountability. Before now, progress on these fronts has been limited, and even though the regime seems to understand that corruption has the potential to kill the economy, many within the party and leadership seem to fear that fighting corruption will certainly kill the party. As a result, many within the party have resisted the sorts of structural reforms needed to deal with the root problem – the party's monopoly on power and the resulting extensive discretionary power wielded by officials – rather than its overt manifestations. Nevertheless, the partial measures, such as mandatory disclosure of officials assets, documentation of the employment of their spouses and children, and requirement that officials account for the origins of property and assets or face prosecution under a new "unexplained assets" law may prove sufficient to keep corruption from getting substantially worse, and thereby may help ensure that the current combination of high levels of corruption and rapid growth continues for some time to come.

Reference

Andrew Wedeman, *Double Paradox: Rapid Growth and Rising Corruption in China* (Ithaca, NY: Cornell University Press, 2012).

Andy Wedeman, Ph.D., is Professor of Political Science at Georgia State University.

China's Cultural Diplomacy: Historical Origin, Modern Methods and Strategic Outcomes

Parama Sinha Palit
Vol.12, No.2
2013

Comprehending behaviors of nation-states has never been easy. Understanding China is particularly difficult given the great divide in terms of language (yu yan) and culture (wen hua). Beijing is conscious of this difficulty in communicating with the rest of the world. To tackle the "hegemony of discourse"– perceived in Beijing as a persistent effort by the West to project a negative image of China and promote "western values" for maximizing its own interests[1] – and to overcome its own weakness of the "power of the word" (hua yu quan), China has embarked on vigorous cultural diplomacy (CD), a strategy used since ancient times for communicating with the rest of the world. China considers culture essential in correcting adverse impressions created by its rapid strategic rise. Consequently, culture has emerged as the third pillar of Chinese diplomacy after economics and politics, with the 18th Congress in 2012 endorsing its relevance and the more recent Third Plenary in 2013 reaffirming its importance. Cultural diplomacy and soft power are important strategies for the Chinese leadership in developing benign impressions about China and securing strategic dividends through "virtuous" policies of engagement.

The employment of culture as a foreign policy tool in present-day politics in China is a combination of both academic effort and the leadership's genuine compulsion to open channels of communication with the international community. This paper tracks use of culture as a soft power tool in Chinese history while underlining the leadership's pragmatic understanding of the concept and underscoring its application worldwide. The Confucius Institutes (CIs) have played a major role in the global transmission of Chinese language and culture. This paper also reflects on the mandate of these Institutes and argues that China's CD is a far more strategically ambitious exercise than the mere export of its rich cultural heritage.

Cultural Diplomacy: An Ancient Chinese Legacy

CD is widely used by modern states for enhancing soft power. Soft power, popularized in the contemporary discourse on international relations by Joseph Nye, focuses on diplomatic engagement for strategic dividends. Several prominent political thinkers, e.g. Foucault, Bourdieu, Gramsci, Habermas and E.H. Carr, also have variously expounded on the concept prior to Nye. As a conceptual identity, soft power and the role of culture in its use are hardly limited to the western political discourse. Indeed, the prevalent impression of China's modern soft power strategy for connecting with the rest of the world being essentially an emulation of similar strategies pursued by major western powers overlooks the fact that soft power was strongly embedded in ancient Chinese history and philosophy. The specific period in Chinese history that can be identified for its distinct emphasis on spread of harmony and amity is the Spring and Autumn era (771 BC – 476 BC), also known as the Hundred Schools of Thought. Marked by significant cultural and intellectual developments, the historical thoughts of the period remain relevant in the modern era and are reflected in the contemporary Chinese articulation of soft power and its emphasis on CD. Thus, recognizing culture as an effective instrument of soft power and modern statecraft is an example of the pragmatism characterizing contemporary Chinese foreign policies.

According to the literature of the Hundred Schools of Thought, China's ancient strategists preferred diplomatic maneuvering to secure state objectives and were averse to territorial expansion by force. Kong Zi or Confucius (551 BC – 479 BC) stressed the limitation and regulation of power. Rather than war, Confucius' teachings focused on education and humanity. Mencius (372 BC – 289 BC), another great thinker of the time, also denounced wars with the idea that benevolent kings who could easily win over masses had no enemies.[2] The Confucius-Mencius political construct rejected the need for possessing large territories for enhancing state prestige. The Chou kingdom (1027 BC – 256 BC), for example, was hardly large but was nonetheless able to retain its dynastic command for eight hundred years – the longest for any Chinese dynasty.[3]

Along with Confucianism, the doctrine of Taoism and Mohism also emphasized "universal love" and the virtues of discussion and persuasion for solving problems. Lao Zi, another ancient Chinese philosopher who wrote the main texts of Taoism along with Zhuang Zi, discounted wars, with the latter emphasizing education and humility. Ideas such as culture winning over an enemy and winning a battle before it is fought are replete in ancient Chinese writings. The celebrated military strategist, Sun Zi (722 BC – 481 BC), in The Art of War, argued for attacking the enemy's mind rather than his fortified cities. Indeed, Chinese ancient philosophy and history rarely espoused hard power and focused on cultivating friends as opposed to engaging in conflicts. Later Chinese history obviously produced different strategies and priorities dictated by national interests of the time. Nonetheless, soft power and CD – conspicuous in modern China's strategic engagement – are essentially products of its ancient history and tradition, not emulations of western experiences.

The Academic Discourse on Culture

China's communication with the world was largely intermittent until the late 1980s. Prolonged isolation by the international community, a vocal discourse in the West labeling China as a destabilizing force, and the increasing spread of the "China collapse" theory after the Tiananmen Square crackdown in 1989 led China to seriously contemplate positive image-building. A nascent interest in soft power began taking shape in the 1990s with scholars and academics deliberating the virtues of dialogue and interaction. Wang Huning was one of the earliest exponents of soft power. Earlier with the Fudan University and currently a member of the Communist Party's Politburo and the Director of the Policy Research Office of the Party's Central Committee, Wang was probably the first contemporary Chinese scholar to argue that culture is the main source of a state's soft power.[4] The view was endorsed by other scholars such as Xiang Shu Yong[5] and Zhao Chang Rong[6] with both identifying culture and language as instrumental in enhancing strategic strength of a nation.

The modern Chinese literature on soft power is conspicuous by its ideological flavor and pronounced emphasis on culture. Discussing soft power, Rong distinguishes between western and Chinese cultures and argues that while the former stresses hegemony, Chinese culture based on Confucianism seeks peaceful solutions to international problems.[7] Several of his peers argue the western culture's focus on materialism, science, individualism, and industrialization are producing clashes and disharmony, while traditional Chinese principles such as "putting people first" and "harmony between nature and mankind"[8] are more effective in solving complex international problems. Modern Chinese writings regard China's indigenous culture imbibing Confucianism, Taoism, Buddhism, Mohism, and other classical schools of thought as embodying the softer aspects of China's national power. In this regard, concepts such as winning respect through virtues, benevolent governance, peace, and harmony without suppressing differences are repeatedly highlighted.

Culture in Official Pronouncements

Chinese culture retains ancient characteristics while accommodating changes. Culture has been influenced by politics and has acquired diverse undertones under different leaders. While Mao Zedong relegated Confucian teachings to the background during the Cultural Revolution (1965-75), the subsequent generation of leaders adopted Confucianism almost passionately. Whether it be Jiang Zemin's "rule by virtue" (yi de zhi guo) or Hu Jintao's "harmonious society" (he xie she hui), Confucian ideals are embedded in modern China's state vision for underscoring and achieving various national objectives. Mao highlighted the congruence of culture and politics decades ago: "There is no such thing as art for art's sake. Proletarian art and literature are... as Lenin said, cogs and wheels in the whole revolutionary machine."[9] In the same vein, he emphasized that the Party would not hesitate to harness literature and art for achieving national interests. Mao's emphasis was on the creation of what he termed a New Democracy—national and anti-imperialistic—for advancing the dignity and independence of the Chinese nation, not the individual. This national and anti-imperialistic flavor continues to condition Chinese contemporary thinking on the role of culture, albeit with modern connotations.

Mao's vision of cultural exclusiveness gave way to a more receptive outlook toward cultural diversity with emphasis on coexistence and harmony during the Hu-Wen period (2003-13). Premier Wen aptly reflected: "...Cultural diversity is an objective reality in this world and only when the diversity of cultures is respected, will civilizations progress."[10] This is a marked departure from past when culture was defined as "class culture," identified more with the "ruling elite," and to be employed for serving workers, peasants, and soldiers. The current new leadership is also showing signs of pursuing an accommodating and pragmatic cultural policy in keeping with larger national interests of holding "high the banner of peace, development, cooperation, and mutual benefit...."[11] The Resolution adopted at the 18th Congress of the Communist Party of China in November 2012 was emphatic about upholding China's cultural heritage: "The country's cultural soft power should be improved significantly"[12] for mutual understanding. Subsequently, the Communiqué of the Third Plenum of the 18th Party Congress held in November 2013 offered similar emphasis. While highlighting "putting people first," the Communiqué stressed cultural openness while strengthening "national cultural soft power."[13] The message is clear. China is eager to project itself as a responsible stakeholder in the international community by employing culture.

The contemporary avatar of culture has been in vogue for a decade or so. While the 18th Congress explicitly highlighted the role of culture in shaping foreign policy, the 11th Five Year Plan (2006-10) urged a bigger presence for China in the international cultural markets.[14] Beijing is determined to push deep into the global culture market in particular to communicate China to western audiences. Efforts for achieving this objective by "connecting people and building platforms for introducing writers…" have been called critical and hailed "as important as high-level government dialogues."[15] China has also tried to project Zheng He's voyages during the Ming dynasty as an example of China's cultural tradition of friendship in international relations. According to Huang Ju, former Vice Premier and a member of the Standing Committee of the Party's Politburo, "Zheng He's voyages facilitated cultural, economic, and trade exchanges across the globe, helped establish friendly ties, and contributed to the world's navigation cause."[16]

China's leadership, however, is still wary of the western "cultural onslaught" and "hegemonism." In Seeking Truth (March 2012 issue) — the Party's flagship magazine — Hu cautioned: "We must clearly see that international hostile forces are intensifying the strategic plot of westernizing and dividing China, and ideological and cultural fields are the focal areas of their long-term infiltration."[17] The Report of the 18th Party Congress underlined similar concerns. Reportedly drafted by a team headed by Xi Jinping, it warns of the continued presence of "hegemonism" and "power politics" in the world in what is probably a veiled reference to the United States and its allies.[18] These perceptions have been influencing China's cultural strategy. Aspiring to play a major power role in future global politics, China realizes that its cultural rise will augment its strategic rise. It is hardly accidental that almost all major world powers are leading global cultural hubs as well. Expanding global cultural presence therefore is a priority. The primary focus, while upping cultural communication with the rest of the world, is to charm the West through a markedly different, Oriental brand of culture. This effort will also add a distinct dimension to global culture and might reduce the western cultural hegemony over time.

Confucius Institutes as Cultural Ambassadors

With culture increasingly identified as "a mission more arduous and critical to guard national cultural security and to boost national soft power and Chinese culture's international influence,"[19] Confucius Institutes have spread globally. The implicit strategic objective behind the proliferation of CIs can be traced to the vision of China nursed by a core group of foreign affairs decision-makers in the Party's Central Committee (zhong yang wai shi gong zuo ling dao xiao zu) emphasizing a globally benign image of China.[20] Confucian teachings and principles with their unequivocal focus on humanity, education and harmony are expected to bind ethnic Chinese all across the world and attract other countries to China, through their non-dogmatic virtuous appeal. Indeed, Confucian thoughts are most representative tenets of a "global" doctrine that the CPC is comfortable in identifying with and disseminating across the world. Taking off in 2004, the CIs were originally designed to promote Chinese language and culture. Over time their mandate expanded from cultural interaction and exchanges to academic collaboration. Their programs now depend on the scope demanded by host countries. The largest number of CIs is in North America. Some of these step beyond their usual domains of promoting cultural interactions to assume advanced academic roles, such as the one at Stanford University, which apart from language training also focuses on research and literature of the Tang dynasty for discerning the cultural saliences of the period. The CIs at Chicago and Columbia Universities also declare themselves "research-oriented."[21] The advanced academic roles are hardly noticeable among CIs in Asia. Aligned with the Chinese Government and its programs overseen by the Hanban (Office of Chinese Language Council International), CIs have emerged as China's cultural ambassadors with varied agendas.

The propagation of CIs began in South Korea, which in many ways was an ideal ground for launching "Brand Confucius" given the Korean peninsula's long history of following the Confucian system of thought, society, and governance. South Korea's significance as an economic partner for China and the importance of not allowing territorial tensions to damage economic ties was also responsible for launching CD through a CI. Furthermore, the fact that South Korea is a major U.S. ally and a conduit for facilitating extra-regional presence in the region made the country and the geography perfect for communicating China's arrival on the world stage, through a dedicated policy of cultural engagement and with a loud and clear message: China was back into the "first world club after a century of semi-colonial status and fifty years of third world membership."[22]

CIs in South Asia – China's western neighborhood with complicated regional dynamics – are much fewer compared with some other parts of Asia. India's dominant presence in the neighborhood and its overarching and deep-rooted cultural influence in the region probably have motivated a relatively low-key cultural engagement strand from China to minimize any potential clash of cultures among the two occasionally estranged neighbors. CIs in the region have confined themselves to teaching Mandarin, organizing limited cultural events, and occasional study tours and education exchanges. CIs have been rather active in their teaching and cultural communication functions in Central Asia – a key region for China given its strategic location and vast natural resources. The CI at the Tajik National University, for example, had 2,000 registered students learning Mandarin in 2011 and is an important platform for cultural exchanges and interactions between China and Tajikistan since its inception in March 2009.[23] CIs have sprung up fast in Africa as well – another strategic continent and region – critical for China's global outreach.

Global Perception of China

China's rise is accompanied by mounting anxiety on the part of the international community. Beijing is conscious of the need to provide an alternate perception of its rise by addressing tensions surrounding it. Premier Li Keqiang spoke to the issue at a press conference held after the annual session of the national legislature in March 2013, saying: "Even if China becomes stronger, we will not seek hegemony." The statement underlines the Chinese effort to project an image as a responsible stakeholder willing to work with other countries. The Code of Conduct to be worked upon for the South China Sea is an example. The Chinese government has demonstrated its willingness to embrace "gradual progress and consensus through consultations" as the cornerstone of the agreement.

Culture has been identified as a key tool for conveying the messages of peaceful development and harmonious coexistence. However the strategy so far has had relatively limited success. A BBC survey conducted in May 2013 across 21 countries revealed perceptions about China at their lowest since 2005.[24] Another survey by the Pew Research Center indicates that while people across the world may accept China's superpower status, they "don't like it."[25] Indeed, CD, and particularly the CIs might be producing counterproductive outcomes by being identified as propagandist arms of the state.[26] Scholar Sheng Ding writes that many Chinese observers believe "despite their neutral scholarly appearance, the new network of Confucius Institutes does have a political agenda.... The Institutes will teach Beijing's preferred version of Chinese, characters that are (not) used in Taiwan. This would help advance Beijing's goal of marginalizing Taiwan in the battle for global influence."[27] Other opinions suggest CIs "have been effective at expanding China's network of relationships, but in terms of cultivating cultural soft power, they have yet to offer anything to substantiate their nominal use of Confucius as a representative of Chinese culture."[28] While aggressive CD is yet to reshape global perceptions, China's massive economic growth has generated enormous interest in its culture. Indeed, economic success has probably acted as a stronger pull for Chinese culture than its CD. In fact the success of the CIs to a large extent has been influenced by this economic pull. Several economically backward countries in Africa and Asia are inspired by China's economic development and are keen on reproducing its economic strategies. However, such awe is much muted elsewhere and accompanied by anxiety. Niall Ferguson argues that the bloody twentieth century witnessed "the descent of the West" and "a reorientation of the world" toward the East, underscoring the future power shift from the West to the East. China's rise, an integral part of this shift, is cause for discomfort in its immediate neighborhoods of Southeast and Northeast Asia, and, needless to say, in the West. CD has hardly been able to erase this strategic discomfort given that the world realizes that China's cultural engagement is far more strategic and national interest-driven than pure virtuous export of cultural heritage. This could be due to several factors including reluctance to introduce domestic political reforms coupled with heavy military build-up including the recent effort for a drone development program.[29] The hard power implicit in these actions continues to overshadow the soft power explicit in CD.

Notes

[1] "Time to break the hegemony of western discourse", People's Daily Online, 5 August 2013 at http://english.peopledaily.com.cn/90777/8352833.html, accessed on 19 September 2013

[2] Ding, Sheng, *The Dragon's Hidden Wings: How China Rises with its Soft Power*, UK: Lexington Books, 2008, p. 24

[3] Wu Teh-Yao, "Southeast Asia and China: Asian Neighbours", NUS Occasional Paper #8, September 1974, p. 4

[4] Huning, Wang, "Zuo wei guo jia shi li de wen hua: Ruan quan li" (Culture regarded as national power: Soft Power). Journal of Fudan University, 1993

[5] Yong Shu Xiang, "Xin guo ji zhu yi yu zhong guo ruan shi li wai jiao" (New country doctrine soft power foreign affairs). Guo Ji Guan Cha (International Observe), 2007

[6] Rong, Chang, Zhao, "Zhong Guo xu yao ruan shi li" (China needs soft power), Liao Wang Xin Wen Zhou Kan, 7 June 2004

[7] Rong

[8] Haiyan, Jiang, "Hong yang zhong hua minzu de you xiu wen hua yu zeng qiang wo guo de ruan shi li" (Promoting the outstanding culture of the Chinese nation and strengthening China's soft power), Journal of the Party School of the Central Committee of the CCP, 2007, pp. 107-112

[9] Tung-Tse, Mao, Selected Works of Mao Tse-tung (2), London: Lawrence and Wishart, 1954

[10] Jiabao, Wen, "Chinese premier calls for respect of civilizations, vows to stick to reform, opening up", 7 December 2005 at http://english.people.com.cn/200512/07/eng20051207_226104.html, accessed on 26 September 2013

[11] Full text of resolution on CPC Central Committee report, 14 November 2012 at http://news.xinhuanet.com/english/special/18cpcnc/2012-11/14/c_131973742.htm, accessed on 25 September 2013

[12] Ibid

[13] Communique of the 3rd Plenum of the 18th Party Congress, 12 November 2013 at http://china-copyrightandmedia.wordpress.com/2013/11/12/communique-of-the-3rd-plenum-of-the-18th-party-congress/, accessed on 26 November 2013

[14] Hongyi, Lai, "China's Cultural Diplomacy: Going for Soft Power", East Asia Institute Background Brief #308. October 2006, p. 6

[15] Chinese media to get boost overseas", China Daily, 10 January 2012 at http://www.chinadaily.com.cn/bizchina/2012-01/10/content_14411347.htm, accessed on 26 September 2013

[16] "Zheng He anniversary highlights peaceful growth", 12 July 2005 at http://www.china.org.cn/english/2005/Jul/134724.htm, accessed on 1 October 2013

[17] "Hu Jintao, China President, says hostile forces to seek to westernize China", 1 March 2012 at http://www.huffingtonpost.com/2012/01/03/hu-jintao-westernize-china_n_1180665.html, accessed on 26 September 2013

[18] Summers, Tim, "China's New Leadership: Approaches to International Affairs", Chatham House Briefing Paper, April 2013 at http://www.chathamhouse.org/sites/default/files/public/Research/Asia/0413bp_chinanewleaders.pdf, accessed on 28 September 2013

[19] "When Soft Power is too soft: Confucius Institutes' nebulous role in China's Soft Power initiative", August 2012 at http://yris.yira.org/essays/644, accessed on 27 November 2013

[20] The author interviewed an Associate Professor at the Nankai University, Tianjin.

[21] Confucius Institute at http://confuciusinstitute.uchicago.edu/, accessed on 19 September 2013

[22] Starr, Don, "Chinese Language Education in Europe: The Confucius Institute", European Journal of Education, 2009, 44 (1), pp. 65-80

[23] Confucius Institute at Tajik National University, Tajikistan, Hanban News, 12 December, 2011

at http://www.chinese.cn/conference11/article/2011-12/12/content_394535.htm, accessed on 28 September 2013

24 "Views of China and India slide in Global Poll, while UK's ratings climb", A Globescan Poll for the BBC, 22 May 2013 at http://www.globescan.com/news-and-analysis/press-releases/press-releases-2013/277-views-of-china-and-india-slide-while-uks-ratings-climb.html, accessed on 23 September 2013

25 "Global Public Opinion Poll reveals an increasingly negative view of China", 25 November 2013 at http://www.scmp.com/lifestyle/arts-culture/article/1329353/global-public-opinion-poll-reveals-increasingly-negative-view, accessed on 25 November 2013

26 Mattis, Peter, "Reexamining Confucian Institutes", The Diplomat, 2 August 2012 at http://thediplomat.com/china-power/reexamining-the-confucian-institutes/, accessed on 2 October 2013

27 Ding, Sheng, The Dragon's Hidden Wings: How China Rises with its Soft Power, UK: Lexington Books, 2008

28 "When oft Power is too soft…"

29 Wong, Edward, "China's push for drones fueled by U.S. secrets", International Herald Tribune, 23 September 2013, p, p1, 4

Parama Sinha Palit, Ph.D, is a Research Associate at the China in Comparative Perspective Network (CCPN) Global, a UK-based Interdisciplinary Academic Society.

China and the Ukraine Crisis

John Garver

Vol. 13, No. 1
2014

China's handling of the Putin-engineered annexation of Crimea from Ukraine into the Russian Federation reflects deeply competing Chinese interests. On the one hand, Beijing values its strategic partnership with Russia – a partnership tracing back to 1996 – especially now, when Sino-U.S. relations are tense over the intertwined issues of Washington's "pivot" to Asia and Chinese cyber-espionage against U.S. advanced weapons research and development. In Washington there is a growing sense that the military gap between China and the U.S. is narrowing rapidly because of Chinese cyber-penetration of U.S. military-industrial firms and approaching a transition point between rising and incumbent paramount powers, which may be especially dangerous. Japan under Shinzo Abe's second government (in office since December 2012) also has begun courting India with unprecedented vigor. Even more startling, New Delhi is responding with an unembarrassed embrace of Tokyo. Beijing's trump card of "the history issue" does not play very well in New Delhi. Given these elemental shifts in the balance of power that are in play, Beijing has no interest in loosening its strategic partnership with Russia. In terms of energy supply, a falloff in European purchases of Soviet natural gas also would not be bad for China, perhaps prompting Moscow to offer China lower prices, easing one of the hurdles to expanded Russo-Chinese energy cooperation over the past decade or so.

These interests may explain why China has decided to call in a $3 billion loan to Ukraine in late February.[1] If China stands by this demand for Ukrainian repayment of this loan as Kiev faces mounting Russian pressure and economic difficulties, this would represent substantial, if low-keyed Chinese support for Moscow in this crisis.

On the other hand, Beijing has long-standing and strongly felt taboos against foreign interference in the internal affairs of sovereign states and secession of territories within sovereign states on the basis of popular elections. Since the end of the Cold War, China has emerged as a staunch defender of strong state sovereignty norms, opposing attempts by one state to bring about political changes within another. This preference for strong state sovereignty norms is rooted in Beijing's apprehensions regarding Taiwan, Tibet, and Xinjiang and fears that "the West led by the United States"[2] might attempt to detach one or all of those regions from the PRC, using the pretext of popular will and elections. From Beijing's perspective, this was what "the West led by the United States" did first with the Baltic republics of the declining USSR, and then with ex-Communist Yugoslavia. Thus, if Beijing openly endorsed Putin's seizure of the Crimea, it would open China to charges of hypocrisy. Such charges could be influential with Western public opinion, which is the main target of China's defense of state sovereignty norms.

In line with these interests, Beijing abstained in the U.N. Security Council when Britain, France, and the United States proposed a resolution condemning the Russian-organized referendum on Crimean secession from Ukraine and entry into the Russian Federation. President Barack Obama telephoned President Xi Jinping before the Security Council vote on March 16 to lobby for China to vote "yes" on the Western-backed proposal.[3] Instead China merely abstained, allowing Russia's veto alone to kill the condemnatory proposal. This was a marked departure from the close cooperation of Moscow and Beijing on a score of issues before the Security Council since the mid-1990s. It also allowed Western powers to claim that Russia was isolated. More important for Beijing, it allowed China to evade endorsement of foreign intervention in another state's internal affairs and succession of territories on the basis of popular will and elections. In terms of formal declared position, Beijing has called for resolution of differences through peaceful discussion and dialogue, and for respect for Ukrainian sovereignty. Chinese Foreign Ministry Spokesman Qin Gang said on March 4:

> "We uphold the principle of non-interference in others' internal affairs and respect international law and widely recognized norms governing international relations. Meanwhile we take into account the historical facts and realistic complexity of the Ukrainian issue"[4]

When pressed to explain what he meant by relevant "historical facts," Qin invited his audience to "please review or refer to the history of Ukraine and this region." That "history" might refer to "the eastward expansion of NATO" condemned routinely by Beijing and Moscow during the 1990s, and/or to the long and close association between Russia and the Ukraine. Or it might not. That is left to one's imagination. When the issue was debated again in the General Assembly (in which no country has veto power), China joined 57 other countries in abstaining from a resolution condemning Russian actions and calling on states to "desist and refrain" from actions recognizing changes in Ukraine's borders achieved through threat or use of force. On this occasion Ambassador Liu Jieyi stated that a General Assembly vote "would only complicate the picture," and he called on all parties to "examine proposals for a political settlement."[5]

At a more fundamental level, it is fortunate for China that the U.S. has been pulled, once again, into a crisis in a region of the world far from the Western Pacific where the U.S. and the PRC are working out a new balance. Beijing recognized the 9/11 attacks as a strategic windfall for China, keeping the United States from fixing on China as its next rival after the demise of the Soviet Union. Beijing views Obama's desire to conclude U.S. involvement in the Iraq and Afghanistan wars as the counterpart of his "pivot to Asia," which it deems to be a type of crypto-containment of China. The Ukrainian crisis, combined with deep cuts in U.S. defense spending, will hinder Washington's ability to give substance to this new crypto-containment effort.

Against those hard realities Beijing weighs the specter of a world dominated by the will of the stronger in which armed seizure of territory becomes common. Some in Beijing certainly understand that that would lead to greater global instability that could undermine both China's economic growth and national security. On the other hand, cooperation with a seemingly declining U.S. to uphold international order may be a step too far for China's realist-minded leaders.

Notes

[1] "China sues Ukraine for breach of US$3b loan-for-grain agreement," *South China Morning Post*, 27 February 2014. http://www.scmp.com/news/china/article/1435976/china-sues-ukraine-breach-us3b-loan-grain-agreement

[2] The term "the West led by the United States" is commonly seen in the official Chinese media.

[3] "Non-interference on the line," *The Economist*, 15 March 2014, p. 44.

[4] Foreign Ministry spokesman,. http://www.fmprc.gov.cn/eng/xwfw/s2510/t1134077.shtml

[5] General Assembly, GA/ 11493, 27 March 2010. www.un.org

John Garver is professor of international affairs at the Sam Nunn School of International Affairs, Georgia Institute of Technology.

The Eighteenth Party Congress Decision: an Introduction

Stephen Herschler, Guest Editor

Vol.13, No.2
2014

China watchers are to Third Plenums of Chinese Communist Party Congresses as film buffs are to the Oscars. One reason is the storied history of Third Plenum Decisions in the post-Mao era. Two of them marked epochal shifts in China's political economy. The first, officially designated by the Party as "history's great turning point," was the Eleventh Party Congress' Third Plenum in 1978. Deng Xiaoping's ascendance became evident in a Decision that touted policies spearheading "Reform and Opening to the Outside World." When it appeared that the events of June 1989 had cut off the engine of reform, in 1993 another Third Plenum trumpeted the establishment of a "Socialist Market Economic System" as the national goal. In the aftermath of that Decision, the Chinese economy revved into a high gear from which it has only rarely downshifted in the subsequent two decades.

While not all Third Plenum decisions are revolutionary, they are all important. They set the national agenda until a new national congress is convened and holds its own Third Plenum, producing its own decision five years later. Hence, they serve as a general "five-year plan" for Party work and thereby for government work as well. A Decision's compositional structure denotes this purpose. Each chapter can be viewed not only as focusing upon a particular area of governance, but also as addressing particular parts of the country's vast political-administrative apparatus. Decisions do not present blueprints but rather guidelines; they indicate priorities as well as behaviors that will receive the state's support or sanction. The timing and details of implementation are the work of other documents, crafted in other institutional arenas and at other administrative levels.

While the production of Third Plenum decisions have become standard operating procedures in the post-Mao era, the most recent Decision, issued in November 2013, differs from any previous one: it is the first that has been put forth under a Party chairman who is neither a Party elder nor an individual personally chosen by an elder. The heads of the third and fourth generation of Party leadership, Jiang Zemin and Hu Jintao respectively, had been approved for Party leadership while Deng Xiaoping was still a force in Chinese politics. The head of the fifth generation of Party Leadership, Xi Jinping, became heir apparently only quite recently. Thus, many watched to see whether this 'new' generation is in fact new in substance as well as name.

Reports indicate that the document has Xi's imprimatur all over it. In April 2013, not long after Xi became Party chairman, a 60-member decision-drafting committee was constituted, headed by Xi. Breaking with precedence, Xi himself presented an "explanation" of the Decision to Central Committee members in November of that year. The buildup, staging, and subsequent government actions conducted under Xi's auspices all indicate that he is no cipher.

The contributors to this section, members of the Atlanta-based China Research Center, draw upon the Decision to assess Chinese governance in a range of policy arenas. Each essay draws its impetus from particular sections of the Decision. The essays do not speak with one voice. Assessments vary as to the effectiveness, feasibility, and intentions of the both the Party's professed aims as well as its actual actions under Xi's leadership. With that in mind:

Yawei Liu's critical appraisal of state-society relations finds prospects for political reform bleak and language suggesting improvements in social justice and societal self-governance to be at odds with recent state actions.

Andrew Wedeman takes up issues of law and order by assessing the scope, length and targets of the recent anti-corruption campaign, in the Party and out, raising questions as to its impetus and ultimate aims.

Baogang Guo places proposed administrative reforms in broader historical context, finding signs of more effective governance in the furtherance of decentralization, red-tape reduction and law-based administration.

Eri Saikawa takes up environmental issues, a topic that for the first time has received its own chapter in the Decision. Her analysis of air pollution problems finds that while new governmental goals are a positive sign, the sincerity and effectiveness of implementation efforts remain to be seen.

John Garver's examination of defense and foreign relations highlights a two-pronged party initiative that seeks to secure China's external development interests, regionally and beyond, as well as preclude ideological subversion domestically.

Xuepeng Liu analyzes the Decision's proposed economic reforms and priorities, helping to decode what it might mean to have the market play a dominant role and yet have the state sector play a decisive role in ongoing market liberalization and expansion.

Penelope Prime hones in on finances, examining the challenge of maintaining high growth rates while concurrently addressing debt, deficits, and currency reform.

Hongmei Li draws upon the Decision's proposals for cultural work to outline countervailing trends in state-media relations that seek concurrently to consolidate state oversight while promoting media expansion, at home and abroad, in a competitive market environment.

Saikawa's question – They talk the talk but do they walk the walk? – reverberates in a number of the other essays, as one might expect of such sweeping policy proposals in most any country. Still, Xi Jinping's relatively recent assumption of Party leadership gives the question a particular edge. If the Party stays on schedule, fall 2018 should see the issuance of another Decision, and with it a chance to assess the Chinese government's progress on these various specific issues as well as to assess Xi's leadership at the start of his second term.

Dr. Stephen B. Herschler is an Associate Professor of Politics at Oglethorpe University.

Where Is Political Reform in Xi Jinping's Reform Scheme?

Yawei Liu
Vol. 13, No. 2
2014

In November 1978, Deng Xiaoping presided over the Third Plenum of the Eleventh National Congress of the Chinese Communist Party (CCP), which launched China's reform and opening up. Thirty five years later, the Third Plenum of CCP's Eighteenth Congress was held with Xi Jinping at the helm. There has been occasional chatter by Chinese government officials and scholars that without political liberalization, reform and opening up would not have been possible, and the consensus is that what happened after the historic meeting in late 1978 was only the beginning of economic reform. Even Deng Xiaoping himself said that all reforms in China would eventually come down to political reform. In other words, without political reform all reform measures were doomed to fail. When Wen Jiabao went to Shenzhen to commemorate the thirtieth anniversary of the establishment of the Shenzhen Special Economic Zone in 2010, he echoed what Deng said many years ago: "We should not only promote economic reform but also political reform. Without the guarantee of political reform, the accomplishments of economic reform will be lost again and the goals of modernization will never be achieved."

Shortly after he was anointed CCP's general secretary in November 2012, Xi Jinping went to Shenzhen to pay tribute to Deng Xiaoping. Xi said that reform had entered into the zone of deep waters and that it was necessary to muster political courage and wisdom to seize the opportunity to deepen reform measures in important areas. Xi declared that in order to remain focused on the correct direction for reform, both ideological shackles and obstruction by special interest groups should be removed. Political commentators were euphoric, and all eyes were fixed on the upcoming Third Plenum. Some were optimistic that there would be significant measures in the political reform arena.

But many were disappointed by the series of remarks made by Xi since he replaced Hu Jintao as CCP's leader. He talked about national rejuvenation and the rise of China and asked all Chinese people to dream the Chinese dream. He lamented that when the Soviet Union collapsed there was not a good man around to stop the fall. He called on the military to be ready to fight and to win wars. There was a glaring absence of the kind of thinking that Xi had presented in 2010. That year, during a speech at the Central Party School in Beijing, Xi said all CCP members should pay attention to the issue of power authorization and the fact that CCP's power was bestowed by the people. The five-character term that "power comes from the people" (权为民所赋) sent a cheerful breeze to the political reform community in China because popular bestowing of power to the CCP would certainly involve a set of procedures that has always been missing from CCP's action, despite the common chant that people are the "masters" of the state. Nonetheless, hope lingered that Xi was an open-minded Communist leader who believed political power derives from the people and a fixed process to bestow that power must be introduced. If such a proposal were to be discussed and written into the Plenum resolution, meaningful political reform would soon unfold in China.

Crushing Disappointment

Those who placed high hopes on Xi Jinping and expected the Third Plenum to engage in icebreaking measures in the arena of political reform were very much disappointed when they read the language on political reform in the Resolution that was adopted. Chapter Eight of the Resolution is entitled "Strengthen the Construction of Socialist Democratic Political System" and it contains three sections detailing how the CCP wants to expand and deepen democratization. The first section focuses on improving China's People's Congress system with high-sounding language, declaring that the congresses at all levels adopt laws and make the most important decisions. It emphasizes that "people's government, people's court and people's procuratorate are elected by, responsible to and supervised by the people's congresses." China has people's congresses at five levels: township/town, country/district, municipal, provincial and national. There are about three million directly (at township/town and county/district levels) and indirectly elected people's congress deputies. This means Chinese people, at least on paper, have no less representation than their counterparts in democratic nations.

If the people's congresses can do what they are charged to do by law and by the Resolution, there would be more accountability and transparency at all levels of the government and the so-called letter and visitation channel through which ordinary people try to file complaints against corrupt, abusive or negligent officials would become obsolete immediately. Sadly, the Resolution has not addressed the actual weakness of the people's congress system. It made no mention of measures to correct the deficiency. The most serious problems of the people's congress system in China are that 1) the Party still runs roughshod over it, and most party secretaries at the provincial level also are chairs of the standing committee of the provincial people's congress; and 2) elections of the deputies, both direct and indirect, are not fair and competitive. When the foundation is soft and the top subject to Party control and manipulation, the people's congress system cannot play a meaningful role. In this sense, the Resolution has simply repeated what had been for the past three decades and broke no new ground.

The second section elaborates on deliberative democracy, which is different from the kind of deliberative democracy that is known in the West. While Western deliberative democracy is usually applied at the grassroots level with societal activists pushing the government to be more transparent and accountable, the Chinese deliberative democracy discussed in the Resolution refers to the united front and its platform, the political consultative conference system. The actors on this stage are retired government officials, members of the eight democratic parties, celebrities, famous people without party affiliations and model workers. They are noisy, sensitive to social and political developments and keen on making policy recommendations but there is very little evidence this high-flying platform is having policy impacts at any level.

The last section talks about grassroots democracy, which includes village self-government, urban resident self-government, and worker self-government. Direct village committee elections and village self-government used to be the beacon of China's expanding democratization. Urban residential committee elections have never been very competitive. Employee committees have always been attached to unions, which have never been rights bargaining mechanisms. The drafters of the Resolution seemed unable to clear a path for real grassroots democracy.

All in all, Chapter Eight of the Resolution calls for expansion of orderly political participation by Chinese citizens but offers little detail in delineating the specific channels through which participation will be allowed and become meaningful. The old wine was poured into a new bottle. The subsequent disillusion and disappointment in the political reform community is palpable. The sense is that Xi Jinping is no longer a credible champion of political reform. Disappointed as they are, Chinese scholars have tried to see the best in a worst-case scenario. Sun Xiaoli, a professor at the National Academy of Public Administration, makes two points when asked by the media why there is little mention of political reform in the Resolution: 1) deepening and expanding economic reform is in itself political; and 2) there is enough space created by the Resolution to plot further political reform.

A New Space in the Making

If Chapter Eight of the Resolution offered disappointment about political reform, Chapter Twelve provides a rhetorical opening for the pursuit of social justice. This section lists a plethora of measures that call for deepening of social reform. The most important seems to be an effort to ensure a more equitable distribution of wealth through a more seriously graduated income tax, and creation of a larger and wider social security net. The following paragraph in the Resolution sounds like a page from President Franklin D. Roosevelt's New Deal:

We will regulate income distribution procedures and improve the regulatory systems and mechanisms and policy system for income distribution, establish an individual income and property information system, protect legitimate incomes, regulate excessively high incomes, redefine and clear away hidden incomes, outlaw illegal incomes, increase the incomes of low-income groups, and increase the proportion of the middle-income group in society as a whole.

The lack of a more equitable distribution of wealth no doubt stirs anger deep within Chinese society, but according to Harvard sociologist Martin Whyte, this has not led to an eruption of unrest. His surveys indicate that Chinese people are more upset by social discrimination that favors the large urban centers. For example, a Beijing high school graduate can enter Peking or Tsinghua University with a 500-point score on the national college entrance exam, but a similar person from Changsha in Hunan Province needs a score of 600 or more to get into these universities. The Resolution makes it clear that authorities will tackle this kind of regional discrimination through reforming the matriculation system and giving universities more authority in admitting students.

It is indeed shameful for CCP to call China a socialist country when it has a healthcare system that builds in the kind of injustice that characterized segregation in the U.S. South before the Civil Rights Movement. Whether one in China can get good and comprehensive healthcare depends on your rank, your income and your residency. Hundreds of millions of Chinese farmers did not have any kind of health insurance until a few years ago when a new rural cooperative healthcare system was introduced. But in comparison to the benefits extended to the urban dwellers, government employees and military personnel, Chinese farmers still have to travel very far to receive proper care. They also must bear a larger financial burden to pay their healthcare costs. Therefore, the CCP vows to "deepen the comprehensive reform of grass-roots medical and healthcare institutions, and improve the network of urban and rural basic medical and healthcare services."

Civil servants, military personnel and Party officials in China have the best pension system and retirement benefits. Ordinary residents of China have inadequate pensions, and many older people are dependent on their children for senior care. The only social security anchor for the farmers used to be the family plot of land. The pension system introduced by the government two decades ago is not entirely portable and management of social security funds is not transparent, making it highly susceptible to misuse and illegal transfer. The primitive nature of this system is highlighted by the proposed measures to reform it:

We will adhere to the basic old-age insurance system that combines social pools with individual accounts, improve the individual accounts system, complete the incentive mechanism in which those who contribute more will get more, guarantee the rights and interests of the insured, place basic old-age pension under unified national planning, and uphold the principle of balance based on actuarial mathematics.

These social reform measures, if fully implemented, would change the nature of the Chinese government overnight, making it more concerned with providing services to its citizens than with regime survival and enforced obedience to its reign. But these reform measures must have popular input, open access to government information, transparency, and accountability to be successfully implemented. In other words, without institutionalizing popular participation in deciding and supervising which social services are going to be provided and how they are going to be provided, these reform measures will either fail or will become window dressing to hoodwink people. If the CCP is serious about implementing what it has proposed in the Resolution, it will need to adopt relevant political reform measures, even if that occurs through an indirect process.

Civil Society

While many praise the proposed economic reform measures, Chapter Thirteen of the Resolution contains language that is innovative and even revolutionary in the context of CCP leaders who see any call related to expanding civil society as subversive and an evil plan cooked in the hallways of the U.S. State Department and bunkers of the Pentagon. This part of the Resolution does begin by saying social governance reforms will be conducted under the leadership of CCP committees and government agencies at all levels. But this is followed by a few paragraphs that rarely appear in CCP's societal governing circulars.

If its language were realized, Section 48 could help liberate society from crushing state domination and infuse a checking and balancing force that modern, progressive states possess. The section calls on authorities to "intensify efforts to separate government administration and social organizations, encourage social organizations to clarify their rights and obligations, and enforce self-management and play their role in accordance with the law." The iron hand of the state is told emphatically to relax or even to move away because now the CCP wants "social organizations to provide public services that they are apt to supply and tackle matters that they are able to tackle." According to the section, "These organizations can directly apply for registration in accordance with the law when they are established. We will strengthen the management of social organizations and foreign NGOs in China, and guide them to carry out their activities in accordance with the law."

Liberating as it sounds, there are challenges to putting these reform measures in place. First, the law that is supposed to govern the registration and management of the NGOs has yet to be submitted to the National People's Congress for review and adoption. At this point, only a few cities in the south allow the registration of NGOs under provincial or municipal regulations. Second, the CCP has made it clear that it wants only certain kinds of NGO: trade associations, chambers of commerce, scientific and technological associations, charity and philanthropic organizations, and urban and rural community service organizations. NGOs with political missions or the intention to hold government accountable are not encouraged to form and can be declared hostile and illegal forces threatening social and political order. It is not a good sign that NGOs whose mission is to conserve nature and protect the environment are not mentioned as preferred social organizations.

What is even more alarming is that seven months after the adoption of the Resolution, there appears to be a concerted effort to investigate which institutes of the Chinese Academy of Social Sciences have been penetrated by foreign NGOs or foundations. This revelation came from a speech made by a member of the Central Commission on Discipline Inspection when he spoke at the Institute of Modern History. The CCP evidently does not want to govern foreign NGOs according to law, as was indicated in the Resolution. It simply desires to see them disappear in China. It is possible that many Chinese universities, colleges and existing NGOs will be subject to the same kind of investigation. Small wonder that many partners of Westerns NGOs have backed out of joint projects since late last year.

Chapter Thirteen ends with a proposal to establish a public security apparatus that includes creating a national security council that will coordinate with all national agencies involved in safeguarding national interests in information-gathering and decision-making. Unlike the U.S. National Security Council, whose sole mission is to stop threats that originate from abroad, the Chinese NSC would also respond to domestic threats to political and social stability. In traditional CCP discourse, all NGOs, domestic or foreign, are seeds of domestic instability, sources of so called "color revolutions" that are funded by Western powers eager to undermine the rise of China or to lead China into the wilderness of disintegration. Wang Zhenyao, former Ministry of Civil Affairs official and current dean of the China Institute of Philanthropic Studies at the Beijing Normal University, told the media that half of the one million NGOs in China are underground because of fear. These NGOs cannot register, dare not register, and will certainly not be able to register because the government sees them as enemies of the state. The stability maintenance apparatus nurtured by Zhou Yongkong – who is currently the subject of a criminal investigation in China – has been more richly funded than the country's defense establishment. Many reform-minded Chinese hope the ouster of Zhou, who has been seen by many as the single most daunting obstacle to the growth of China's civil society, may create an opening to expand civil society. When the Resolution was made public there was initial euphoria and media hoopla about the potential of this reform measure. It is too early to say that social reform is dead but not too late to say political reform will never be real and meaningful when there is no vibrant civil society and NGOs are always met with iron fist of the state.

The final balance sheet

In an interview with a newspaper in 2012, Zhou Ruijin, a retired media professional who is a strong advocate of political reform in China, said China's reform, although interconnected and interwoven to a large extent, will have to be divided into three phases, namely economic, social, and political. The first phase of economic reform began in 1978 and was somewhat completed by 2004. The social reform phase began in 2010 and shall be completed by 2025. The final and the most important phase of the reform may kick in by 2030.

No Chinese leader, from Mao Zedong to Xi Jinping, has ever set a timetable for political reform. When asked in 1945 how the CCP would avoid the notorious dynastic cycles of the previous emperors, Mao said to Huang Yanpei proudly but vaguely that the CCP had found a miraculous mechanism to ward them off: democracy. During his negotiation with British politicians on the transfer of sovereignty of Hong Kong to China in 1986, Deng Xiaoping predicted that China might adopt national presidential elections by 2050 after overcoming the wealth, educational, economic, and geographic gaps between urban dwellers and rural residents. A year later, at CCP's Thirteenth National Congress, Zhao Ziyang submitted a seven-point political reform package. This is the first time the CCP had introduced a political reform action plan. It did not have a five-year-plan kind of timetable and was quickly shelved after the political turmoil in 1989. It was not until 2008 when another top Chinese leader, Wen Jiabao, brought up a political reform plan that had implementable specifics. In a meeting with John Thornton, former chairman of Goldman Sachs, Wen outlined a three-prong action proposal: 1) direct elections moving up from villages to towns and to counties; 2) restraining government power via independent judiciary oversight; and 3) enhancing government accountability through a freer and more autonomous media. It appeared this proposal was more of Wen's own personal aspiration than a CCP institutional push. He made his ambitious statement only to foreigners and never conveyed it to his own people.

Almost six years passed between Wen's lofty plan and the adoption of the Resolution of the Third Plenum. In between, Xi came to power, Bo Xilai, a Politburo member of CCP's Seventeenth Congress, was sentenced to life in prison, and two former high CCP officials – General Xu Caihou, a vice chairman of the Central Military Commission, and Zhou Yongkang – were placed under Party investigation and will eventually go to jail. The legitimacy of the CCP is under unprecedented self-inflicted assault. Will serious political reform be entertained? Prospects may seem unlikely, but if Xi Jinping is serious about keeping the CCP in power by making it less corrupt, more responsive to the people and more easily accountable to the people, political reform cannot wait until 2030 as was suggested by Zhou Ruijin. After all, there is a timetable that Xi and his Party are racing to keep. The goal is that China will become a democratic, prosperous, and wealthy nation in 2049 at the People's Republic's centennial. China watchers can measure whether the Xi Administration is moving closer to the timetable by examining how the Party is implementing proposed measures to 1) redistribute wealth via a new tax scheme and cast a wider social security net that includes all people regardless of differences in employment, residency, race, or age and 2) allow NGOs and other societal forces to participate in building China into a fairer and more just state. If the CCP can achieve this goal without instituting any political reform measures such as free speech, free elections, free press, and a judicial system free from CCP manipulation, the world will need to take a second look at China's development and governance model. There may indeed be such as thing called Chinese exceptionalism. But that prospect seems dubious. Chinese leaders likely will find that democracy cannot be ushered in without thorough and deep political reform.

Yawei Liu, Ph.D., is Director of the China Program at The Carter Center, Atlanta, Georgia.

Xi Jinping's Tiger Hunt and the Politics of Corruption

Andrew Wedeman
Vol. 13, No. 2
2014

The Communist Party of China has been grappling with corruption almost from its birth. Corruption was one of the major issues during the 1989 anti-government demonstrations. The leadership, in fact, responded to public anger over corruption and what was then known as "official profiteering" by launching a major campaign, in the course of which the number of individuals charged with corruption jumped from 33,000 in 1988 to 77,000 in 1989, and 72,000 in 1990. Since the 1989 campaign, the leadership has waged an ongoing "war" against corruption and routinely prosecutes substantial numbers of officials. Between 1997 and 2012 the Supreme People's Procuratorate reported that it indicted 550,000 individuals on either corruption or dereliction of duty charges, including three members of the powerful Politburo.[1]

These prior efforts notwithstanding, upon assuming the office of General Secretary of the party in November 2012, Xi Jinping announced yet another campaign, which was formally approved by the Third Plenum of the Eighteen Party Congress in early November 2013. At first, the campaign appeared to be a repeat of the same old song and dance. Many of the steely toned slogans about the necessity to fight a life-and-death struggle against corruption and the need to put an end to extravagant spending by officials and cadres had been raised many times before. Announcements of new regulations mandating fewer dishes at official banquets, banning the purchase of luxury sedans and their use for unofficial business, and the construction of lavish government buildings all reiterated orders issued in past years. Eighteen months on, however, it appears that far from a smoke and mirrors attempt to create the impression of action, Xi Jinping's anti-corruption campaign may well be the most sustained and intensive drive against corruption since the start of the reform era.

By the Numbers

Measuring the intensity of an anti-corruption campaign is, admittedly, a tricky business given that we cannot even roughly estimate the true extent of corruption. Instead, we can at best guess at the extent by asking experts for their impressions of how bad things are or tracking changes in the number of officials who suddenly stop being corrupt because they get caught. Indices such as the popular Corruption Perceptions Index (CPI) published by Transparency International would have us believe that rather than getting worse, corruption in China has actually been on the decline for at least a decade, with its score falling from 7.6 (out of a maximum of 10, where 10 is the most corrupt and 1 the least corrupt) in 1995 to 6.0 in 2013, which would put China just below the 75th percentile and hence not among the worst of the worse.1

Data on prosecutions tell a different story. The number of criminal indictments was up 9.4 percent in 2013, with the total number of corruption and dereliction cases increasing from 34,326 in 2012 to 37,551 in 2013 (see Figure 1). The number of officials holding position at the county and departmental levels who were indicted rose from 2,390 to 2,618, a 9.5 percent increase. The number of officials the prefectural and bureau levels who were indicted shot up more dramatically, from 179 in 2012 to 253 in 2013, a 41.4 percent jump. Although nine percent increases in the total number of cases and in the number of county and department officials indicted may seem modest for a highly trumpeted campaign, these increases followed a decade in which the total number of indictments had been slowly decreasing. Increases in 2013, moreover, follow more modest increases in 2012. As a result, the total number of indictments in 2013 was 16.2 percent more than in 2011, and the number of country and department officials indicted was up 12.6 percent compared to 2011. More critically, the 41 percent increase in prefectural and bureau level officials indicted is the largest such increase since 2004, and represents a 27.8 percent rise over 2011. Finally, eight officials at the provincial and ministry levels were indicted, compared to five in 2012. The party's Discipline Inspection Commission (DIC) also reported a 13.3 percent increase in the number of party members who faced disciplinary action.

Note: To provide a long-term perspective, I have transformed the raw data on cases filed into an index anchored on the years 1997-8. I do this because the 1997 revision of the criminal code decriminalized a large number of low-level offenses. The dramatic drop in cases filed thus creates the misleading impression that either corruption fell dramatically, which it did not, or that enforcement suddenly slacked off, which it did not either.

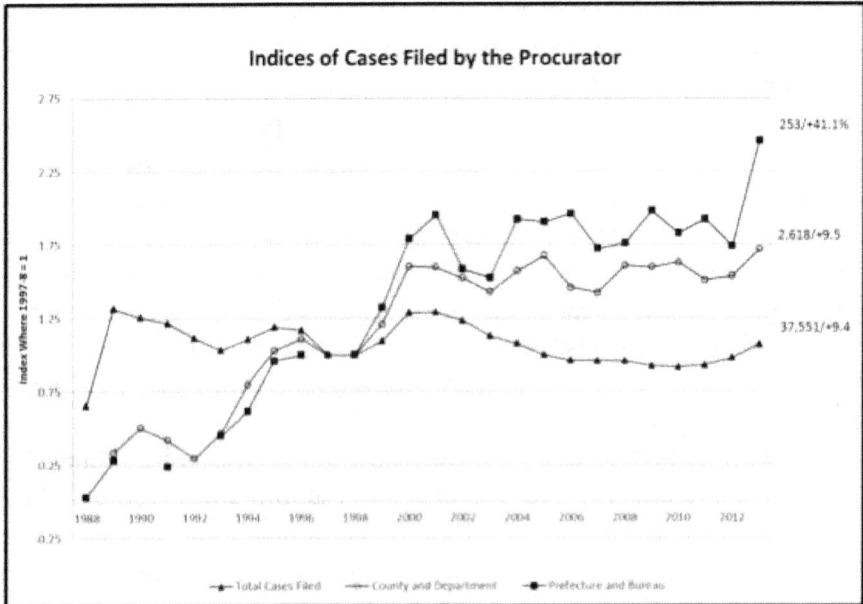

Indices of Cases Filed by the Procurator

Sources: *Zhongguo Jiancha Nianjian [Procuratorial Yearbook of China], (Beijing: Zhong-guo Jiancha Chubanshi, various years) and Zuigao Renmin Jiancha Yuan Gongzuo Baogao [Work report of the Supreme People's Procuratorate], 3/18/2014, available at http://www.spp.gov.cn/tt/201403/t20140318_69216.shtml, accessed 6/12/2014.*

Targeting

It is also possible to look at the type of corruption a campaign is targeting and who is getting caught to get a more nuanced sense of whether Xi's roar is that of a paper or a real tiger. China's ongoing efforts to curb corruption are often described as a "war" and it is thus convenient to use war as a way to deconstruct the current campaign. The campaign can be decomposed into four distinct fronts. At the grassroots level the regime is fighting a guerrilla war in which whistleblowers and netizens have used social media to expose brazen examples of corruption and degenerate official behavior. Videos of officials laughing at the site of fatal highway accidents, photos of them sporting luxury watches, smoking outrageously priced cigarettes, documents identifying poorly paid low-level bureaucrats as the owners multiple of luxury condominiums and villas, videos of cadres playing sex games with their mistresses, drinking, and cavorting with Thai transvestites have gone viral within China despite the efforts of the army of "ten cent" Internet, forcing the party to move with unheard of speed to sack and indict officials. But the internet front of Xi's war on corruption is a bush war in which most of the corrupt officials exposed are low-level officials who were so foolish, so arrogant, or so greedy that they failed to remember that corruption should kept discrete.

Parallel to the internet guerrilla war, the regime continues to wage a protracted war of attribution against low- and mid-level corruption. This part of the push against corruption resembles trench warfare: an ever-lengthening list of casualties but scant evidence of real advances. In recent years, prosecutors have indicted about 35,000 individual on economic crime charges each year, the bulk of whom are officials holding posts below the county and departmental leadership levels. The fighting on this front in 2013 seems a bit more intense than in past years. Based on a survey of cases reported in the press and on the Discipline Inspection Commission's website, it appears that more "tiger cubs" – senior party cadres and officials holding posts just below the county and department levels – have been bagged. At present, however, there is no reason to believe the number of corrupt officials has been reduced by much.

The third front in Xi's attack is a drive against "commercial bribery" in the domestic and foreign business sectors. Although official corruption receives the bulk of public attention, corruption often involves both a supply side (officials willing to use their authority for illicit private gain) and a demand side (private parties willing to pay officials to use their authority for illicit private gain). Corporate actors, moreover, can use the authority delegated to them to pursue illicit gains. Procurement managers, for example, can demand kickbacks from potential venders. Although the data are thin, it appears that inter-firm corruption is widespread in China and that a corporate "culture of corruption" exists in which bribery and corruption are viewed as a normal part of doing business. Chinese prosecutors began cracking down on corruption in the business sector in about 2006. In the spring of 2013, they intensified these attacks and expanded their targets to include foreign businesses. Chinese prosecutors are not alone. In recent years, prosecutors in both the United States and the United Kingdom also have gone after American and British companies for paying bribes to Chinese officials and companies. Chinese prosecutors have gone after evidence that foreign pharmaceutical and medical equipment vendors frequently turn a blind eye to the illicit means used by their sales forces to book orders and the complex dodges used by "consultants" and other middlemen to secure contracts and close deals. Charges were leveled against GlaxoSmithKline, Abbott Labs, Astra Zeneca, Sanoli, Norartus, Eli Lilly, and others. Prosecutors detained almost two dozen GlaxoSmithKline employees and consultants, including Peter Humphrey, a Shanghai-based British risk consultant, and his wife. JP Morgan, Goldman Sachs, Citibank, and Deutsche Bank have been accused of hiring the sons and daughters of senior Chinese officials with some expectation that such hires might benefit them financially.

The final aspect of Xi's war on corruption is a highflying aerial combat in which corruption often becomes a weapon in factional infighting. Any scandal involving a senior official is inherently political. At a minimum, prosecutors have to receive high-level political approval to look into allegations of corruption among top officials. The inner leadership itself must presumably clear investigations of very senior officials. To go hunting a big tiger, therefore, investigators must first get a license. It is widely assumed, therefore, that factional politics play a major role in decided who gets investigated and who gets swept quietly under the rug.

Factional Politics

High-level scandals also create political opportunities. Xi's current campaign is no different. Triggered by the exposure of Neil Heywood's death and allegation that Bo Xilai's wife either killed him or had him killed, the current drive has spawned a series of investigations into corruption in the oil sector and Sichuan that seem to implicate former Politburo Standing Committee Member and former Chairman of the Central Committee's powerful Politics and Law Committee Zhou Yongkang. According to insiders, in the run up to the November 2012 Eighteenth Party Congress, Zhou had been pushing Chongqing Party Secretary, Politburo Member, and so-called "Red Princeling" Bo Xilai as a leftist counterweight to Hu Jintao's heir apparent Xi Jinping.2 Bo's abrupt fall from power clearly removed a potential political rival, while investigations into corruption involving PetroChina Chairman Jiang Jiemin, Chengdu Party Secretary Li Chuncheng, Hainan Vice Governor Li Hualin, Vice Minister for Public Security Zheng Shaodong, former Sichuan Vice Governor Guo Yongxiang, and former Chairman of the Hubei Party Committee's Politics and Law Committee Wu Yongwen – all of whom worked with Zhou at one point or another – enabled Xi or others to take out many of the now retired Zhou protégés.

In late July 2014, the official media announced that the Central Committee had approved a formal investigation of Zhou Yongkang. Zhou and his involvement in corruption had been the subject of rumors almost since the Bo Xilai case became public. For months, rumors circulated that Zhou and Bo had been plotting a coup, that Zhou had ordered three failed attempts on Xi Jinping's life, that Zhou had his first wife killed after they divorced; Zhou's son Zhou Bin had been detained; that his son had ties to Liu Han, a Sichuanese business tycoon who was sentenced to death in May after being convicted of leading an organized crime syndicate; that Zhou had had affairs with 400 women. For months there was also talk that Xi was afraid to put Zhou on trial because he feared that Zhou would speak out and expose the secrets he had learned during his days in charge of the internal security apparatus. Other rumors said that Xi had been unable to get permission to go after Zhou from former General Secretary and still party strongman Jiang Zemin. Despite talk that Xi might not be brave enough or strong enough, he ultimately did move against Zhou, but only after a series of Zhou's former secretaries, protégées, and cronies had been detained and charged with corruption. Authorities also arrested Zhou Bin and a half dozen other members of Zhou's extended family. Zhou has yet to be formally indicted and it is not entirely clear exactly what he will be charged with when the Procuratorate issues a formal indictment. The announcement that Zhou would face a formal investigation may signal the beginning of some sort of end game. Although the campaign has afforded Xi the opportunity to take down a series of rival political leaders, assert himself as party leader, and show the public that he is willing and able to do something about China's corruption problem, the politics of the campaign also have a downside. Zhou is not the only rotten apple and he alone did not cause the rot to spread to other apples in the barrel. Moreover, Zhou has long been seen as a member of the "Shanghai Gang," the cadre of officials linked to former General Secretary Jiang Zemin. Even before Zhou was formally taken down, the rumor mill was full of speculation about who the "real target" of Xi's tiger hunt was and who would be the next retired leader to find himself detained by investigators from the Central Discipline Inspection Commission. There was also talk of a building backlash against Xi, who many senior leaders felt was going "too far" and was becoming dangerously like former Chairman Mao Zedong. Xi thus has incentives to use the indictment of Zhou as an opportunity to declare "victory" and begin scaling back the campaign or at least easing off on his attack on high-level corruption.

Scaling back also had a downside. One of the core objectives of an anti-corruption campaign is to demonstrate to the public that the leadership is determined to fight corruption. Bagging big tigers helps show such determination. But bagging too many big tigers can backfire if the public becomes convinced – if it is not already – that the party's jungle is full of big tigers, senior leadership is full of corrupt tigers, and that the only big tigers being hunted are Xi's political enemies and the politically unlucky and unloved whom Xi had sacrificed.

Finally, in recent months evidence of corruption among the senior military command has surfaced. General Gu Junshan, Deputy Commander of the PLA General Logistics Department, who was in charge of barracks construction, was indicted in March 2014 on bribery charges. According to various sources, Gu had received huge bribes and kickbacks from developers seeking rights to land controlled by the PLA and had used part of his illegal income to bribe senior officers, including possibly two Vice Chairmen of the Central Military Commission. One of them, General Xu Caihou was allegedly arrested in a hospital bed where he lay dying of bladder cancer. Corruption among the military has long been suspected, but before now, military corruption has remained largely hidden from view. Evidence of more extensive corruption among senior military officers could thus prove a major political liability for the party and could generate resentment among the officer corps.

Regardless of whether Xi opts for a slow winding down or an abrupt claim to have won, it seems unlikely that he will convince the Chinese public that the campaign had achieved its goals of significantly reducing corruption and ending official extravagance. Neither goal is, in fact, achievable in the short-term. Making real inroads into corruption will take time, sustained effort, and a combination of political and administrative reforms.

Conclusion

The scale and scope of the high-level, heavily political portion of Xi's campaign differentiates the current campaign from its predecessors. The current campaign is clearly more sustained and intense. It is now 18 months old and by all indications more senior officials and cadres, perhaps as many as 31, have been investigated, expelled from the party, sacked, indicted by the Procuratorate, or tried than in any other post-1978 period. How many are ultimately brought down by Xi's campaign remains to be seen and it may be months before the ultimate scale and intensity of the campaign become clear. It is also likely that many of those detained on corruption charges over the past year-and-a-half will not go to trial for some time. Regardless of what the coming weeks and months bring, however, it seems clear that Xi Jinping's anti-corruption campaign is no tempest in a teapot.

Gauging the long-term and broader political impact of Xi Jinping's anti-corruption campaign is difficult. Anti-corruption campaigns seek to achieve three goals. First, they seek to cull out corrupt officials. Second, they seek to deter those who are now tempted. As evidenced by the number of indictment and investigations, it is possible that Xi campaign has cut into the ranks of the corrupt, but how far is uncertain. Even more uncertain is whether the bagging of this crop of tigers will scare off other potential tigers and flies. Third, anti-corruption campaigns seek to convince the public that a regime is serious about fighting corruption, particularly in the highest places. Bringing down Zhou, or even his protégées, along with other senior officials, may convince ordinary Chinese that this time the regime is really determined to deal with corruption. Ultimately, however, the real proof will be in the follow-through. Should the fight against corruption fall off when all of the sound and fury of the current campaign comes to an end, then it is likely that the public will sink deeper into cynicism and dismiss the campaign as political knife fight in which a lot of flies and tiger cubs were killed to cloak the true factional reasons for the drive.

Note
[1] *Chen Xitong in 1997, Chen Liangyu in 2006, and Bo Xilai in 2012*

Suggested Reading

Roderic Broadhurst and Wang Peng, "After the Bo Xilai Trial: Does Corruption Threaten China Future?" *Survival* (June 2014): 53:3.

Jerome Doyan, "A new impetus for the fight against corruption," *China Perspectives* (June 2013), 2; 74-5

Kilkon Ko and Cuifen Wen, "Structural Changes in Chinese Corruption," *China Quarterly* (September 2012) No. 211: 718*740.

Peter Kwong, "Why China's Corruption Won't Stop," *The Nation* (4/22/2013); 17-21.

Alice L. Miller, "The Road to the Third Plenum," *The China Leadership Monitor* Fall 2013, (42): *http://www.hoover.org/sites/default/files/research/docs/clm42am-2013.pdf*

TI scales its index from 1 (least honest) to 10 (most honest). Because I find it counterintuitive to have an increase in a country score correspond to a decrease in corruption, I have chosen to invert the TI index.

The rumor mill went much further, suggesting – without substantiating evidence – the Zhou and Bo had plotted a coup in hopes of seizing power before Xi could take over from Hu Jintao as General Secretary or that Zhou had been behind repeated assassination attempts against Xi and other members of the leadership.

Andy Wedeman, Ph.D., is Professor of Political Science at Georgia State University.

New Trends in China's Administrative Reform

Baogang Guo
Vol. 13, No. 2
2014

State-building seems to be a never-ending task for the People's Republic of China (PRC). Since its founding, the government has revamped its administrative system more than 10 times. Reform has sped up recently, with a goal to transform governmental functions and improve administrative efficiency. Notably, the new leaders in Beijing have promoted the modernization of its governance system and administrative capability as the fifth modernization along side of the goal of modernizing China's agriculture, industry, science and technology, and military.

The Third Plenum of the Eighteenth Party Congress held in November 2013 called for accelerating China's administrative reform by building a law-based and service-oriented government. More specifically, it demanded deepening reforms of the administrative system, innovating administrative methods and enhancing the credibility and execution of the government. In the upcoming fourth plenary session to be held in October 2014, the rule of law – including building a government ruled by law – will refine the direction of the administrative reform even further. A number of new trends in China's administrative reform are worth noting: streamlining governmental administrative approval processes, curtailing the excessive administrative powers, promoting plural governance, and strengthening the administrative litigation system.

Background of the Administrative Reforms

China's latest administrative reform is motivated by a number of key concerns. The existing system of public administration is still based on the command-and-control approach inherited from the era of the planned economy. It has distorted the political and legal environment for doing business in China in the new age of the market economy and is largely responsible for the widespread rent-seeking and corrupt behaviors of government officials. Administrative redundancy and bureaucratic red tape also have hindered China's competitiveness and economic vitality.

Over-centralization of power is long-held as a major problem in China's administrative system. Therefore, China's administrative reform has focused on three main areas: the decentralization of power and delegation of rights, simplification and rationalization of administrative power, and building a government ruled by law. The reform involves three overlapping stages. The first one is to reorganize government institutions and decentralize administrative powers. The second stage is to change governmental functions in order to assist the transformation from a planned economy to a market one. The third stage is to transform the government's administrative methods.[1]

Seven rounds of institutional reform have been carried out since 1982. Government ministries and agencies have gone through sizable reorganization. Many industry-related ministries have been phrased out or converted into industry associations. The number of ministries in the central government has been cut in half and several new "super ministries" have been created to simplify administrative management. The regulatory power of the central government over the economy has been gradually shifted from micro-management to macro-management. A new civil service system has been in place since 1993.[2]

The decentralization drive has caused major change in state-local relations. Although the latest anti-corruption campaign has led to some recentralization of judicial and party disciplinary power, fiscal decentralization has characterized the new central-local governmental relationship and produced de facto fiscal federalism. Starting in 1994, a new "separated tax system" scheme (分税制) was implemented and local governments have acquired significant amounts of taxation, fee collection, investment, and legislative powers.

Today, the government is again in the process of streamlining the tax revenue-sharing system. The main problem with the existing system is that the reforms carried out in the last two decades, such as the elimination of agricultural tax and the restriction on collecting local fees, have a negative impact on local revenues. At the same time, more unfunded mandates, such as new programs on education, public welfare, and social and income security, are handed down from the top. Unable to pay for these new mandates, local governments are increasingly relying on borrowed money and land sales. Land sales in particular have directly and indirectly contributed to an overheated housing market and skyrocketing housing prices,[3] and led to rapid increases in the number of anti-land-grab protests staged by farmers.[4]

Another major delegation of rights has taken place in the areas of community governance. The 1982 Constitution codified the concept of local self-rule. There are 588,000 rural village committees and 95,000 urban neighborhood communities in China.[5] In 1987, the National People's Congress (NPC) adopted two organic laws for these two types of grassroots organizations.[6] Self-rule and direct election are all integrated elements. In recent years the number of homeowners associations also has grown rapidly and played an important role in community governance.

However, contrary to the development of community self-governance, we have seen the latest development of a "city grid management" model being promoted in many cities. It is an attempt by the government to extend its reach to local communities and enhance its capability of community control. This move may compromise the achievement of recent community governance reform and seriously restrict the space for more community autonomy.[7]

Curtailing Administrative Powers

One of the most important administrative reforms is to curtail excessive administrative powers. This reform actually started as early as in September 2001 when the Leading Group for the Reform of the Administrative Examination and Approvals was established. In October 2002, 789 administrative approval requirements were appealed. In August 2003, the NPC adopted the Law of Administrative Licensing to standardize the administrative power and procedures over issuing administrative licensing. The law requires that government at the local level create administrative service centers to allow license applicants to get their applications approved in one central office without having to visit many government offices and go through a lengthy and complicated review process.[8]

Starting from 2013, the priority of the administrative reform has been placed on eliminating and delegating administrative review and approval powers. The new consensus seems to be that any administrative approval requirement that is not authorized by law should be repealed and that business and social activities not clearly forbidden by law should be permitted. It appears that the direction of the reform is to create a new system of retroactive supervision, which will eventually replace most of the prospective review and inspection requirements. The Plan for the Institutional Restructuring of the State Council and Transformation of Functions, which was adopted by the NPC in 2013, further specifies that many requirements concerning investment, production, operations, licensing, and accreditation shall be canceled or delegated to lower-level governments. The Plan also specifies that administrative charges and government-funded items that are illegal and improper shall be repealed or delegated.

So far, seven rounds of elimination and delegations have been conducted and

463 items have been repealed at the national level since 2013. That involves about one-third of all items that needed central governmental approval. This was done on top of five similar reductions and simplifications between 2002 and 2012. The remaining approval items are expected to be further reduced in the years ahead. Government departments at all level are now required to publish a list of existing items that need administrative approval. In addition, the screening of the existing 369 national non-administrative approval items has begun. It is hoped that these items also will be gradually eliminated.

Similar administrative reforms are being carried out at the provincial and local levels, but the extent to which administrative simplification is implemented varies greatly. Zhejiang Province, for example, has eliminated 181 administrative approval items and 464 non-administrative approval items since 2013. But the reduction in the number of the administrative approval items represents only 11 percent of the 1,617 existing administrative approval items.[9] In Dongguan, the city government eliminated 81 administrative approval items, and delegated 58 in June 2014. This was done after a 55.1 percent of reduction in administrative approval items in 2013 and the elimination or delegation of another 135 items in March 2014.[10]

Promoting Plural Governance

Another trend in China's administrative reform is a move toward plural governance. Since the Sixteenth Party Congress, China has been moving away from the traditional emphasis on social control and unitary governance. Hu Jintao embraced the notion of social management in 2011, which was still a state-centered approach. The Xi-Li administration, however, embraces the notion of social governance, which calls for shared governance with an intention to minimize the unitary role of the central government.

The current system of registration and approval of civic organizations is very much outdated and restrictive.[11] The regulations require a non-governmental organization (NGO) to be managed by two government departments (a sponsoring department and the civil affairs department). Only one professional organization is allowed in each professional field, and no inter-provincial or cross-regional associations are permitted. Officially, 440,000 social organizations are registered, but according to one estimate, 1.5 million others cannot obtain official approval and operate on an unregistered basis.[12] Many unregistered organizations advocate labor rights, women's rights, farmers' rights, and environmental action, reflecting the rapid growth of these types of organizations and concerns.

The new regulations will remove some of the unwanted barriers. The government wants to invite NGOs to participate in or perform some of the social management functions for the government. Government agencies are encouraged to purchase social services from these organizations. But it is unlikely that the state will reduce its control of political-oriented civic organizations and grant full freedom of association. According to the MCA, the reform will be restricted mostly to the registration of four types of NGOs: professional and business, science and technology, charity, and community services.[13]

The reform has encountered several problems. The effectiveness of the reform seems to diminish as the policies move down the layers of bureaucracy. Many government departments or agencies refuse to give up important regulatory power. Premier Li Keqing openly voiced his frustration over the resistance to the administrative reform and blasted local officials for inertia in carrying out central government directives in a cabinet meeting in May 2014.[14]

Strengthening the Law-Based System of Public Administration

Building a law-based public administration is another important area in which we have seen some progress. For years, the practice of China's public administration could be characterized as "administration according to policy" and "administration according to party directives or documents." In an effort to legitimize administrative decision-making power and procedures, the NPC has adopted some much needed-laws in the area of public administration.

A large number of administrative laws also were formulated by the State Council to regulate market, enterprise activities, market exchange, economic contracts, intellectual property rights, taxation etc. In order to comply with WTO requirements, the state made a swift cleanup of all the so-called "red-heading documents," or government internal directives. Some 188,000 provincial and city level "red-heading documents" were invalidated.[15] In March 2004, the State Council published the Opinion on Pushing Forward Implementation of Administration According to Law. It stressed the need to safeguard people's procedural rights, enhance administrative accountability and responsibility, and develop a "sunshine" government.

The enactment of the Administrative Litigation Law was a high point in China's legal history. Encouraged by the law, hundreds of thousands of people began to file lawsuits to challenge local government acts or decisions.[16] Since the law's inception in the late 1990s, the court has heard more than two million administrative litigation cases.[17] Urban construction disputes such as land management, city planning, sales of land, and housing demolition now make up almost 20 percent of all cases.[18] Despite the sheer number of the cases, a plaintiff may still find it difficult to have a case accepted in the first place, to win these cases, and to enforce court decisions. In 2005, the court heard more than 127,000 cases. Among them, 25,317 resulted in rescinding or changing official decisions; in 15,796 cases, official decisions were upheld.[19] Overall the percentage of cases resulting the plaintiffs' winning is only about seven percent.[20] Another issue is that as many as 40 percent of administrative cases do not conclude with judicial rulings; plaintiffs simply withdraw their cases for various reasons.[21]

The lack of true separation of courts from local governments is one of the main reasons for these difficulties. Judges sometimes must seek local government approval if a lawsuit is unfavorable to the government before accepting these cases. Local party organizations may order courts to avoid accepting cases involving "hot issues" or sensitive matters. The low acceptance rate of administrative litigation cases may also be linked to the lack of qualified judges. Increasing numbers of judges have resigned because of long working hours, mounting case loads, and poor salaries. Another factor to consider is that administrative litigation remains a costly and unpredictable option for many people. Many people still prefer the administrative petition system ("letter-writing and office visits") to get grievances resolved.

To solve these issues, the NPC is in the process of revising the Administrative Litigation Law to improve its effectiveness. The proposed revisions include reducing administrative interference, enlarging the scope of administrative decisions subject to administrative litigation, restricting discretionary power of courts to reject cases, trying cases in unrelated cities or counties, introducing simplified procedures for less controversial cases, and making administrators legally liable for enforcing court orders.[22] Some core issues, such as how to make local agencies or chief administrators appear in the court, still lack enforceable measures. The proposed revision already has gone through the public comment phase. The revision process has been slowed after the first reading at the NPC in December 2013. The revision process may not conclude until sometime in 2015.

Concluding Thoughts on China's Administrative Reforms

In general, China's administrative reforms are in line with similar reforms carried out in many other countries. Its goals are to use scientific management to improve efficiency, to wage war on wasteful spending, to standardize administrative procedures aimed at making them fair and open, and to structure and limit administrative power to prevent corruption and reduce bureaucratic red tape.[23] Returning the power to the people and strengthening the governance by law are at the heart of the reform.

One of the familiar criticisms of China centers on the lack of progress in political reform.[24] Although there is certainly some truth to the claim,[25] there is no doubt that China's political landscape, at least the system of state governance, has undergone major changes because of continued administrative reforms. The creation of an effective, efficient, limited and service-oriented administrative system may involve only low-risk political changes, but we have reason to believe that good governance is one of the crucial prerequisites of higher-level political reform, such as electoral reform.[6]

China's administrative reform is clearly moving in the right direction. With a leaner and more efficient government, a reduction in governmental regulatory powers, a new plural governance structure, and law-based administrative system, China is in a better position to manage an increasingly more complex society. By pursuing a strategy of good governance, the Chinese Communist Party (CCP) has managed to consolidate its political legitimacy.

The author wishes to express his thanks for the generous support of the East Asia Institute, Singapore National University for conducting this research, and for the helpful comments made by Yongnian Zheng, Lance Gore and He Li.

Notes

[1] Zhou Guanghui, "Toward Good Governance: Thirty Years of Administrative Reforms in China," in Yu Keping ed., *The Reform of Governance* (Leiden, the Netherlands: Koninklijk Brill BV, 2010), p. 138.

[2] Kjeld Erik Brodsgaard & Chen Gang, *China's Civil Service Reform: An Update*, EAI Background Brief No. 493, 16 December, 2009.

[3] Zhou Zhihua, *The Land Supply System for Urban Development in China*, EAI Background Brief No. 769, 18 October, 2012.

[4] Cary Huang, "Land Grabs are Main Cause of Mainland Protests, Experts Say," *South China Morning Post*, 20 December, 2012.

[5] Ministry of Civil Affairs, PRC, "Quarterly Statistic Release of Social Services (March 2013)," http://files2.mca.gov.cn/cws/201404/20140428173249870.htm, accessed 10 June, 2014.

[6] *The Organic Law of Village Committees of the PRC* (1987) and *The Organic Law of Urban Neighborhood Committees* (1989).

[7] Tian Yipeng and Xue Wenlong, "Chengshi guanli 'wanggehua' moshi yu shiqu zizhi chuyi [The 'block management' model in urban management and its impact on community self-rule]," *Xuehai*, March 2012, http://www.sociology2010.cass.cn/upload/2012/12/d20121204154042925.pdf, accessed 10 June, 2014.

[8] *BBC Monitoring Asia Pacific*, "Licensing law said 'driving force' behind China's administrative reform," 6 February, 2014.

[9] *Zhejiang News*, http://zjnews.zjol.com.cn/system/2013/08/10/019525636.shtml, accessed 30, June 2014.

[10] See *Nanfang City Daily*, http://epaper.oeeee.com/I/html/2014-03/24/content_2041348.htm, accessed 9 June, 2014.

[11] The regulation in use was adopted in 1989 and amended in 1998. It requires a minimum 50 members, and minimum activities fund of 30,000 yuan. It must be sponsored by one of the government institutions. See Sonia Wong, *Non-Governmental Organizations and Government in China: Enemies or Allies*, EAI Background Brief No. 704, 8 March, 2012.

[12] "Chinese Civil Society: Beneath the Glacier," *The Economist*, April 12, 2014.

[13] Li Liguo, Minister of Civil Affairs, "Chuangxin shehui zhili tizhi [Reinventing the System of Social Governance]," *Qiushi*, no. 24, 2013, http://www.qstheory.cn/zxdk/2013/201324/201312/t20131212_301550.htm, accessed 15 June, 2014.

[14] Wang Xiangwei, "After Power Start, Li Keqiang's Frustration Grows with Resistance to Reforms," *South China Morning Post*, 9 June, 2014.

[15] Cai Dingjian, op cit, p. 253.

[16] Kevin J. O'Brien and Lianjiang Li, "Suing the Local State: Administrative Litigation in Rural China," *The China Journal*, no. 54, 2004, p. 76.

[17] Ye Zhusheng, "'Min gao guan' zai chufa [A New Beginning of the Administrative Litigation]," *South Review*, 10, January, 2014, http://www.nfcmag.com/article/4515-s.html, accessed 10

June, 2014.
[18] He Haibo, "*Kundun de xingzheng susong [Problems of Administrative Litigation]*," *Journal of East China University of Politics and Law*, No. 2, 2012, pp. 86–95.
[19] Cai Dingjian, op cit., p. 262.
[20] Chinese courts also handled more than 300 million cases filed by government departments or agencies against individuals or enterprises under the administrative litigation category in the same period. The government won more than 90 percent of these cases. See Ye Zhusheng, op cit.
[21] He Haibo, "Litigation without a Ruling: the Predicament of Administrative Law in China," *Tsinghua China Law Review*, 3, no. 2 (Spring 2011), pp. 258–281.
[22] Ye Zhusheng, op cit.
[23] Chang Mengzhong, "Crossing the River by Touching Stones: a Comparative Study of Administrative Reforms in China and the United States," *Public Administration Review*, special issue on comparative Chinese/American public administration, 69, sp1, (December 2009), pp. 82–87.
[24] Richard L. Grant, "Political and Economic Reform in China," *The World Today*, 51, no. 2, Februry, 1995, pp. 37–40; Hong Shi, "China's Political Development after Tiananmen; Tranquility by Default," *Asian Survey*, 30, no. 12, December 1990, pp. 1206–1217.
[25] Lance L. P. Gore, *Status Quo Interests Stall China's Reform*, EAI Background Brief No. 748, 23 August, 2012.
[26] Zheng Yongnian, *Zhongguo Gaige Sanbu Zou [China's Reform: a Roadmap]* (Beijing: People's Oriental Publishing & Media Co., Ltd, 2012); Wang Yukai, "paichu gaige zuli xuyao gengda yongqi he zhihui [More Courage and Wisdoms Are Needed to Overcome Obstacles of Reform]," http://www.zgdzgblt.com/index.php/manage/showmagcontent/mid/124/newsid/37, accessed 15 June, 2014.

Baogang Guo, Ph.D., is Associate Professor of Political Science at Dalton State College, Dalton, Georgia.

China's War on Air Pollution

Eri Saikawa
Vol. 13., No. 2
2014

Introduction

In 2008 and 2009 if I asked a Beijing taxi driver or anyone on the street about air quality on a hazy day, I was normally told that it was fog. No matter how much I tried to convince them that it was air pollution, most would just laugh and tell me that I did not know anything. Now, there is not even a need to ask what it is. In fact, when President Xi Jinping walked in Nanluoguxiang district on February 25, 2014, Xinhua's headline read: "Xi Jinping Visits Beijing's Nanluoguxiang amid the Smog: Breathing Together, Sharing the Fate."[1] Some people even commented about it on social media, asking why he was not wearing a face mask, which has become popular recently. Extremely bad air pollution events, especially linked to fine particles known as $PM_{2.5}$, have contributed to changing Chinese perceptions of their air quality and to raising awareness.

Environmental problems and air pollution incidents in China are not at all new. Ever since China started with a rapid economic growth model, there was an underlying policy of industrializing first and cleaning up later. What is new is the magnitude of the problem, and the urgency within the government to solve it. Prime Minister Li Keqiang in March 2014 "declared war on pollution," acknowledging that pollution is the major problem in the country.[2] Li wrote in a report he delivered at China's annual parliamentary meetings that heavy pollution "is nature's red-light warning against the model of inefficient and blind development," and added: "We must strengthen protection of the ecological environment and resolve to take forceful measures."[3]

This is also illustrated in the Decision of the Third Plenum of the Eighteenth

Party Congress that the government will "improve local government's performance in" and "allocate more law-enforcement resources to the primary level in such key areas as...environmental protection."[4] Most importantly for air quality, the plenum also explicitly states that it will "establish and improve an environmental protection system that strictly supervises the emission of all pollutants, and independently conduct environmental supervision and administrative law enforcement." As they promised to publicize environmental information, they also opened a new website where they post the real-time air quality index in various Chinese cities.[5]

How bad has China's air quality been, you might ask. The Ministry of Environmental Protection announced that only three of China's seventy-four cities met the national standard for "fine air quality" in 2013.[6] The three cities were all in remote areas: Lhasa – the capital of Tibet; Haikou – the capital of Hainan; and Zhoushan in Zhejiang province. These were the only cities that had an average air quality index (AQI) value of less than 100. Although AQI is based on six different pollutants (sulfur dioxide SO_2, nitrogen oxides NO_x, coarse particulate matter PM_{10}, fine particulate matter $PM_{2.5}$, carbon monoxide CO, and tropospheric ozone O_3) and is determined by taking the worst value among them, it is safe to assume in China that $PM_{2.5}$ usually determines the general AQI. The Chinese AQI value of 100 translates into annual average $PM_{2.5}$ concentrations of less than 75 micrograms per cubic meter ($\mu g/m^3$). Taking into consideration that the World Health Organization (WHO) guideline for the annual average is $10\mu g/m^3$,

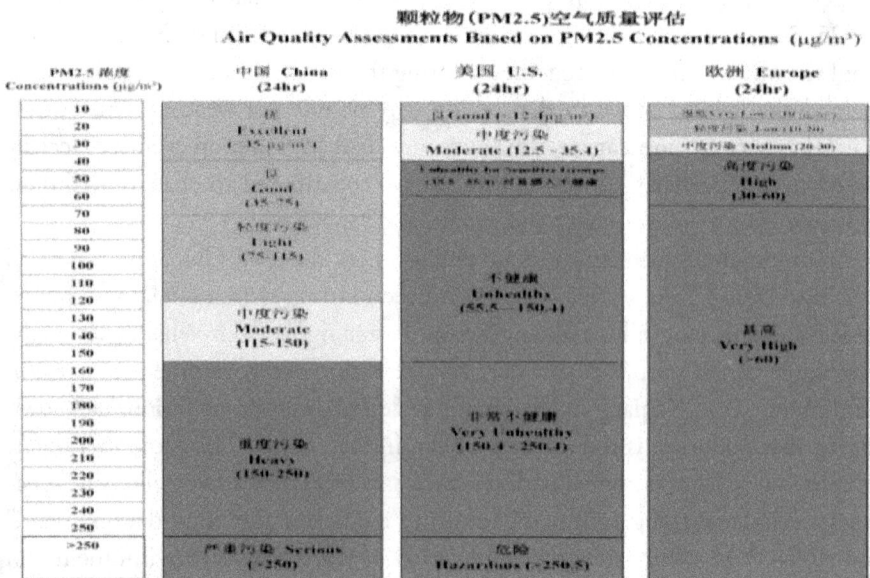

Figure 1. Comparisons of Air Quality Assessments in China, U.S., and Europe.

and the U.S. and EU standards are 12 and 10μg/m^3, respectively, AQI of less than 100 is not necessarily considered "fine air quality" in other parts of the developed world. Even then, the northern region including Beijing, Tianjin, and Hebei had only 135 days in year 2013 that met this criterion.[7] The figure below taken from Andrews (2014) compares China's standards to those of the U.S. and Europe.

The WHO announced a report linking outdoor air pollution to 3.7 million annual premature deaths worldwide.[8] Approximately 350,000-500,000 Chinese are estimated to die prematurely due to air pollution per year based on studies by the World Bank, WHO, and the Chinese Academy for Environmental Planning.[9] This is no surprise, since PM2.5 concentrations can be even higher than 500μg/m^3, which is even not listed on the figure above. In addition, 450,000 deaths were already estimated in 2000 due to China's PM$_{2.5}$ concentrations from its own emissions.[10]

Air Pollution Policy

Although China has been putting development first for a long time, it started including emissions reduction in the 10th five-year plan for 2000 through 2005. The first target included 10 percent emissions reduction for SO$_2$ from the 2000 level by 2005. This goal failed miserably. SO$_2$ emissions actually increased 28 percent from 2000 levels.[11] In the 11th five-year plan (2006-2010) SO$_2$ emissions reduction goal of 10 percent appeared again. This time the target was met successfully.[12] In the 12th five-year plan (2011-2015) China for the first time included politically binding targets not only for SO$_2$ (eight percent below 2010 levels), but also for NO$_X$ (10 percent below 2010 levels) and CO2 intensity (17 percent reduction in emissions per unit of GDP relative to 2010 levels).

As air pollution began to be more visible and cause problems for longer periods of time, the Chinese government started to change course on air pollution regulation. On February 29, 2012, China's State Council approved its first national environmental standard for PM$_{2.5}$ at 35μg/m^3 annual average.[13] Furthermore at the end of 2012, the government issued the 12th five-year plan on Air Pollution Prevention and Control in Key Regions, which for the first time provided a comprehensive plan for three key regions (Beijing-Tianjin-Hebei, Yangtze River Delta, and Pearl River Delta) and 10 city clusters, involving 19 provincial level jurisdictions and 117 cities. There were three reasons why this was important. First, this issued ambient concentration targets for the first time for SO$_2$, PM$_{10}$, NO$_2$, and PM$_{2.5}$. The reductions required for these pollutants were 10 percent, 10 percent, seven percent, and five percent below 2010 levels, respectively by 2015. For the three key regions, PM concentrations were required to be reduced by six percent rather than five percent. Second, it set higher emissions reduction targets than the national target. For example, SO$_2$ reduction and NO$_2$ emissions reduction targets are four and three percent higher than the national target. It also required non-attainment cities to develop air quality attainment plans, which needed to be publicly available.

After severe haze events in January 2013, the Premier Li Keqiang pledged to use an "iron fist" on the country's pollution at his first news conference after the annual legislative session in March.[14] Ten Measures on Air Pollution Control was then issued in June 2013 to indicate his seriousness about that promise. The measures he outlined were quite vague. However, one specific goal was included: to improve public transport and clean energy production, reducing the ratio of atmospheric pollutant emissions to GDP by 30 percent or more by 2017.

This was not the end of regulation in 2013. On September 12, the government further implemented the Action Plan on Air Pollution Prevention and Control, which included much stricter standards, higher goals, and more concrete measures. Its target for PM10 concentrations is now to reduce by at least 10 percent by 2017 compared to the 2012 level. A much larger emphasis was put on the three key regions (Beijing-Tianjin-Hebei, Yangtze River Delta, and the Pearl River Delta) and $PM_{2.5}$ concentrations are to be reduced by 25 percent, 20 percent, and 15 percent in each of the regions respectively, within the same period. For the first time, there was a specific target for annual $PM_{2.5}$ concentrations to be kept at $60\mu g/m^3$. Here again, there was a mention of reducing emissions in the transport sector such as eliminating old, high-emitting "yellow label" vehicles, promoting public transportation and alternative energy vehicles, and upgrading fuel quality.

Following the Third Plenum's increased interest in pollution control, Beijing on January 16, 2014, passed the "Regulation on Prevention and Control of Air Pollution in Beijing" on January 21, 2014. This featured not only stringent emission controls but also higher penalties in order to mediate haze events. For the first time in history, the Beijing Municipal People's Congress voted in favor of the regulation and replaced a guideline that was issued in 2000.[15] Beijing is now required to limit and gradually reduce the major air pollutant emissions using annual quotas for district, county government, and for individuals. Quotas are also in place for coal burning, and a plan is in place for regulating vehicle emissions.[16] It is the first time Beijing has set a cap on total pollutant emissions rather than on growth rate, and these new regulations make clear the intention of the government to clean up its air.

Auto Industry and Air Pollution

From the recent regulations, it is clear that the target sector is coal-fired power plants and road transport. Why is the regulation of tailpipe emissions so important? One main and obvious reason is the sheer number of cars, which has increased exponentially in China starting in the 1990s.[17] China has been promoting its automobile industry as a "pillar industry" since 1986.[18] As a way to introduce cleaner, more advanced technologies from developed countries, it has been strategic in adopting stringent emission standards.[19] Since it adopted its first emission standards in 2000, China has successfully been tightening the regulation at a very rapid pace.[20] The problem here and in some other developing countries is the fuel quality. It has always been the case in China that emission standards are adopted first, followed by fuel quality standards with some delay, although it is inefficient to run vehicles with low-quality fuel.[21] In the past, this even caused some of the vehicles to break down, without customers knowing it was because of high sulfur content in their gasoline.

Because China's emission standards have advanced far, it is not possible any more to meet stringent emission standards with lagging fuel quality. Low sulfur fuel is required for vehicles with clean technologies, and without high quality fuel, vehicles are destined to fail. In fact, Euro IV emission standards, planned to be in effect in late 2011, had to be delayed because of the lack of high-quality fuel then.[22] Oil companies are more often than not reluctant to make investments in clean fuel and they play a powerful role in emissions regulations in the road transport sector.[23] Whether the new Xi-Li administration can exert its will against the powerful oil companies is the big question.

Air Pollution and Climate Change

What is the main challenge for reducing emissions from power plants? Coal is cheap and China has been using coal to produce 69 percent of its energy.[24] With a very rapidly increasing energy demand and being the largest global energy consumer since 2010, China has been investing in alternative energy including solar power and wind. China was the world leader in clean energy investment in 2013, with $54 billion invested in renewables and leading by a large amount from the second largest investor, the U.S., with an investment value of $36.7 billion.[25] As China installs more electricity generation capacity from renewable energy, the hope is that coal dependence will be much lower.

China's large investment in renewables is great news for the other countries as well. Although China's main motive is its economic development, its shift to renewables could not only reduce air pollution and adverse health impacts within China, but also reduce the impact of global climate change. When China's major energy source becomes renewables, then the current growth in plug-in hybrids in China will also produce much sought-after emissions reductions both from tailpipes and power plants.

New Politics

What does it mean to have new political leadership for environmental protection in China? So far, it appears that the new leaders are more serious and concerned about mitigating air pollution. For China and other countries that have prioritized rapid economic growth over everything else, now is the time to reverse such trends. Increasing the weight of environmental damage in development progress evaluation, as stated in the Third Plenum's Decision, needs to become a norm for moving forward. With good air pollution goals in place, a workable implementation strategy is now needed. The new environmentally friendly China with new leaders began by showing the world that it is capable of creating stringent standards for its environment. Now is the time to also illustrate that China is serious by implementing effective policies as well.

Notes

[1] *Huang, 2014*
[2] *Li, 2014*
[3] *Li, 2014*
[4] *Decision of Third Plenum, 2013*
[5] *http://113.108.142.147:20035/emcpublish/*
[6] *Wong, 2014*
[7] *Wong et al., 2014*
[8] *WHO, 2014*
[9] *Moore, 2014*
[10] *Saikawa et al., 2009*
[11] *Schreifels et al., 2012*
[12] *Schreifels et al., 2012*
[13] *Zhang et al., 2012*
[14] *Wu, 2013*
[15] *Zhu, 2014*
[16] *Zhu, 2014*
[17] *Saikawa et al., 2011*
[18] *Thun, 2006*
[19] *Saikawa and Urpelainen, 2014*
[20] *Saikawa, 2013*
[21] *Saikawa, 2013*
[22] *Zhang et al., 2012*
[23] *Saikawa, 2013*
[24] *EIA, 2014*
[25] *Magill, 2014*

References

Andrews, Steven Q. "China's air pollution reporting is misleading." China Dialogue. March 27, 2014. Retrieved online on May 13, 2014.

Decision of the Central Committee of the Communist Party of China on Some Major Issues Concerning Comprehensively Deepening the Reform, (January 16, 2014), http://www.china.org.cn/china/third_plenary_session/2014-01/16/content_31212602.htm Retrieved online on July 31, 2014.

Huang, Rui. "Xi Jinping visits Beijing's Nanluoguxiang amid the smog: breathing together, sharing the fate (in Chinese)." Xinhua News Agency, February 25, 2014. http://news.xinhuanet.com/politics/2014-02/25/c_119498782.htm Retrieved online on August 1, 2014.

Li, Keqiang. "Report on the work of the government." March 5, 2014. http://online.wsj.com/public/resources/documents/2014GovtWorkReport_Eng.pdf Retrieved online on July 28, 2014.

Kaiman, Jonathan. "China's toxic air pollution resembles nuclear winter, say scientists." *The Guardian.* February 25, 2014. Retrieved online on April 21, 2014.

Magill, Bobby. "U.S. Lags Behind China in Renewable Investments." *Climate Central.* April 3, 2014. Retrieved on May 14, 2014.

Moore, Malcolm. "China's 'airpocalypse' kills 350,000 to 500,000 each year." *The Telegraph.* January 7, 2014. Retrieved on May 14, 2014.

Saikawa, Eri, Vaishali Naik, Larry W. Horowitz, Junfeng Liu, and Denise L. Mauzerall. "Present and potential future contributions of sulfate, black and organic carbon aerosols from China to global air quality, premature mortality and radiative forcing." *Atmospheric Environment, 43* (17): 2814-2822, 2009.

Saikawa, Eri, Jun-ichi Kurokawa, Masayuki Takigawa, Jens Borken-Kleefeld, Denise L. Mauzerall, Larry W. Horowitz, Toshimasa Ohara, The impact of China's vehicle emissions on regional air quality in 2000 and 2020: a scenario analysis, Atmospheric Chemistry and Physics, 11, 9465-9484, 2011

Saikawa, Eri. Domestic politics and environmental standards: China's policy-making process for regulating vehicle emissions, J. Sato (ed.), "Governance of natural resources: Uncovering the social purpose of materials in nature", Chapter 3, pp. 74-97, The United Nations University Press, 2013.

Saikawa, Eri and Johannes Urpelainen, Environmental Standards as a Strategy of International Technology Transfer, Environmental Science and Policy, 38, 192-206, 2014.

Schreifels, Jeremy J., Yale Fu, and Elizabeth J. Wilson. "Sulfur dioxide control in China: policy evolution during the 10th and 11th Five-year Plans and lessons for the future." *Energy Policy,* 48: 779-789, 2012.

Thun, Eric. Changing lanes in China: foreign direct investment, local government, and auto sector development, New York: Cambridge University Press, 2006.

U.S. Energy Information Administration (EIA). "China." http://www.eia.gov/countries/cab.cfm?fips=CH Retrieved on May 12, 2014.

Wong, Edward. "Most Chinese Cities Fail Minimum Air quality Standards, Study Says." *The New York Times.* March 27, 2014. Retrieved on April 21, 2014.

World Health Organization (WHO). "Ambient (outdoor) air quality and health." http://www.who.int/mediacentre/factsheets/fs313/en/ Retrieved on May 14, 2014.

Wu, Changhua. "China announces ten 'tough measures' to combat atmospheric pollution." *The Climate Group.* June 25, 2013. Retrieved on April 27, 2014.

Zhang, Qiang, Kebin He, and Hong Huo. "Cleaning China's air." *Nature,* 484: 161-162, 2012.

Zhu, Ningzhu. "Beijing passes regulation on air pollution control." *Xinhua news.* January 22, 2014. Retrieved online on April 22, 2014.

Eri Saikawa, Ph.D. is an assistant professor in the Department of Environmental Sciences and the Rollins School of Public Health at Emory University.

Foreign and Security Affairs in the Third Plenum

John Garver
Vol.13, No.2
2014

Stress on Internal Stability and National Security

The political direction outlined by the Third Plenum in November 2013 for China's international relations embodied a contradiction. It coupled a call for deepening integration of China's economy with the global economy with an intensified struggle against ideas carried into China by that very process of deepening globalization – ideas that are antithetical to the authority of the Chinese Communist Party and its monopoly on state power. To realize its and the Chinese people's aspiration of making China rich and strong, the CCP must open China to the world. But that very opening brings in powerful ideas of human liberty that have already toppled scores of undemocratic regimes in recent years. Xi Jinping's and the Third Plenum's answer to this conundrum is rejection of political liberalization and intense ideological struggle among China's people against liberal democratic ideas, coupled with the judicious use of assertive nationalism to rally popular support for the CCP regime.

The Communiqué issued by the Third Plenum affirmed the work of the Politburo since the previous Congress, work conducted, it said, "in the face of extremely complex international circumstances."[1] The nature of those "extremely complex international circumstances" was not specified, but the stress of the Communiqué was on maintaining internal stability. The Plenum resolved to "safeguard national security, guarantee that the people can live and work in peace and contentment, and that society is stable and orderly." The Communiqué also warned against marching "the evil road of changing banners and allegiances" and falling from the path of "Socialism with Chinese characteristics." This was an allusion to the Soviet experience and warning against political liberalization à la loosening of the Party's control. To this end the Plenum decided to set up a National Security Commission and "prefect national security system and a national security strategy to guarantee national security." It was imperative, the Plenum decided, to build strong armies for the Party, "people's armies which listen to the Party's instructions, [and] can be victorious in battle." "New era" military strategies and "modern military force[s] with Chinese characteristics" were to be built.

Xi Jinping elaborated on the nature of security threats during an explanation after the Plenum of the decision to set up a National Security Commission. China faced two security challenges, Xi said, which would be addressed via strengthened unified leadership of state security work to be provided by the new Commission. The first challenge involved the need to safeguard China's sovereignty, security, and "development interests." The second involved the need to ensure domestic political security and social stability. [2]

Challenges to Sovereignty and Development Interests

In the several years leading up to the Third Plenum, challenges to China's "sovereignty" came mainly from Japan in the East China Sea and Vietnam and the Philippines in the South Sea. Starting in 2010 an escalating cycle of Chinese and Japanese military assertion of presence around and over the Sengaka/Diaoyu Islands and the disputed middle zone of the East Chinese Sea moved Chinese and Japanese military forces to an increasingly sharp confrontation that is, fortunately, still without firing. In 2010 the number of Chinese fishing boats entering the waters close to the disputed islands increased dramatically. Chinese boats also became less compliant with orders by Japanese coast guard ships to leave the area. In September one Chinese fishing boat, rather than leave the area as ordered by a Japanese coast guard ship, rammed the Japanese vessel. When Japan detained the offending captain, Beijing responded with a number of forceful moves, including severe restriction of export of Chinese rare earths to Japan. Large emotionally charged anti-Japanese demonstrations erupted in China, and Beijing catered to that opinion with strong moves.

When the Japanese government in September 2012 purchased several of the Sengakus still privately owned (reportedly as a way of preempting provocative actions there by freelancing Japanese nationalists) Beijing responded forcefully. China accelerated PLA-N operations in the seas around Japan, in effect warning Tokyo to desist from challenges to what Beijing deemed China's territorial sovereignty in the East China Sea.[3] Japan responded to China's moves with increased military moves of its own, and throughout 2013 Chinese and Japanese coast guard ships and aircraft confronted one another in the seas and airspace around and over the Sengakus. In the South Chinese Sea, Philippine and Vietnamese ef-

Figure 1: Maritime East Asia

Source: Dr. Jean-Paul Rodrigue, Department of Economics and Geography, Hofstra University, June 2004. <people. Hofstra.edu/jean-paul_Rodrigue/ GESA/maplibrary.html>

forts to survey and exploit the energy resources under the sea floor were countered by PLA-Navy moves.

China's "developmental interests" requiring "new era" military capabilities include evacuation of Chinese citizens (including Taiwanese, according to Beijing's policy) working abroad but finding themselves in conflict situations. China's first military operation to evacuate citizens endangered by internal disorder came in Libya during the uprising there in early 2011. More than 35,000 Chinese citizens were evacuated from Libya in a period of weeks, constituting the largest and most complicated evacuation of Chinese nationals up to that point. A PLA-N frigate on anti-piracy duty in the Gulf of Aden was dispatched to assist and safeguard the Chinese evacuation. The growing international presence of Chinese firms and personnel, combined with mounting instability in countries where Chinese firms operate, mean that Beijing called these rescue operations a major category of "military operations other than war." By conducting these operations effectively and professionally, Beijing demonstrates to its citizens that it protects China's interests and reputation as a strong country.

China's most strategically vital "developmental interest" involves the sea lines of communications (SLOCs) over which moves China's vast merchandise, energy, and raw materials trade. Broadly speaking, as China has globalized its economy, the SLOCs, which carry 90 percent of all world trade, have become more important to China.[4] The implications of this are profound, ranging from rising ship insurance costs for vessels transiting the pirate-ridden Gulf of Aden, to the hypothetical ability of the United States Navy to blockade China in the contingency of a U.S.-PRC war that became protracted.[5] There is a huge gap between PLA-N requirements and capability to protect China's SLOCs.[6]

Beijing's ability to defend these Chinese interests is linked to legitimization of the CCP regime and internal stability. Since the upheavals of 1989-1991, nationalism has become China's dominant popular ideology and de facto legitimization of the CCP regime. This requires that the regime demonstrate its ability to defend China's interests and honor. Having founded its claim to continued political tutelage on its ability to make China rich, strong, and esteemed among the nations of the world, the CCP cannot appear to be weak-kneed. Thus the Third Plenum Communiqué affirmed CCP rule since 1978 and proclaimed the objective for the future as "creat[ing] a wealthy, strong, democratic, civilized and harmonious Socialist country, and realize the Chinese Dream of the great rejuvenation of the Chinese nation."

Enemies Within and Without

In the run-up to the Third Plenum, the CCP devoted considerable effort to ideological work aimed at unifying thinking. In May 2013 an internal document was issued by the Party's General Office for study by Party organs. The contents of the document leaked to the foreign media.[7] The secret study guide identified seven dangerous Western values that had to be struggled against as a matter of life and death. It was especially important to prevent communication of these dangerous ideas via the Internet. The seven dangerous and subversive Western ideas were:[8]

Constitutional democracy
Universal human rights
Media independence (from Party guidance)

Judicial independence (from Party guidance)
Civil society (made up of autonomous organizations)
Pro-market neo-liberalism

"Nihilist" criticism of past errors by the Party

Xi Jinping reiterated in an "important speech" to a National Propaganda and Ideology Work Conference convened in Beijing on August 19 (about a month before the Third Plenum), the importance of ideological class struggle against external and internal enemies. [9] In effect, Xi was fleshing out the "extremely complex international circumstances" alluded to vaguely in the Third Plenum Communiqué. Powerful foreign forces were conducting a propaganda campaign, especially via the Internet, but including all forms of media and communication, to create the ideological base for overthrow of the CCP regime, Xi said:

Hostile forces are doing their utmost to propagate so-called 'universal values'... their objective is...to overthrow the leadership of the Chinese Communist Party and China's Socialist system. If we allow [this]...those false efforts will...endanger the Party's leadership and the security of the Socialist national regime.... Western anti-China forces continue to vainly attempt to use the Internet to 'topple China' ... On this battlefield of the Internet, whether we can stand up, and gain victory, directly relates to our country's ideological security and regime security.

The ideological class struggle was crucial. Alluding to the upheavals of 1989-1991 Xi continued:

History and reality have repeatedly proven that whenever or not ideological work is done well relates to the Party's future fate...we cannot even for a moment slacken and weaken ideological work. In this area we have gained deep lessons. The disintegration of a regime often starts from the ideological area, political unrest and regime change may perhaps occur in a night.... If the ideological defenses are breached, other defenses become very difficult to hold. We must grasp the leadership power...in ideological work closely in our hands...otherwise, we will make irredeemable historical mistakes.

"Western countries see our country's development and expansion as a challenge to their value views, systems, and models, and intensify ideological and cultural infiltration of our country," Xi said further. There were a range of "mistaken viewpoints" within China upon which the Western ideological offensive could build: embrace of Western values, discussion of party or national history, denial of reform or the Four Cardinal Principles. There were also "social contradictions and problems" in Chinese society that were creating fertile soil for foreign hostile ideological subversion.

Xi Jinping's August 2013 "important talk" on ideological class struggle was followed by the release of a six-part, 100-minute video program titled "Silent

Contest."[10] Mandatory viewing for all CCP cadre above a certain level, the program apparently was produced by the General Staff Department of the PLA along with the PLA's National Defense University and the Chinese Academy of Social Sciences. The program argued in detail that the U.S. defeated its greatest enemy, the Soviet Union, by non-military means, including especially ideological subversion, and was now trying to do the same thing with China. Gorbachev's "New Thinking" that had erased Soviet Communist Party members' awareness of domestic and foreign class enemies and attempted "westernization" that produced Soviet weakness, had all facilitated a sustained and long-term campaign of U.S. subversion. The result was the dissolution of the Soviet Union. This resulted in the U.S. shifting its spearhead toward China. The years 1978-1989 had been a "honeymoon" in U.S.-PRC relations because of common opposition to the Soviet Union. The United States was using a vast array of weapons to subvert China: radio and television broadcasts, cultural and academic exchanges, the Internet, support for Tibetan or Xinjiang rebels, and even the village election program of the Carter Center in Atlanta.

"Silent Contest" grew out of a decade-long debate in China over the cause of the Soviet disintegration. A leadership consensus was reached in 2004 that, in line with comments by Deng Xiaoping from 1989, a major reason for the Soviet collapse was the abandonment of core Marxist principles.[11]

Deep Internal Insecurity and Assertive Nationalism: Concluding Thoughts

The efforts of the CCP to anathematize expression of doubts about Marxism-Leninism and the Four Cardinal Principles are linked to debates within China, and probably within the Party itself, about whether to undertake basic reform in China's political system. Discussion of that would, however, take this essay away from its proper focus on China's international relations. In terms of China's diplomacy, several conclusions follow from the previous discussion.

The deep insecurities of CCP leaders regarding domestic stability and legitimization will, first of all, lead Beijing to be careful to avoid genuine military conflict with its neighbors. In a conflict with Japan over a dispute in the East China Sea the PLA-N could well be defeated by the very high tech and very well-trained Japanese Maritime Self Defense Force. Chinese defeat in a naval clash with Japan would touch off anti-Japanese protests that could become very dangerous for the CCP. Hatred of Japan is easy to mobilize in China these days, but once anti-Japanese demonstrators are in the streets, it is extremely easy for popular anger to be directed against the government rather than against Japan. Under normal conditions Party authorities are able to turn down or off popular anti-Japanese fashions once they threaten state objectives.[12] But the spilling of Chinese blood by Japanese forces could well unleash a wave of emotion that overwhelmed controls that worked well enough during earlier upwellings of anti-Japanese emotion. In such circumstances, escalation into a larger scale clash with Japan might be deemed preferable to backing down. This could confront the CCP with a bigger war, with one of China's main economic partners that might derail the economy and/or lead to a Chinese confrontation with the United States – with Japan at the U.S. side. On the other hand, assertive Chinese moves that generate tension but remain below the threshold of use of armed force, and which allow the CCP state to demonstrate its bold resolution in defense of China's interests, could be very attractive to China's rulers.

By defining liberal democratic ideas as "Western" the CCP is better able to anathematize them as part of a hostile Western ideological attack on China. In the first instance it must be observed that the linkage of democracy with the West is bogus. While many of these ideas did originate in Europe, they are today embraced by many non-Western countries: South Korea, Mongolia, Japan, Taiwan, the Philippines, Indonesia, Thailand, Bangladesh, India, Turkey, and so on. Scores of non-Western countries are struggling toward adoption of some variant of these universal ideas: Iraq, Iran, Afghanistan, Nepal, Egypt, the Ukraine, Tunisia, etc. Ideas of human liberty and democracy have spread across the globe. To call these ideas today "Western" makes as much sense as to call science "Western." Yet in China, convincing China's people that these ideas are "Western" goes a long way toward persuading them that they come from power centers hostile to China and are outside China's 4,000-year-old tradition.

The period between the spring 1989 internal challenge to the CCP regime and the collapse of the Soviet Communist state in December 1991 was pivotal. With old Marxist-Leninist ideas drained of popular appeal, the CCP state stood exposed as founded on naked brute power, unadorned by popularly appealing ideas. Confronted by this deep crisis of legitimacy, the CCP turned to aggrieved nationalism to rally popular support. Ideological indoctrination and mobilization was one thing the CCP regime was still good at. Over the next two decades China's populace was intensively indoctrinated with the ideology of "China's century of national humiliation" focusing on all the putative injustices inflicted on China when China was weak – i.e., before the CCP came to power. Expression of contrary ideas within China was repressed. The CCP's new ruling strategy was remarkably effective in re-legitimizing CCP rule, especially among China's more educated urban classes, a group that historically was attracted to ideas of nationalism. The turn-around from a deep legitimacy crisis in 1989 to strong nationalist support for the CCP regime today (as indicated by many opinion polls) is truly remarkable. And perhaps troubling. Lacking the legitimization of free popular election – the immensely powerful legitimizing mechanism of modern liberal democracy – the CCP has appealed to nationalism.

The intense, popular nationalist belief fanned by decades of CCP indoctrination apparently has begun to exercise significant influence on China's foreign policy moves. Forceful moves against putative foreign miscreants injuring China's interests or opposing China's unquestionably just "rise" are popular, especially when directed against Japan, the number one villain of China's national humiliation narrative. The idea that "little countries" like the Philippines or Vietnam should be allowed to trample on China's unquestionable territorial sovereignty in the South China Sea – which is how the CCP's ideological apparatus frames the issue – go down well with popular nationalist opinion.[13] Moreover, attempts to settle territorial disputes with China's neighbors via negotiation not backed by demonstrations of China's now-great power and by concessions and compromise – as are perhaps inevitable in any negotiation – are decried as cowardly and naïve, or perhaps downright treasonous. China's Ministry of Foreign Affairs, more attuned to foreign views than other organs of China's government, has occasionally been criticized for lack of patriotic ardor.[14] A Chinese leader who aspires to high position, such as Xi Jinping, cannot afford to seem weak in rebuffing foreign transgressions.

The PLA officer corps may be a second constituency particularly enamored of China's new aggrieved nationalism and favorable to forceful action to rebuff foreign offenses against China's honor or interests. Since the upheaval of 1989-1991, the CCP has paid special attention to indoctrination of the PLA, and China's soldiers are probably less exposed to challenges to the CCP's orthodox national humiliation narrative than are China's urban intellectuals. The PLA's budget and status are also linked to an active role in defense of China's interests. This is not to say that PLA leaders favor war, especially against countries allied with the United States. But the use of China's carefully cultivated and ever-greater military power in support of China's interests in ways short of war – i.e., in the sort of demonstrations in the vicinity of the Sengaku's in 2009-2014 – may well accord with PLA recommendations.

These hawkish forces in China are balanced by extremely powerful groups with vested interests in minimizing conflict with China's neighbors let alone with the United States. China's state-owned enterprises, private sector entrepreneurs and development-oriented provinces, plus broad swaths of China's slowly emerging civil society, are deeply interested in participation in the global economy and recognize that this would be hindered by international tension. CCP leaders also understand that it is they who will bear the possible risk of embarrassing defeat in foreign adventures, and/or the potentially internally destabilizing aspects of economic losses associated with foreign conflicts. The international trajectory of China's rise is not ordained. Yet the question looms: how will an undemocratic and even anti-democratic but intensely nationalist China behave as its power waxes over coming years and decades?

Notes

1 *Communiqué of the Third Plenum of the 18th CCP Central Committee, (Full Text). http://www. c3sindia.org/china-internal/3787*

2 *Xi Jinping expounds security commission role, Xinhuanet. November 15, 2013 http://news. xinhuanet.com/english/china/2013-11/15/c_132892155.htm*

3 *A detailed review of PLA-N activities in the seas around Japan is in Defense of Japan 2013, White Paper, Ministry of Defense, Japan. www.mod.go.jp, Part 1: Security Environment Surrounding Japan, 41.*

4 *See, Rose George, Ninety Percent of Everything (New York: Metropolitan Books, 2013).*

5 *A major factor prompting Beijing to decide in late 2008 to deploy PLA-N warships to join in international anti-piracy operations in the Gulf of Aden was the fact that Chinese companies were threatened with bankruptcy from escalating ship-insurance costs and disruption of delivery schedules because PRC ships needed to round the Cape of Good Hope rather than transit the Suez Canal. See Andrew S. Erickson and Austin M. Strange, No Substitute for Experience; Chinese anti-piracy Operations in the Gulf of Aden (Newport: China Maritime Studies Institute, China Maritime Studies monograph Number 10, November 2013).*

6 *For a review of PLA-N anti-piracy operations in the Gulf of Aden and growing PLA-N attention to "military operations other than war," Erickson & Strange, Ibid.*

7 *Chris Buckley, "China Warns Officials against 'Dangerous' Western Values," The New York Times, May 13, 2013; Chris Buckley, "China's New Leadership Takes hard Line in Secret Memo," The New York Times, August 19, 2013.*

8 *Raymond Li, "Seven Subjects Off Limits for Teaching, Chinese Universities Told," South China Morning Post, September 19, 2013.*

9 *"Xi Jinping's 19 August speech revealed?" (Translation), China Copyright and Media. http://chinacopyrightandmedia.wordpress.com/2013/11/12xi-jinpings For a discussion of the authenticity of the leaked CCP document see Cary Huang and Keith Zhai, "Xi Jinping rallies party for propaganda war on internet," South China Morning Post, September 4, 2013. http://www. scmp.com.*

10 *Jeremy Page, "China Spins New Lesson From Soviet Fall," The Wall Street Journal, December 11, 2013, 1.18; Jane Perlez, "Strident Video by Chinese Military Casts U.S. as Menace," The New York Times, October 31, 2013. The program was available on November 2013 at https:// www.youtube.com/watch?v=m_81sjicoswb but was later removed.*

11 *Page, "China Spins New Lesson From Soviet Fall."*

12 *For an insightful discussion of the relation between CCP authority and semi-autonomous nationalist activism see, James Reilly, Strong Society, Smart State; the Rise of Public Opinion in China's Japan Policy (New York: Columbia University Press, 2012).*

13 *One study found that a Google search of the Chinese media yielded 210,000 uses over a several year period of key three-phrase descriptions of putative Vietnamese and Philippine violations of China's sovereignty and resources in the South China Sea. Zheng Wang, "Bad Memories, Good Dream: the Legacy of Historical Memory and China's Foreign Policy," The Asan Forum (July 25, 2014): 10, http://www.theasanforum.org*

14 *Jeff Bader, a key Obama China aide during his first term, recounts in his memoir the intimidation of less militant-minded voices in China's elite during the 2009-2010 debate. Jeffrey A. Bader, Obama and China's Rise; An Insider's Account of America's Asia Strategy (Washington: Brookings Institution, 2012, 109. 122. 104-05).*

John Garver, Ph.D., is Professor of International Affairs at the Georgia Institute of Technology, Atlanta, Georgia.

Market vs. Government in Managing the Chinese Economy

Xuepeng Liu
Vol. 13, No. 2
2014

One issue that stands out in the *Decision* concerns the relationship between market forces and the power of government in the Chinese economy. In previous government statements or reports, the market was expected to play a *fundamental* role; while in this report, market will play a *decisive* role and have the final say in resource allocation. As stated in Chapter III of the *Decision*, "Establishing a unified, open, competitive, and orderly market system is the basis for the market to play a *decisive* role in the allocation of resources." (emphasis added by author) The changing role of the market means China is seeking to inject vitality into the economy by allowing market forces freer reign. We would expect to see a more level playing field for businesses, a more important role played by private sectors, and an improved market mechanism such as a unified urban and rural construction land market and a more open financial market system. To some extent, this transition has met the expectation for market-oriented reforms from both within and outside China.

The articles on protecting property rights and developing a healthy non-public sector are in line with China's commitment to continued free market reform. Despite the determination of the Chinese government in implementing and deepening the market reforms, government will still play a leading role in the economy. The *Decision* says in Chapter II:

The basic economic system with public ownership playing a *dominant* role and different economic sectors developing side by side is an important pillar of the socialist system with Chinese characteristics and is the foundation of the socialist market economy. We must unswervingly consolidate and develop the public economy, persist in the dominant position of public ownership, give full play to the *leading* role of the state-owned sector, and continuously increase its vitality, controlling force and influence. (Emphasis added by author)

Even after several decades of market reform, the government today still has control of the commanding heights of Chinese economy, usually the upstream sectors such as resource and energy sectors.[1] By analyzing the domestic value-added content of Chinese exports, Tang, Wang and Wang (2014) shows that state-owned enterprises (SOEs) are consistently more upstream than small and medium-sized enterprises. This finding suggests that SOEs indeed still play an important role in shaping China's exports.[2]

The *dominant* role played by state ownership stated above seems to contradict somewhat with the *decisive* role of the market. Such an inconsistency just reflects the mixed feelings about the role of government in China's economy. Over the last several decades, along with the economic boom, China has developed a mixed economy with cross holding by and mutual fusion between state-owned capital, collective capital, and non-public capital. The problems of socialist policies had been well understood, and the government has gradually loosened its grip on the economy. At the same time, we also observed many issues with privatization in Russia and Eastern European countries, such as insider trading and voucher privatization,[3] and their much less impressive economic progress. All of these, together with the 2008 world financial crisis, have spawned new critiques of privatization and free market economy, giving us an impression of the crucial role of government in the economy. They also gave rise to the so-called "China Model" or "Beijing Consensus," with both market and government playing key roles in an intertwined way, as opposed to the neoliberal "Washington Consensus."

On one hand, China has demonstrated the effectiveness of a gradual and determined reform that releases the vitality of the market in a controlled way to maintain fast economic growth and a stable society. China's pragmatic use of innovation and experimentation has achieved an "equitable, peaceful high-quality growth" and "defense of national borders and interests" (Ramo, 2004).[4] This is exemplary for many developing and transitional economies. On the other hand, however, some may be suspicious of such a type of "China Model." To a large extent, the dominance of state capital is simply a leftover of the socialist era. The true impetus to China's economic growth over the past decades is not government control but the introduction of market mechanisms. In other words, China's economic success should be attributed to less, not more, government controls. But the coexistence of the still relatively high share of state assets and China's economic success tends to give people a false sense of the importance of public ownership and an underestimation of the inefficiencies of government controls.

Since the reform of the agricultural sector in 1978, Chinese government has been retreating from the commanding heights of the economy, and private sectors have been playing a larger and larger role. Because China adopted a gradual approach to reform, unlike the shock therapy in the USSR and Eastern Europe, the change in public ownership has been gradual. Promoting this kind of mixed economy may have been a good move for China; it is debatable whether it has been the optimal choice. This point is especially important when other countries consider copying China's approach to transform their own economies.

Although the Chinese government considers the dominant role of public ownership a feature of its socialist market economy "with Chinese characteristics," it can be better understood from classic economy theories of market failures. As we know, government controls may be able to improve market outcomes in the cases of market failures. But public ownership is rarely the best option. The appropriate role of government in economics is not as a player, but as a referee that guarantees a level playing field. There is much evidence in the literature of the inefficiency of SOEs. For example, Dollar and Wei (2007) find that even after a quarter century of reforms, state-owned firms still have significantly lower returns to capital than private firms. By their calculation, if China succeeds in allocating its capital more efficiently, it could reduce its capital stock by eight percent without sacrificing economic growth.[5]

Another serious problem associated with the state ownership in some key industries in China is "red" capitalism, a symbiosis between large businesses and high-level government officials, their delegates, or family members. This nurtures an environment for corruption and rent-seeking, discourages innovation and fair business practice, and hence is against the objective of enhancing the role of free market in the economy. Of course, this is also a political problem. Although the step-down of government from the commanding heights may not eliminate this problem, it can at least help to alleviate it. It can also help to transform the functions of the government.

I am not saying that China should privatize its state-owned sectors completely and immediately. The lesson from the shock therapy in Russia and Eastern Europe should be remembered. The importance of stability should never be underestimated, and the gradual approach adopted by China can be indeed conducive to long-term economic prosperity. My point is on the direction of change regarding the roles of market versus government in the economy. The *Decision*, emphasizing the decisive role of market on one hand but the dominant role of state-ownership on the other, is rather confusing. The Chinese government is obviously correct in promoting modern corporate governance for SOEs. At the same time, it is also important to point out that a stronger SOE sector does not necessarily imply a *bigger* SOE sector.

History can be a good guide for the future, so it is useful to review the rise and fall of the roles played by government versus market over the last 100 years. At the turn of the 20th century, the market dominated western economies. With the Great Depression and two world wars, however, the advent of state-dominated economies was seen. The state gradually extended its sphere of influence into areas originally controlled by the market. At the extreme, the Communist states planned their economies so that government would be an omniscient entity. Many industrial countries in the West and in developing countries around the world were building "mixed economies" in which the government dominated but still allowed a functioning market system. The goal of such reforms was to provide justice, opportunity, and a good life for all. Until 1970s, this "mixed economy" remained practically uncontested and government was unceasingly enlarging. However, starting from the 1970s, government started to lose ground. Led by Margaret Thatcher in the U.K. and Ronald Reagan in the U.S., western governments were casting off power and tasks as the spotlight was shifting to "government failure" rather than "market failure." Privatization or deregulation became the goals of governments as they rushed to sell state-owned assets to the public and took hands off the operation of businesses. After the failure of Communism in 1990s, the system disappeared in Eastern Europe and what had been the Soviet Union and had been replaced by a more market-oriented economy in China. Today all over the world, government planning has decreased, regulation has decreased, and markets have grown. Markets began the 21st century again in a dominating position.[6] During the 2008 world financial crisis, however, the role of governments expanded again in many countries through ambitious rescue plans, and fiscal and monetary policies.

In sum, economic development and reform remain the major focus of this report. To achieve continued economic growth and prosperity, radical reforms are still needed. The *Decision* recognizes the importance of finding a good balance between government and market in the economy. A revolutionary breakthrough on this issue in the *Decision* is the recognition of the key role played by the market in resource allocation, but the dominant role of state-owned sectors as stated in the report may cause some confusion. The planned deeper market reform is encouraging, while its true effect remains to be seen and will rely on its successful implementation. Several current economic difficulties can well prevent the government from following the rules of market. For instance, under the backdrop of a potential significant slowdown of Chinese economy after the 2008 world financial crisis, the government had already carried out stimulus plans and may step in again to avoid the collapse of its housing market. In addition, many new concerns such as environment protection and building the social security system also require the government to play a key role. Therefore, we may continue to see ups and downs of government in China in the years to come.

Liberalizing International and Domestic Trade

The *Decision* shows the continued commitment of China to open economic policies by further relaxing control over investment access; by providing equal treatment to both domestic and foreign investment; by providing stable, transparent, and predictable policies; by promoting the orderly opening up of finance, education, culture, healthcare, and other service sectors; and by further liberalizing general manufacturing. Although many people claim China has given up the "crossing the river by stepping on the stones" strategy and started to embrace whole heartedly the free market and open economic policy, I would still expect to see gradual changes. The reforms in the above areas may be carried out in a faster pace than before, but will not happen immediately.

A good example is the establishment of the China (Shanghai) Pilot Free Trade Zone. It is a major step that China has taken to deepen reform and open up in the face of new circumstances. Different from the special economic zones and export processing zones established in earlier years aimed mainly at promoting manufacturing, this new type of free trade zone focuses instead on financial and business services, which China has been very reluctant to open. A competitive services sector, as a typical feature of a modern economy, is crucial to sustained growth of China. If the experiment carried out in this free trade zone is successful, we would expect to see its expansion soon to the whole country.

Trade liberalization is usually achieved through various trade agreements. Besides the multilateral liberalization approach under the GATT/WTO, free trade agreements (FTA) have been on the rise, especially after the 1990s, partially because of slow progress made under the WTO in the last two decades. China also intends to speed up the construction of FTAs with neighboring countries, covering many traditional and non-traditional trade and investment related issues. FTAs may serve as an experiment for China to carry out some deeper liberalization initiatives in the areas such as investment, property rights, and services trade. In these areas, China and many other developing countries have been reluctant to open their domestic markets for fear of the fierce competition from advanced economies. Different from the multilateral approach adopted by the WTO, however, FTAs are by their very nature discriminatory because the preferential treatments apply only to member countries within the bloc, not to countries outside the bloc. This is a major exemption to the most favored nation clause of the GATT.

One pitfall of FTAs is the potential trade diversion effect when a country switches from a highly efficient non-FTA member country to a less productive FTA partner that enjoys preferential tariffs. In addition, the complex rules of origin and overlapping FTA networks, called "spaghetti bowls" by Jagdish Bhagwati, is another undesirable feature of regionalism. As a result, China should be cautious when moving away from the multilateral approach under the WTO to the bilateral approach. China has to balance well the potential benefits and costs of forming FTAs with neighboring countries.

Opening the Hinterland

The *Decision* also discusses how to further open up inland and border areas. China intends to promote the development of inland industry clusters by using preferential policies and promoting cooperation among regions. China will also accelerate the construction of infrastructure connections to neighboring countries and regions to build a Silk Road Economic Belt and a Maritime Silk Road, so as to form a new pattern of all-round opening. All of these policies are conducive to the economic development of the inland region.

When it comes to trade barriers, people tend to focus on international barriers and ignore domestic ones, even though domestic trade barriers can be significant. It is encouraging to see that the *Decision* also emphasizes developing transportation and logistics infrastructure to form a "corridor" of foreign trade that links different regions *within* China. Together with the market reform policy to "combat regional protection" in Article 9 of the *Decision*, this policy initiative intends to address the high cost of doing businesses among different regions within China. Although this issue is touched in the *Decision*, the economic cost of barriers within China and the potential impact of lowering such barriers may not be fully understood. Despite China's impressive export performance in recent years, internal trade barriers remain surprisingly high but are less well understood. For example, it was reported that,

> ...a kilogram of cargo shipped from Shanghai to New York costs 1.50 yuan while the same weight shipped from Shanghai to Guizhou (the capital city of an inner province that is 2,000 km away) costs between 6-8 yuan. This makes the total cost of shipping from Shanghai to Guizhou four to five times as expensive as shipping to New York, which is 11,862 km away. Transportation costs added to storage, and distribution management costs, lead to logistics costs 18 percent of GDP, that's more than twice as much as the U.S. ... Any western fashion brand from Gap to Versace, *even clothing made in China*, are priced 30 percent to several times more than the same product in the U.S.[7]

Much work has been done to examine national borders as impediments to international trade, but less attention has been paid to inter-state/provincial border effects. The internal trade barriers in China are significant and the domestic market segmentation is substantial, but these have been largely concealed by the country's impressive export performance. These barriers not only explain why many Chinese-made products are sold in China at higher prices than in the U.S., but also help to demonstrate why China's growth relies heavily on exports rather than domestic demand (arguably a contributing factor to global trade imbalance). A reduction in intra-China trade barriers and a less segmented national market is critical to a successful transition of an export- and investment-driven economy to a domestic consumption-driven economy.

Conclusion

To conclude, the *Decision* reconfirms China's dedication to further liberalization of international and domestic trade in not only manufacturing sectors but also services sectors. Because policy making in a globalized economy becomes more complicated, the coordination of various policies remains to be a challenging task for China. It is inevitable to see some policy inconsistencies, loopholes and even setbacks during this process. For both policy makers and researchers, it is important to evaluate these policies appropriately and provide policy remedies in a timely manner.

Notes

[1] *Upstream industries refer to sectors that process raw material into an intermediary product for the final production of finished product by the downstream industries. For instance, petroleum refineries refine crude oil into intermediary chemicals which can be used to produce plastics by other firms.*

[2] *Tang, Heiwai, Fei Wang and Zhi Wang, "The Domestic Segment of Global Supply Chains in China under State Capitalism", CESifo Working Paper No. 4797, May 2014.*

[3] *Voucher privatization is a privatization method in which citizens are given or can inexpensively buy a book of vouchers that represent potential shares in any state-owned company. See http://en.wikipedia.org/wiki/Voucher_privatization*

[4] *Ramo, Joshua Cooper, 2004. "The Beijing Consensus," The Foreign Policy Centre. http://fpc.org.uk/fsblob/244.pdf*

[5] *Dollar, David, and Shang-Jin Wei, 2007. "Das (Wasted) Kapital: Firm Ownership and Investment Efficiency in China," NBER Working Paper No. 13103. http://www.nber.org/papers/w13103*

[6] *For more detailed discussion, please refer to The Commanding Heights: The Battle for the World Economy, by Daniel Yergin and Joseph Stanislaw, Published by Simon & Schuster, New York, 2002.*

[7] *Li, Waiching, 2011. "Why 'Made in China' Costs More in China." http://econintersect.com/wordpress/?p=11897*

Further Readings:

Ramo, Joshua Cooper, 2004. *"The Beijing Consensus," The Foreign Policy Centre. http://fpc.org.uk/fsblob/244.pdf*

Williamson, John: *What Washington Means by Policy Reform, in: Williamson, John (ed.): Latin American Readjustment: How Much has Happened, Washington: Institute for International Economics 1989.*

Yergin, Daniel and Joseph Stanislaw, *The Commanding Heights: The Battle for the World Economy, Published by Simon & Schuster, New York, 2002.*

Xuepeng Liu, Ph.D., is Associate Professor of Economics at Kennesaw State University, Kennesaw, Georgia.

New Approaches in Banking, Currency and Public Finance

Penelope B. Prime
Vol. 13, No. 2
2014

Reforming the Financial Industry

The Eighteenth Party Congress' Third Plenary Session's Decision of November 2013 lists a new round of financial reforms aimed at introducing more market forces into the economic system. Two of the most important facets of this stage of reform are market-determined interest rates and permitting the value of the RMB to float. Both are a necessity for the leadership to attain the goal of making the yuan a world reserve currency to rival the U.S. dollar. But looks can be deceiving. Forces are arrayed on both sides of the question of reform, with uncertainties about China's future economic growth rate. As a result, implementation of these financial reforms is likely to come in fits and starts, but the changes could end up being significant.

China faces the same conflicting pressures that other countries do. Polices are needed to stimulate growth but debt and deficit financing must be kept in check. China's financial system must support growth by providing credit to companies and funding investment by local governments, but it also must manage resulting deficits and debt. For years, capital costs have been subsidized for state companies and governments by fixing interest rates. Now the People's Bank of China, China's central bank, has been advocating market-determined interest rates to improve the allocation of investment capital by conveying the true cost of borrowing. Rates would likely rise, however, which would dampen new investment, affect growth, and raise the costs of refinancing outstanding loans. The construction industry has been a main driver of domestic growth, but it is sensitive to the cost and access of loans. Hence, numerous interests within China are wary of moving in this market-oriented direction.

To make matters more complicated, China is in a period of slowing economic growth, which enhances the risk to some projects. Slow sales of housing, commercial property, and manufactured goods have increased the chances of default on related loans. Property prices in many parts of China have softened. For some, this sounds all too similar to the beginning of the U.S. financial crisis when housing prices began to fall in mid-2006.

Market-determined Interest rates

One difference between China and the U.S., however, is that China's key financial prices are not yet fully market determined. For example, interest rates for loans in China are capped in the formal banking sector, as are deposit rates. Because there is more demand for loans than banks are willing, or can, offer, there is a thriving "shadow" banking sector where the costs of borrowing are much higher. This sector has grown substantially over time, and even state banks and large companies have diverted funds to these channels to earn higher returns.

Reforms envisioned in the Decision would lessen the need for shadow lending. While the shadow sector has served a useful purpose – supplying capital to many companies that would not have access otherwise – there is a strong argument for letting the formal credit market determine rates. As the cost of borrowing in the formal sector would most likely rise, this would focus borrowers on good quality, reasonable risk projects, since they would have to pay more for access to credit. This should help investment efficiency by improving the quality of projects in China's domestic economy.

To achieve the reforms laid out in the Decision, the development of new financial products carrying different rates of return will be essential. For example, banks are experimenting with offering certificates of deposit to individuals and corporations at higher interest rates than savings accounts. Another major step is allowing corporations to offer corporate bonds to individuals and companies, rather than just to financial institutions. Pursuing these reforms would help create the conditions for interest rates to vary according to demand. Chinese banks currently hold large household savings deposits that could potentially be used for investment, and holders of the deposits could earn higher returns, if they were willing to take on more risk. Certificates of deposit would open new sources of investment funds for banks, and expanding the scope of corporate bond issuance would take pressure off banks to make loans at a time when concerns about are intensifying about bad loans on bank balance sheets.[1]

Evidence of demand for new investment products by households can be seen in services being created by Alibaba and the telecom companies to offer a return on funds held by these companies for deposits. Alibaba began its online investment service in 2013. China Unicom is planning to offer a similar service, starting with its Shenzhen contract phone customers.[2] The rates of return are higher than those offered by banks on savings accounts. For example, Alibaba advertises a five percent annual return and China Unicom has said its service will earn six percent, while a one-year term deposit at the commercial banks is capped at 3.3 percent.[3]

Currency Rates and International Capital Flows

A related piece of China's financial market liberalization is the value of the yuan, or RMB. As long as the RMB value is fixed by the People's Bank, and not by the market, the Central Bank cannot use the money supply as a policy tool. For example, in the current fixed exchange rate system, if the Central Bank decreases the money supply by raising banks' reserve requirements – which would raise interest rates – there would be upward value on the RMB, and the Central Bank would simply have to increase the amount of RMB in circulation again to keep the RMB value stable. Hence, an important aspect of the Decision is a set of changes leading eventually to a market-determined exchange rate and more policy leverage for the Central Bank.

With a market-determined exchange rate, the value fluctuates with the relative demand and supply of that currency. This will mean volatility in the currency's value. Chinese policy makers have thus far not been willing to accept such volatility, in part because China's finance system does not have adequate tools to help companies hedge this type of risk. The Decision emphasizes making changes in an "orderly way" along with establishing risk management systems. The specifics of these challenges are not addressed explicitly.

Another risk factor in play here is the flow of money into and out of China. So far, access to foreign exchange or RMB for trade in goods and services is open and does not need special permission; however, access to currency for investments in China or in other countries is highly restricted. Again policy makers are concerned about volatility of capital flows, especially the possibility of "hot money" flowing quickly in and out of China to take advantage of short-term portfolio investment opportunities. These types of short-term portfolio flows add to currency and equity value volatility and have caused serious problems for many countries such as in Mexico in 1994 and Thailand in 1997.

Volatility concerns need to be considered. However, access to RMB and to foreign currency is increasingly important to the development of Chinese companies as global players. In addition, the RMB can potentially become one of the important international currencies, but this cannot happen without cross-border access to the currency.

Dealing with financial and public debt

Related to the growth equation is the issue of debt. According to one estimate, China's bank credit to GDP ratio rose by 69 percent of GDP between 2009 and 2012.[4] And although non-performing loans currently are not seen as a crisis issue, they have been rising for several years.[5] In tandem with this concern are worries about the financial health of local governments. Local officials have been major players in supporting growth since the early days of China's reforms. Vigorously responding to incentives to develop their cities, towns, counties, and provinces, they had to manage with major constraints in access to capital. Public finance reforms implemented in the mid-1990s left them with larger expenditure responsibilities than local revenue could support. According to the Asian Development Bank, local governments' share of revenue is 50 percent or less of total revenue collected but they are responsible for 85 percent of the expected government expenditure.[6]

How has this been possible? Local governments have worked with development corporations that can borrow funds for local projects on the governments' behalf. The Asian Development Bank estimates that local government debt is about 30 percent of GDP and is rising.[7] According to Public Finance International, local direct and indirect debt is about 50 percent of GDP as reported by Moody's.[8]

To partially address this issue, the Decision includes reforms to allow local governments to issue municipal bonds to raise needed funds instead of relying on the indirect loans from non-bank entities. This would be another financial instrument that would affect interest rates and investment options across the economy. There is also a call to clarify center-local expenditure responsibilities. In addition, instituting real estate taxes has been discussed for some time now, both to increase local governments' revenue streams but also to help manage the demand for housing, and this is included in the Decision.

Opening financing to the private sector

The slowing of China's economy adds to the risk of default on outstanding loans held by both the public and private sectors. This brings us back to the delicate balance between trying to stimulate growth but not by increasing new loans too much or too fast. One of the goals of the Decision is to give more help to the private sector to increase its role as a driver of growth. During the summer of 2014, the Central Bank made a concrete move in this direction. The Bank exempted smaller banks from an attempt to slow loans by raising banks' reserve requirements. In fact, a "targeted cut" was proposed for banks that lend to rural and small companies. In other words, those banks could lower their reserve requirements and thus increase their loans.[9] Talk of helping the private sector is not new in China, but there have not been many concrete measures. This policy may not make a large difference to small, private firms, but it is at least in their favor and may be a sufficient incentive for banks to loan to them.

Conclusion

Financial reforms, growth and deficit/debt reduction represent a triplet of policy challenges that will not easily move forward together. Ultimately which one dominates in the short-run will be influenced by the need for political leaders to ensure growth above all. Annual growth estimates vary but tend to be between seven and 7.5 percent. If the actual growth falls much short of this, reforms will likely be put on a back burner, given the political sensitivity to a slowing economy. As of this writing, official growth rates are holding. Second quarter growth in 2014 was 7.5 percent –up from 7.4 percent in the first quarter.[10] The good news underlying these figures is that growth has not collapsed as some had predicted, and no doubt many others feared in silence.

Still, these growth targets do not allow for much experimentation. Most likely the interest rate pilot reforms will be the most robust, followed by exchange rate values determined increasingly by demand and supply of the currency. A completely open capital account will likely be the last step in China's financial system development, but is certainly being discussed as a long-term goal along with the market determination of the currency. (See "China's Currency Reforms from a Banker's Perspective," China Currents Vol. 13, No. 1, 2014.)

Notes

[1] Jiang Xueqing, "CD Liberalization 'A Step Forward,'" *China Daily,* May 27, 2014, Business & companies p. 15, and Jiang Xueqing, "Analysts urge broader range of channels for sales of domestic corporate debt," *China Daily,* May 24-25, 2014, business weekend, p. 10.

[2] Meng Jing, "Telecoms dialing up financial products," *China Daily,* May 27, 2014, Business & Companies, p. 16.

[3] Jiang Xueqing, "CD Liberalization 'A Step Forward,'" *China Daily,* May 27, 2014, Business & companies p. 15.

[4] Niall Ferguson and Moritz Schularick, "The U.S. and China both need economic rehab," *The Wall Street Journal,* November 5, 2013, http://online.wsj.com. Accessed November 8, 2013.

[5] Zheng Yangpeng, "Watchdog sure of nation's bad-loan figures," *China Daily,* May 31- June 1, 2014, p.2.

[6] Takehiko Nakao, "The road to public finance reform," *China Daily,* March 25, 2014.

[7] Ibid.

[8] Vivienne Russell, "Chinese local government debt risks stability of public finance," *publicfinanceinternational.org,* January 6, 2013. Accessed June 10, 2014.

[9] William Kazer, "China's Central Bank Unveils Cuts in Reserve Ratios for Some Banks," *The Wall Street Journal,* June 9, 2014, online.wsj.com. Accessed June 11, 2014.

[10] Michael J. Casey, "In China, Warnings Flash Despite Better Data," *FX Horizons, The Wall Street Journal,* July 27, 2014. Online. Wsj.com. Accessed July 28, 2014.

Penelope B. Prime, Ph.D., is Professor of International Business at Georgia State University, Atlanta, Georgia and director of the China Research Center.

Chinese Media and Culture: Dancing with Chains

Hongmei Li
Vol. 13, No. 2
2014

The Eighteenth Party Congress' Third Plenary Session's Decision maps out the country's plan for cultural and media development. There is nothing on the surface that suggests a radical departure from the tight control the Chinese party-state exerts. The Decision is full of paternalistic clichés about the development of socialist culture under the guidance of Marxism, media controls, and the unification between social benefits and economic benefits. But new elements embedded in the Decision contain potential seeds for at least a partial reordering of the dynamic tension between impulses demanding control and those calling for expression in the Chinese cultural and media realm, with control perhaps gaining ground. These elements also figure in China's recent effort to develop culture industries and rebalance domestic media control and international cultural expansion and influence.

This essay does not aim to provide a comprehensive commentary on China's recent cultural policies as they relate to the Decision. Instead, it focuses on the intersection between cultural and media policies and the push and pull between the party-state and aggressive market-oriented media producers. Specifically, the essay will highlight some potential changes in the following six areas: (1) control mechanisms, (2) the prescribed nature of a media organization, (3) media censorship, (4) media consolidation and economies of scale, (5) the entry of private capital into the Chinese media industries, and (6) China's soft power and public diplomacy.

First, the Decision stresses the government's role as administrator rather than player in managing cultural agencies. This is framed as a measure to further cultural reforms that aim to separate operations of the government from those of the enterprise. Specifically, the Decision proposes to establish unified management organizations linking party and state to administer cultural staff, affairs, capital, and orientation. This opens the possibility of changing what has been a dual-track media control system in China.

Generally speaking, Chinese media have been regulated and controlled both by a Party and an administrative system. The Party system is represented by the Central Propaganda Ministry and its branches at the provincial, district and county levels. The administrative system is represented by various ministries under the State Council and the nationwide branches of each ministry. For example, TV and radio have been regulated by the State Administration of Radio, Film and Television (SARFT); print media, audio, and video by the General Administration of Press and Publication (GAPP); and the Internet by the Ministry of Industry and Technology Information. In 2013, SARFT merged with GAPP to form a new body called the State Administration of Press, Publications, Radio, Film, and Television. The new body, whose name has been widely criticized by netizens for its lack of creativity, aims to streamline China's regulation over both print and broadcast media.

China's Central Propaganda Department and its branches monitor media content and can stop problematic programs at any time by issuing formal or informal notices or oral directives. Since the founding of the People's Republic of China in 1949, shaping culture has always been a key official mission of the government and the Party. Except for a few years during the Cultural Revolution (1966-1976), the Chinese Communist Party has maintained tight, centralized control over Chinese media.[1] Various ministries also participate in controlling media content. For example, China's State Language Affairs Commission, which seeks to standardize Chinese language and enforce proper pronunciation in China, can file official complaints about problematic content. Given the tradition of the Communist Party's pervasive ideological control involving many different government agencies, a transition away from the current structure is likely to encounter resistance at various levels.

Second, the Decision emphasizes the dual role of a Chinese cultural organization as both an instrument of social control and a business, with social benefits prioritized over economic benefits. While this kind of positioning is not new, the statement could be viewed as a corrective measure, aiming to rectify media practices in China that overemphasize economic benefits, as discussed below.

In the era of reform, media organizations have been told to simultaneously serve as an official organ of the state and at the same time rise or fall based on market forces.[2] In the last few decades, the Chinese government has gradually reduced subsidies and the vast majority of Chinese media now rely predominantly or solely on advertising as a source of income. The market now plays a key role in dictating media content, as evidenced by the importance of the ratings system and the booming entertainment culture.

The media ratings system was introduced in China in the late 1990s. Now, CCTV-controlled Yangshi Suofurui, with its shortened English name CSM, is the most important media research firm in China. Firms that monitor print media, radio, outdoor media, and the Internet have also been established since the early1990s. Among them, Hui Cong, established in 1992, is one of the most important, currently monitoring more than 1,400 print outlets and more than 7,000 Internet sites. Ratings have become a common currency of exchange and the most important criterion in dictating a TV station's programming and daily practices. CCTV even implemented a system called "the last rated program out" in 2002, which means the lowest rated program gets canceled first. Although the CCTV system was replaced by a more comprehensive evaluation mechanism in 2011 that stresses four dimensions, including a program's leadership power, influence, communicative power, and professionalism, ratings still take up more than 50 percent of the weight in the equation.[3]

An entertainment culture has boomed since the late 1990s with the rise of media metrics. Entertainment programming often is less controlled and more profitable that other types of content. Many provincial satellite TV channels have launched entertainment programs to increase their competitiveness in an economy that depends on eyeballs. Hunan Satellite TV (HSTV) in particular has become a successful model. Starting with its flagship program Happy Camp, a variety show that debuted in July 1997, and its subsequent dating program The Promise of Rose (running from July 16, 1998 to August 25, 2005), HSTV has distinguished itself by celebrating happiness and youth culture. Other stations followed suit and attempted to differentiate themselves either through TV dramas, martial arts, localized storytelling or other types of programming.

Chinese authorities often show ambivalent attitudes toward media entertainment, fostering the boom on the one hand but attempting to control it on the other. A number of policies and regulations have been issued by China's SARFT to control the "over-entertaining" trend in Chinese media. Entertainment is often criticized by the authorities as promoting vulgarization, infotainment, and celebrity gossip. For example, SARFT issued an order requiring that no satellite TV channel, starting in July 2011, should air entertainment programs more than three times a week in prime time from 17:00 to 22:00. This example demonstrates an inherent contradiction in the dual functions of Chinese media.

Third, the Decision speaks to censorship. It aims to improve ideological control mechanisms, enhance the management of media infrastructure and content, establish "a unified mechanism to prevent and strike online crimes," and "improve the mechanism to handle unexpected events over the Internet" so as to "form a working framework that combines direct guidance and administration under the law." It further calls for "the institutionalization of news releases, tightening of the journalist qualifications, management of new media,[4] and the regulation of the communicative order." In a way, the Decision proposes to tighten ideological controls and online censorship, probably as a response to the fragmentation of the Chinese media market and the threat posed by new media, such as social media and mobile phones.

Indeed, many observers and analysts have pointed out that since Xi Jinping took power, control over the Internet has been increased. Most recently, China issued a document called "Temporary Rules for Managing Instantaneous Communication Tools and Public Information Service Development," which aims to manage and censor information distribution. However, authorities have always been struggling with the issues of control over media. There has never been a clear line about what is allowed and what is not. There is no single media law in China, and scholars have been discussing whether the state should adopt one. Chinese media are now regulated by scattered regulations, orders, and circulars, and the control regime is ambiguous, combining formal and informal controls. Arguably, the lack of formal boundaries makes censorship effective. Media workers often censor themselves to a degree that goes further than the often unclear official guidelines.

Other controls are being put in place. Chinese people have long had to obtain state-issued work certificates (shanggang zheng) to work in media organizations, and regulations are being tightened. Recently, regulations were implemented to prevent people on social media from distributing news unless they are licensed to do so. As the least controlled sector, advertising traditionally has been under less scrutiny. However, a 2007 decree issued jointly by the Ministry of the Personnel (currently the Ministry of Human Resources and Social Security) and the State Administration of Industry and Commerce initiated the practice of certifying ad workers. This decree specifies criteria used to evaluate and grant the certificates of "assistant advertising expert," "advertising expert," and "senior advertising expert" through annual exams overseen by the Chinese Advertising Association. In 2011, the first qualifying exam was held and the subjects tested include advertising laws and regulations, practices, copywriting, design, and planning. The practice makes China the only country that grants official certifications to advertising workers.

Fourth, the Decision continues to stress media consolidation and economies of scale. It states that "a special shareholding policy will be applied to state-owned media that are reformed according to state policies." It also stipulates that China will "push consolidation and acquisitions of cultural enterprises across geography, industry, and different kinds of ownership and improve the scale, concentration, and professionalism of the cultural industries." This is a response to the exponential media growth in China in the last few decades and to the competition posed by large foreign media. A staple slogan in Chinese media industries since the late 1990s calls for enterprises to "become larger and stronger." In the last two decades, Chinese media have been characterized by a rapid expansion as well as a simultaneous consolidation under the direction of the government as a way to enhance their competitiveness prior to China's entry into the WTO.

Media consolidation started in 1996 with the formation of the Guangzhou Daily Newspaper group. By 2003, China had established 69 media groups, including 38 newspaper groups, 13 broadcasting groups, one magazine group, nine book publishing groups, five distribution groups, and three film groups.[5] In May 2011, China News and Publishing Group was founded. Not officially allowed to form cross-media groups, most conglomerates are based on single medium and related entities, or geography. The Decision means that in the future cross-media groups can be formed. Media organizations from different industries and different places can be consolidated. Consolidation is a means to achieve economies of scale as well as a way to support government control over previously fragmented media.[6]

Fifth, the Decision aims to further promote the development of private capital in China's media market. It encourages private cultural enterprises, lowers the threshold of entry, and allows private capitalists to be involved in overseas publishing and online publishing businesses and in holding shares of state-owned film production, cultural, and arts organizations. It also states that China will increase government subsidies, cultural purchases, and copyright protections. This is evidence of China's effort to develop its culture industries domestically and internationally.

While allowing private capital into media industries is not entirely new, it can potentially lead to new practices. In the past, private capital was mainly allowed in the areas of production and distribution. Since the late 1980s, TV stations have started to purchase programs on the market, inaugurating a system that separates the producer from the broadcaster. Since the 1990s, state authorities have begun to more aggressively promote the system and allow private capital to enter the TV market. TV drama is the first area that has witnessed the penetration of private capital. It is a common practice now for TV stations to buy programs produced by others. Now, the stages seems to be set for a broadening of the embrace of private capital in media.

While Chinese TV producers initially only cloned successful foreign programs, starting with HSTV's highly influential show Super Girl, they have in recent years begun to purchase global programming, such as Ugly Betty (debuting in 2008 and licensed from Televisa), If You Are the One (debuting in 2010 based on the UK program Take Me Out), China's Got Talent (deputing in 2010 and licensed from UK-based FremantleMedia), Daddy, Where Are We Going? (debuting in October 2013 and licensed from a South Korean producer), Voice of China (debuting in July 2012 and licensed from the Dutch program The Voice of Holland), Chinese Dream Show (debuting in April 2011 and licensed from BBC) and so forth.

Fashion magazines have long entered the Chinese market through licensing or partnership with a local publisher.[7] For example, the Hearst Corporation from the U.S. started to publish a Chinese version of Cosmopolitan in 1993. Harper's launched the Chinese version of Harper's Bazaar in 2001, and the Chinese version of Vogue was introduced in 2005. Japanese magazines such as Vivi, With, Style, Oggi and CanCam have also launched Chinese versions in the 2000s. Given that most of these magazines are advertising vehicles, content is less controlled than news programs. In the book publication area, U.S. publisher Simon & Schuster started to collaborate with Chinese publishers in the late 1990s in licensing or co-publishing deals.

Lastly, the Decision stresses China's public diplomacy. Since the turn of the 21st century, China has attempted to increase its comprehensive power, which includes a higher international profile and soft power. In addition to increasing China's international aid and participation in global affairs, an important step has been the spread of Chinese culture through Confucius Institutes. China has founded more than 300 Confucius Institutes worldwide. Interestingly, promotion of Chinese culture overseas emphasizes ideology as well as economic benefits. Recently, Confucius Institutes in the U.S. has been under increasing scrutiny.

While there is no doubt that China's international influence has increased recently, there is a general consensus that China's soft power mainly emanates from its conformity to international norms rather than its power to shape global policies.[8] Li (2009) argues that China's soft power concerns "the soft use of power." China has not yet taken a leading role in international affairs except in the case of climate change. Also, there is a deep suspicion toward China in the West. While China has allocated huge amounts of money for state-owned media such as Xinghua News Agency, China Central TV, and Shanghai Media Group to increase their international influence, gaining credibility is a major challenge for these media outlets. Competition for viewers in other countries is always contentious,[9] but China faces a unique challenge because of its Communist ideology, state control, and the West's anxiety about China's rise.

In this essay, I discussed potential changes in China's media control mechanisms, the dual role of China media, censorship, media consolidation, the entry of private capital into the Chinese media industries, and China's soft power and public diplomacy. In summary, it seems that the Decision largely aims to further promote the economic function of culture and media industries and control their ideological function. It would not be surprising if we see China implementing tighter controls over the Internet and social media and simultaneously encouraging entrepreneurship and creativity. To a large extent, culture and media industries are dancing with chains. They are allowed to become economic entities that only disseminate non-threatening cultural contents. Chinese media aiming to expand internationally will encounter even more challenges. After all, they may continue to be viewed as the Chinese Communist Party's mouthpieces. Their dual roles will be constantly tested and contested in the domestic and international markets. One more note: the Decision only prescribes the rules for the media and cultural industries, but the practices may be different.

Notes

[1] *Zhao, 2008*
[2] *Zhao, 1998, 2008*
[3] *Chinanews.com, 2011, Aug. 12*
[4] *Many observers believe the party-state's aim is to converge new and old media so as to maintain the dominance of traditional outlets and thereby maintain ideological control.*
[5] *"Zhongguo chuanmeijituan fazhan baogao," 2004*
[6] *Zhao, 1998, 2008*
[7] *Fritha & Yang, 2009*
[8] *Li, 2009*
[9] *Price, 2002*

References

Chinanews.com (2011, Aug. 12). *Shoushi lu bu zai shi wei yi, yangshi gaige feichu lanmu mowei taotai zhi.* http://www.chinanews.com/yl/2011/08-12/3253041.shtml. Accessed Feb. 1, 2013.

Fritha, K., & Yang, F. (2009). Transnational cultural flows: An analysis of women's magazines in China. *Chinese Journal Of Communication, 2(2),* 158-173. doi:10.1080/17544750902826681

Li, H. (2010). *Chinese Diaspora, the Internet, and the image of China: A case study of the Beijing Olympic torch relay.* In J. Wang (ed.), *Soft power in China: Public diplomacy through Communication* (pp. 135-156). New York, NY: Palgrave Macmillan.

Li, H. (2013). China's media transformation and audience studies. In A. N. Valdivia (Gen. Ed.) & R. Parameswaran (Ed.), *The international encyclopedia of media studies. Vol. 3: Audience and interpretation in media studies* (pp.341-364). Oxford, UK: Wiley-Blackwell.

Li, M. (2009) (ed.). *Soft Power: China's Emerging Strategy in International Politics.* Lanham, MA: Lexington Book.

Price, M. (2002). *Media and sovereignty: The global information revolution and its challenge to state power.* The MIT Press.

Wang, J. (2011). *Soft Power in China: Public Diplomacy through Communication.* New York: Plagrave Macmillan.

Zhao, Y. (1998). *Media, Market and Democracy in China.* University of Illinois Press.

Zhao, Y. (2008). *Communication in China.* Rowman & Littlefield

"Zhongguo chuanmeijituan fazhan baogo" (2004, May). *Zhongguo chuanmeijituan fazhan baogao.* Changsha, China: Hunan Jiaoyu Chubanshe.

Hongmei Li, Ph.D., is Assistant Professor of Communications at Georgia State University, Atlanta, Georgia.

About the Editors

Penelope B. Prime: Beginning with her first visit to China in 1976, Penelope Prime has more than 30 years of experience studying the dynamic Chinese economy. After majoring in Chinese studies and studying Mandarin as an undergraduate, she earned a Ph.D. in economics at the University of Michigan. Dr. Prime is currently Professor in the Institute of International Business in the J. Mack Robinson College of Business, Georgia State University, and Director of the China Research Center. Dr. Prime's research focuses on China's economy and business environment, including topics such as China's foreign trade and investment, domestic market reforms, and provincial and local-level development, as well as applied business and economics cases on China and Asia.

James R. Schiffman: Dr. Schiffman is Assistant Professor in the Mass Communication Department at Georgia College & State University in Milledgeville, Georgia. Previously, he served as Chief Copy Editor at CNN International, where he was involved in editorial decision making, network style, hiring, and training. Prior to joining CNN, Dr. Schiffman was a staff correspondent for The Wall Street Journal in Atlanta and The Asian Wall Street Journal in Hong Kong, Seoul, and Beijing. As a correspondent in Beijing between 1986 and 1988, Dr. Schiffman reported extensively on Chinese economic reforms, the role of foreign investment, and Chinese politics and culture at a time of rapid change and turmoil. Dr. Schiffman speaks Mandarin Chinese, and lectures occasionally to academic and community groups. He earned a Ph.D. in Communication at Georgia State University in May 2012 and is the editor of China Currents.

www.ingramcontent.com/pod-product-compliance
Lightning Source LLC
Chambersburg PA
CBHW060844280326
41934CB00007B/912